An Important Message to Our Readers

This product provides information and general advice about the law. But laws and procedures change frequently, and they can be interpreted differently by different people. For specific advice geared to your specific situation, consult an expert. No book, software or other published material is a substitute for personalized advice from a knowledgeable lawyer licensed to practice law in your state.

6th edition

How to Form a
California
Professional
Corporation

by Attorney Anthony Mancuso

Keeping-Up-to-Date

To keep its books up-to-date, Nolo issues new printings and new editions periodically. New printings reflect minor legal changes and technical corrections. New editions contain major legal changes, major text additions or major reorganizations. To find out if a later printing or edition of any Nolo book is available, call Nolo at 510-549-1976 or check our website at www.nolo.com.

To stay current, follow the "Update" service at our website at http://www.nolo.com/update. In another effort to help you use Nolo's latest materials, we offer a 35% discount off the purchase of the new edition of your Nolo book when you turn in the cover of an earlier edition. (See the "Special Upgrade Offer" in the back of the book.) This book was last revised in November 2000.

SIXTH EDITION	
Second Printing	NOVEMBER 2000
Editor	SHANNON MIEHE
Book Design	JACKIE MANCUSO
Illustrator	MARI STEIN
Production	SARAH TOLL
Index	THÉRÈSE SHERE
Printing	VERSA PRESS

Mancuso, Anthony.
  How to form a California professional corporation / by Anthony
Mancuso — 6th ed.
    p.   cm.
  Includes index.
  ISBN 0-87337-496-7
  1. Professional corporations—California. I. Title.
  KFC545.5 .M36   1998
  346.794'0668—dc21

                                                        98-35443
                                                        CIP

For information on bulk purchases or corporate premium sales, please contact the Special Sales Department. For academic sales or textbook adoptions, ask for Academic Sales. Call 800-955-4775 or write to Nolo.com, Inc., 950 Parker Street, Berkeley, CA 94710.

Acknowledgments

Thanks to Jake Warner, publisher, Shannon Miehe, editor, and the entire Nolo staff for helping me provide nuts-and-bolts legal information to California professionals.

About the author

Attorney Anthony Mancuso is a corporation and limited liability company expert and author of Nolo's best-selling corporate and LLC law series. He is the author and programmer of *LLC Maker* (software to form an LLC in each state), and many Nolo business formation books, including: *How to Form Your Own Limited Liability Company*, *Nolo's Quick LLC*, *Your Limited Liability Company: An Operating Manual*, *How to Form Your Own Corporation* (California, New York, and Texas editions), *How to Form a Nonprofit Corporation* (National and California Editions), *Nolo's California Quick Corp*, *The Corporate Minutes Book: The Legal Guide to Taking Care of Your Corporation*, and *How to Create a Buy-Sell Agreement & Control the Destiny of Your Small Business*. His books and software have shown over a quarter of a million businesses and organizations how to form an LLC or incorporate. He is also a guitarist and licensed helicopter pilot.

CONTENTS

Introduction

CHAPTER 1
Background Information on California Corporations

A. DIFFERENT WAYS OF DOING BUSINESS 1/1
    1. Sole Proprietorship 1/1
    2. Partnership 1/1
    3. The Corporation 1/3
B. KINDS OF CORPORATIONS 1/4
    1. Nonprofit Corporations 1/4
    2. Profit Corporations 1/5
C. CORPORATE POWERS 1/5
D. CORPORATE PEOPLE 1/5
    1. Incorporators 1/6
    2. Directors 1/7
    3. Officers 1/8
    4. Shareholders 1/10

CHAPTER 2
The Professional Corporation

A. INTRODUCTION 2/1
B. PROFESSIONS REQUIRED TO INCORPORATE AS PROFESSIONAL
    CORPORATIONS 2/1
C. WHY BECOME A PROFESSIONAL CORPORATION? 2/2
D. HOW WILL YOUR CORPORATION BE SET UP? 2/2
E. CALIFORNIA LAW COVERING PROFESSIONAL CORPORATIONS 2/3
F. WHAT AGENCY SUPERVISES YOUR PROFESSION? 2/3
G. SPECIFIC REQUIREMENTS COVERING THE INCORPORATION OF
    YOUR PROFESSION 2/3

CHAPTER 3

Advantages, Disadvantages, and Other Considerations

A. ADVANTAGES 3/1
    1. Limited Liability 3/1
    2. Taxation 3/3
    3. Fringe Benefits 3/9
    4. Establishing Order in Your Business 3/10
    5. Formality 3/10
    6. Perpetual Existence 3/11
    7. New Tax Year 3/11

B. DISADVANTAGES 3/12
    1. Paperwork 3/12
    2. Costs 3/12

C. OTHER INCORPORATION CONSIDERATIONS 3/13
    1. Capitalization 3/13
    2. Piercing the Corporate Veil
       (if you want to be treated like a corporation, it's best to act like one) 3/16
    3. Reallocation of Income 3/17
    4. Paying Yourself Too Much Salary 3/18
    5. Accumulated Earnings Credit 3/18
    6. Personal Holding Company Penalty 3/19
    7. Federal S Corporation Tax Status 3/20
    8. Corporate Accounting Periods and Tax Years 3/25
    9. Becoming a Close Corporation 3/28
    10. Sale of Stock 3/28
    11. Dividends 3/29
    12. Section 1244 Stock 3/29
    13. IRC Section 351 Tax-Free Exchange Treatment of Your Corporation 3/30
    14. Tax and Financial Considerations When Incorporating a Prior Business .. 3/34
    15. Dissolution of the Corporation 3/36

CHAPTER 4

Specific Requirements for Professionals Who Incorporate

A. LICENSING 4/1

B. CERTIFICATE OF REGISTRATION 4/2

C. NAMES 4/2

D. WHO MAY BE SHAREHOLDERS? 4/3

E. WHO MAY BE DIRECTORS AND OFFICERS 4/3

    1. Directors 4/4

    2. Officers 4/4

F. TRANSFERRING SHARES 4/5

G. SECURITY-MALPRACTICE 4/5

H. REPORTS 4/6

I. THE PROFESSIONAL CORPORATION STOCK QUALIFICATION EXEMPTION 4/6

J. FEDERAL SECURITIES LAW 4/7

Retirement Plans

A. INTRODUCTION 5/1

B. INDIVIDUAL RETIREMENT ARRANGEMENT (IRA) 5/2

C. KEOGH 5/3

D. SEP (SIMPLIFIED EMPLOYEE PENSION PLANS) 5/3

E. CORPORATE RETIREMENT PLANS 5/3

    1. Defined Benefit (Pension) Plan—Fixed Plan 5/4

    2. Defined Contribution (or Money-Purchase Pension) Plan 5/4

    3. Targeted Benefit Pension Plans 5/5

    4. Profit Sharing Plans 5/5

F. BORROWING UNDER A CORPORATE PLAN 5/5

G. THE RETIREMENT PLAN AND EMPLOYEES 5/6

H. TOP-HEAVY PLANS 5/6

I. CAFETERIA PLANS AND 401(k) PLANS 5/6

J. WHERE DO YOU GO FOR A PENSION PLAN? (WHETHER IRA, KEOGH,
    SEP OR CORPORATE) 5/7

Steps to Form a Professional Corporation

A. CHOOSE A NAME 6/2

B. PREPARE ARTICLES OF INCORPORATION 6/4

C.: FILE YOUR ARTICLES OF INCORPORATION 6/7

    1. Make Copies 6/7

    2. Pay Fees 6/7

    3. Send in Articles and Fees 6/9

D. ORDER CORPORATE SEAL AND SET UP A CORPORATE RECORDS BOOK 6/9

E. ORDER STOCK CERTIFICATES OR A CORPORATE KIT 6/10

F. PREPARE THE BYLAWS 6/10

G. HOLD THE FIRST MEETING OF THE BOARD OF DIRECTORS 6/12

H. PREPARE THE MINUTES OF THE MEETING 6/13

    1. Fill in Waiver of Notice and Consent to Holding of First Meeting 6/13

    2. Fill in the First Page of the Minutes of the First Meeting
       of the Board of Directors 6/13

    3. Fill in Pages 2 and 3 of the Minutes of the First Meeting 6/13

    4. Fill Out Pages 4–6 of the Minutes of the First Meeting 6/13

    5. Fill Out Last Page of Minutes 6/14

    6. Fill Out Pages 7–13 of the Minutes of the First Meeting 6/15

    7. Include Pages 14–16 of the Minutes of the First Meeting 6/17

    8. Include Page 17 of the Minutes of the First Meeting 6/18

I. ISSUE SHARES OF STOCK 6/18

    1. If Applicable, Comply With California's Bulk Sales Law 6/18

    2. Taking Title to Stock 6/19

    3. Filling Out the Stock Certificate 6/19

    4. Distributing the Stock Certificates 6/20

J. FILE YOUR CERTIFICATE OF REGISTRATION (IF REQUIRED) 6/28

CHAPTER 7

After Your Corporation Is Organized

A. FINAL FORMALITIES AFTER FORMING YOUR CORPORATION 7/1

    1. File California Annual Domestic Stock Corporation Statement 7/1

    2. File and Publish Fictitious Business Name Statement (if appropriate) 7/2

    3. File Final Papers on Prior Business 7/3

    4. Notify Creditors and Others of Dissolution of Prior Business 7/4

B. TAX FORMS—FEDERAL 7/4

    1. S Corporation Tax Election 7/4

    2. Federal Identification Number 7/5

    3. Employee's Withholding Certificates 7/5

    4. Income and Social Security Tax Withholding 7/5

    5. Quarterly Withholding Returns and Deposits 7/6

    6. Annual Wage and Tax Statement 7/6

    7. Federal Unemployment Tax 7/6

    8. Corporate Income Tax Return 7/7

    9. S Corporation Income Tax Return 7/7

    10. Corporate Shareholder and Employee Returns 7/7

    11. Estimated Corporate Income Tax Payments 7/8

C. TAX FORMS—STATE 7/8
    1. Corporate Estimated Tax Return 7/8
    2. Annual Corporate Franchise Tax Return 7/9
    3. Employer Registration Forms 7/9
    4. State Withholding Allowance Certificate 7/10
    5. Personal Income Tax Withholding 7/10
    6. California Unemployment and Disability Insurance 7/10
    7. Withholding Returns 7/10
    8. Annual Wage and Tax Statement 7/11
    9. Annual Reconciliation of Income Tax Withholding Forms 7/11
  10. Sales Tax Forms 7/11

D. WORKERS' COMPENSATION 7/12

E. PRIVATE INSURANCE COVERAGE 7/12

CHAPTER 8

Lawyers and Accountants

A. LAWYERS 8/1
B. ACCOUNTANTS 8/2

APPENDIX 1

Secretary of State Contact Information
Cover Letters
Articles of Incorporation

APPENDIX 2

Bylaws

APPENDIX 3

Minutes
Stock Issuance Receipts

APPENDIX 4

Special Provisions for Professional Corporations

APPENDIX 5

How to Use the Forms CD-ROM

INTRODUCTION

THE BUSINESS ACTIVITY of the United States was, at one time, primarily one of individual and family enterprises. Things have changed a lot since then, and now many of these small businesses have joined up with the big guns to take advantage of the formality and economic flexibility of being a corporation. Professionals, however, were traditionally not permitted to incorporate (presumably because the legislature did not want to distance the relationship between professional and client).

But times have changed, and in 1968 California passed the Moscone-Knox Professional Corporation Act. The list of professions which may incorporate under the Act has expanded since then, and we suspect additional professions will be included (perhaps even by the next edition of this book).

If your profession is listed on the back cover or in the beginning of Chapter 2, and you wish to incorporate, this book is for you. If your profession is not included, you may still be able to incorporate under the General Corporation Law. Check with the agency supervising your profession. If you are so permitted, see, *How to Form Your Own California Corporation*, by Anthony Mancuso, also published by Nolo.

This book will provide you with the forms necessary to organize a California professional corporation. We also discuss general information on the advantages and disadvantages of incorporating, as helpful background information.

Generally, lawyers charge from $1,000 to $2,000 for an incorporation. This book is intended to minimize your reliance on attorneys' services with respect to filling in standardized "boilerplate" forms, and to help you ask specific, informed questions related to the specific needs of your professional corporation when it becomes necessary to seek a lawyer's advice. Although not required by law, we recommend that you consult an attorney to check over your incorporation papers after you draft them and before you file with the state. (Chapter 8 provides some assistance in finding an attorney.) Despite the trend of higher and higher attorneys' fees, the process outlined in this book, including consultations with a lawyer, should make the cost of incorporating extremely reasonable.

This book is a tool to be used to comply with the legal formalities necessary to form a valid professional corporation. It does not and cannot substitute for a careful examination of the economic realities facing each business. Only you can make informed decisions regarding the consequences of organizing your business as a professional corporation.

Since accountants can often assist you with decisions regarding the tax consequences and other financial aspects of incorporating your business, we have also included a section on choosing an accountable accountant.

Chapter 1

BACKGROUND INFORMATION ON CALIFORNIA CORPORATIONS

BEFORE WE GO INTO the details of professional corporations, we thought it would be helpful to review the other two basic forms of doing business, and provide some general background on California corporations, including the cast of characters. The following chapters will deal with the specific points you need to know about if you intend to become a professional corporation.

A. Different Ways of Doing Business

There are several legal structures or forms under which a business can operate, including the sole proprietorship, partnership, limited liability company and corporation. In addition, two of these structures have important variants. The partnership form has spawned the limited partnership and the registered limited liability partnership. And the corporation can be recognized, for tax purposes, as either the standard C corporation, in which the corporation and its owners are treated as separate taxpaying entities, or as an S corporation, in which business income is passed through the corporate entity and taxed only to its owners on their individual tax returns.

Choosing the legal structure for your business is one of your important decisions. The analysis we present here should help you make a good decision.

1. Sole Proprietorship

A sole proprietor is the sole owner of a business. Employees may be hired and may even receive a percentage of the profits as wages. The owner is personally liable for all the debts and taxes of the business, as well as for any injuries caused to or by the employees acting within the scope of their employment. The owner is entitled to retain the profits of the business and must include them on his or her individual income tax returns and pay taxes on them.

2. Partnership

A partnership is a business owned by two or more people. The owners may or may not have a written partnership agreement specifying their respective rights and liabilities. A simple verbal agreement is enough to create a partnership. Either partner is an "agent" for the partnership and can individually hire employees, borrow money and do any act necessary to the operation of the business. Unless otherwise agreed upon, the partners share equally in the profits and, although the partnership entity is required to report its income on a separate, informational tax return, the partners themselves include these profits on their individual tax returns and pay taxes on them.

Each partner is personally liable for the debts and taxes of the partnership. This means that if the partnership assets are insufficient to satisfy a creditor's claim, the partners' personal assets are subject to attachment and liquidation to pay the business debts. A partnership, unless otherwise agreed to, terminates upon the death, disability or withdrawal of any one of the partners.

One final point about partnerships—the law allows a special kind of partnership, called a *limited partnership*. A limited partner, in conjunction with one or more general partners (the kind discussed above), is allowed to invest in a partnership without the risk of incurring personal liability for the debts of the business. If the business goes under, all she can lose is her capital investment (the amount of money or other property she paid for her interest in the business). However, as a general rule, the limited partner is not allowed to participate in the management of the business. This kind of partnership cannot be set up by verbal agreement alone; the state requires a bit of paperwork to get it started.

LLCs and RLLPs: Two new business entities have arrived on the scene in California. One is the *limited liability company*, an entity that is taxed like a partnership but gives limited liability protection to all owners (like a corporation). Unfortunately, the trial lawyers lobby has been successful in blocking the use of this entity for professionals, and anyone who renders licensed professional services in California cannot, at present, form an

LLC (but watch for changes in the law to open the LLC up for use by professionals too). Of course, lawyers and accountants carry clout in the California legislature, and were able to pass legislation that allows *attorneys and accountants* to register their general partnerships as *registered limited liability partnerships* (RLLPs). Recently, architects were added to the short list of professions that could convert their general partnership to an RLLP. The RLLP, like the LLC, gives the limited liability protection to all employees in the firm, and protects these professionals from vicarious personal liability for the malpractice of other professionals in the RLLP practice (but not for their own malpractice or for those whom they supervise). The net result: to achieve legal benefits similar to forming an LLC or RLLP, all other professionals must still form a professional corporation. This doesn't get you the benefit of partnership taxation, but does let you achieve the same measure of protection from personal liability for normal business claims and the malpractice of others in your firm.

Summing Up Non-Corporate Alternatives: These non-corporate ways of doing business (the sole proprietorship or partnership) have the advantage of requiring little, if any, preliminary red tape. Complete control of the management of the business is held in the hands of the business owners. However, doing business this way can be risky. This is because the owners (except in the case of a limited partner) are personally liable for the debts of the business. One substantial malpractice award or business claim can wipe out most, or all, of the professional partners' personal assets. In addition, non-corporate ways of doing business often result in reduced flexibility in tax planning (e.g., all profits of the partnership are passed through and taxed to the partners each year).

The death of the owner or owners of a small business also raises problems for the sole proprietorship or partnership. It often means the end of a business which has been built up after years of hard work. While the death of a central figure is also likely to cause problems for the small corporation, the formal structure of the corporation often makes the continuance or sale of the business easier.

It is true, particularly with the partnership form, that some of the problems associated with non-corporate business forms can be solved by careful planning and by the use of custom-tailored, written business agreements (if you are interested in doing this, see the very excellent *The Partnership Book*, by Denis Clifford & Ralph Warner, (Nolo) or *Nolo's Partnership Maker* software, a program that allows you to prepare a partnership agreement on your computer). However, this sort of good planning and attention to detail is rare, particularly during the beginning stages of the partnership. All too often, the lack of minimal day-to-day business formalities contributes to hasty business decisions and poor planning. Let's look at the characteristics of the corporate form and see how they overcome some of these problems.

3. The Corporation

A corporation is a statutory creature, created and regulated by state laws. If you want the *privilege* (that's what the courts call it) of turning your business enterprise into a California corporation, you must follow the requirements of the California Corporations Code (professional corporations also have to comply with additional laws as explained in Chapter 2). However, what sets the corporate entity apart from all other types of businesses, and what makes it special for legal, practical and tax purposes, is that the corporation is a legal entity separate from any of the people who own, control, manage or operate it. It is, in fact, a legal *person* capable of entering into contracts, incurring debts and paying taxes. It is this separateness, this distinction between the business entity and the people who own the business (the shareholders), from which many of the advantages of the corporate entity flow.

For example, unlike sole proprietorships and partnerships, the corporation is a separate taxable entity. Business income can be sheltered in the corporation and reported and taxed at the business (corporate) level only, in accordance with the separate tax year of the corporation. The decision as to how much money should be kept in the business and how much should be paid out to the owners is, moreover, still left in the hands of the real people who own the business. In addition, since the corporation is a separate taxable person, the instant you incorporate your business, you become an employee of your own business, eligible for tax deductible employee fringe benefits. In effect, once you incorporate, you are truly working for yourself.

In addition to allowing you to place some distance between yourself and business income kept in the corporation, incorporation allows you to step back from many of the lawsuits and claims made against your business. Normally, except for the malpractice participated in by a professional (see Chapter 3, Section A1), the liabilities of the business are those of the separate corporate person, not of the real people behind the corporation. These business claims can only reach as far as the business assets of the corporation, not the personal assets of the people who own and operate the corporation. As a result, this double-sided nature of the corporate way of life is a unique, and often advantageous, way to operate a business. We look at the specific advantages of the corporate form in Chapter 3.

B. Kinds of Corporations

California classifies corporations in several, sometimes overlapping, ways. The first classification is *domestic* versus *foreign*. A domestic corporation is one which is formed under the laws of California by filing Articles of Incorporation with the California Secretary of State. A corporation which is formed in another state, even if it is physically present and is doing business in this state, is a foreign corporation.

Corporations can also be classified as stock or non-stock. A stock corporation is simply one which is authorized by its Articles of Incorporation to issue shares of stock. A non-stock corporation is any corporation not so authorized.

In addition to these general classifications, there are special kinds of corporations (divisions of these larger groupings, such as professional and nonprofit corporations). There are special provisions and rules relating to these subgroups.

1. Nonprofit Corporations

A nonprofit corporation is a non-stock corporation formed under the California Nonprofit Corporation Law by one or more persons, for the benefit of the public, the mutual benefit of its members or religious purposes.

Except with respect to mutual benefit nonprofit corporations, the Corporations Code prohibits the distribution of profits to members. Most nonprofit corporations dedicate all corporate assets to another nonprofit corporation upon dissolution to comply with the stricter provisions of state and federal tax laws and to obtain exemptions from payment of corporate income tax (the main reason for organizing a nonprofit corporation). A nonprofit corporation is generally formed for religious, charitable, literary, scientific or educational purposes.

Nonprofit corporations, like regular stock corporations, have directors who manage the business of the corporation. Instead of shares of stock, memberships can be issued whose purchase price, if any, is levied against the members and paid as enrollment fees or dues. Like regular corporations, a nonprofit corporation may sue or be sued, incur debts and obligations, acquire and hold property, and engage, generally, in any lawful activity not inconsistent with its purposes and its nonprofit status. It also provides its directors and members with limited liability for the debts or liabilities of the business and continues perpetually unless steps are taken to terminate it.

Additional Reading: For more information on nonprofit corporations, see *How to Form a Nonprofit Corporation in California*, by Anthony Mancuso (Nolo). Order information can be found at the back of this book.

2. Profit Corporations

There are several types of profit corporations. You are probably most familiar with the large ones with listings on stock exchanges and many thousands or millions of shares of stock. Professional corporations are a special kind of profit corporation, as are close corporations (we review the relationship of close corporations to professional corporations in Chapter 3, Section C9).

C. Corporate Powers

The California Corporations Code gives profit corporations carte blanche to engage in any lawful business activity. Generally, this means that a corporation can do anything that a natural person can do. The Code, by way of illustration and not limitation, lists the following general corporate powers:

- To adopt, use and alter a corporate seal.
- To adopt, amend and repeal Bylaws.
- To qualify to do business in any other state, territory, dependency or foreign country.
- Subject to certain restrictions, to issue, purchase, redeem, receive, take or otherwise acquire, own, hold, sell, lend, exchange, transfer, or otherwise dispose of, pledge, use and otherwise deal in and with its own shares, bonds, debentures and other securities.
- To make donations, regardless of specific corporate benefit, for the public welfare or for community fund, hospital, charitable, educational, scientific or civic or similar purposes.
- To pay pensions, and establish and carry out pension, profit-sharing, share-bonus, share-pension, share-option, savings, thrift, and other retirement, incentive and benefit plans, trusts and provisions for any or all of the directors, officers and employees of the corporation or any of its subsidiary or affiliated corporations and to indemnify and purchase and maintain insurance on behalf of any fiduciary of such plans, trusts or provisions.
- Except with respect to certain restrictions as to loans to directors, officers and employees which we discuss later, to assume obligations, enter into contracts, including contracts of guarantee or suretyship, incur liabilities, borrow and lend money and otherwise use its credit, and secure any of its obligations, contracts or liabilities by mortgage, pledge or other encumbrance of all or any part of its property, franchises and income.
- To participate with others in any partnership, joint venture or other association, transaction or arrangement of any kind, whether or not such participation involves sharing or delegation of control with or to others.

As you will see, there are some restrictions on professional corporations in exercising the above powers, where the integrity of the profession is involved. (See the limited liability section in Chapter 3, and the ownership of another corporation's shares in Chapter 4).

D. Corporate People

While a corporation is a legal person capable of making contracts, paying taxes, etc., it needs real people to carry out its business. These corporate people are classified in the following ways:

- Incorporator
- Director
- Officer
- Shareholder

Note: Distinctions between these different roles often become somewhat blurred in a small professional corporation, since one person may simultaneously serve in more than one, or all, of these capacities.

The courts and the Corporations Code have given these corporate people varying powers and responsibilities. Here we discuss these Code provisions and a few court-developed rules.

1. Incorporators

Legally, an incorporator is a person who signs the Articles of Incorporation which are filed with the Secretary of State when the corporation is formed. In a practical sense, the incorporators are the promoters of the corporation. They are the people who make arrangements for obtaining money, property, people and whatever else the corporation will need to make a go of it. A corporate promoter is considered by law to be a fiduciary of the corporation. This means he or she has a duty to make full disclosure to the corporation of any personal interest in, and potential benefit from, any of the business he or she transacts for the corporation.

EXAMPLE: If the promoter arranges for the sale of property to the corporation in which he or she has an ownership interest, the fact of his or her ownership interest and any personal benefit he or she plans to make on the deal must be disclosed.

The corporation is not bound by the promoter's contracts with third persons prior to actual formation of the corporation unless they are later ratified by the board of directors, or the corporation accepts the benefits of the contract (e.g., uses office space under a lease). A promoter, on the other hand, may be personally liable on these pre-incorporation contracts unless he signs the contract in the name of the corporation only and clearly informs the third party that the corporation does not yet exist, may never come into existence and, even if it does, its board of directors may not ratify the contract.

So, a bit of advice. If you want to arrange for office space, hire employees, or borrow money before corporate formation, make it clear that any commitments you make are for and in the name of a proposed corporation and are subject to ratification by the corporation when it comes into existence. The other party may, of course, refuse to do business with you under these conditions and tell you to come back after the corporation is formed. In any case, it's neater this way.

2. Directors

Except for certain specific decisions which require shareholder approval, the directors are given the authority and responsibility for managing the corporation. The directors meet and make decisions collectively as the board of directors. However, the Corporations Code does permit the board to delegate, by resolution, most of the management of the corporation to an executive committee consisting of two or more directors. This arrangement is often used when one or more directors are unable or unwilling to assume an active voice in corporate affairs and the remaining directors wish to assume full control. The passive directors should still keep an eye on what the other directors are up to as courts sometimes hold them liable for the mismanagement of the active directors. The board of directors may also delegate management of day-to-day operations of the corporation to a management company or other person provided that these people remain under the ultimate control of the board.

Directors, like promoters, are fiduciaries of the corporation and must act in its best interest and exercise care in making management decisions. What does this mean? The Code [Corporations Code Section 309(a)] doesn't help much. It says a director must act "in good faith, in a manner [which the] … director believes to be in the best interests of the corporation and its shareholders and with such care, including reasonable inquiry, as an ordinarily prudent person in a like position would use under similar conditions" (ever wonder what law students find to talk about for three years?). In effect, the Code leaves it up to the courts to define what duty a director owes a corporation. Courts, in turn, usually decide cases on an individual basis. Broadly speaking, however, the courts say honest errors in business judgment are okay, while fraudulent or grossly negligent behavior isn't. The Code specifically allows a director to rely on the apparently reliable reports of attorneys, accountants and corporate officers in arriving at decisions, unless there is some indication of the need for independent inquiry by the director.

The director owes the corporation his loyalty and usually must give the corporation a "right of first refusal" as to business opportunities he becomes aware of in his capacity as a corporate director. If the corporation fails to take advantage of the opportunity after full disclosure (purchase of cheap land, for example), or would clearly not

be interested in it, the director can go ahead for himself.

Directors normally serve without compensation, as their work is usually done in consideration for increasing the earning potential of their stock. Reasonable compensation is allowed, however, if given for the performance of real services to the corporation. A director may be authorized to receive advancement or reimbursement for reasonable out-of-pocket expenses (i.e., travel expenses) incurred in the performance of any of her corporate duties. Any compensation, advancement or reimbursement paid to a director should be authorized in advance of such payments.

The board of directors may properly vote on a matter in which one or more of the directors has a personal interest, provided the following conditions are met:

- The director's interest in the transaction is fully disclosed or known to the board;
- The vote to pass the resolution is sufficient without counting the vote of the interested director;
- The contract or transaction is just and reasonable as to the corporation.

The Code contains additional rules and procedures which can be used to validate actions which benefit directors (see Corp. Code Section 310).

Subject to some exceptions, if the corporation lends money or property to, or guarantees the obligations of, directors, these transactions must be approved by the shareholders (by a majority vote of the shares not counting those held by benefited directors or by the unanimous vote of all shareholders)—see Section 316 of the Corporations Code. Of course, full disclosure of the nature and extent of the benefit to the directors should be made to the shareholders prior to taking the shareholder votes.

If a director violates one of the above rules, in that she grossly mismanages or takes advantage of the corporation, receives unauthorized or unwarranted compensation, or participates in unauthorized or unfair transactions, she can be subject to personal financial liability for any losses to the corporation, shareholders and creditors of the corporation. In addition to actual damages, she can also be subject to monetary penalties awarded as a part of a lawsuit (punitive damages), be temporarily or permanently ousted from the directorship and, in certain cases, be subject to criminal penalties.

It is interesting, and possibly a little comforting, to note that a corporation can purchase insurance to cover legal expenses, judgments, fines, settlements and other amounts incurred in connection with a lawsuit brought against a director for breach of duty to the corporation, its creditors or shareholders, or simply because of his status as a director of the corporation. Insurance coverage or not, however, the corporation must reimburse (indemnify) a director for legal expenses if he is sued and wins the suit, except for suits brought by or in the name of the corporation.

The statutory indemnification rules (contained in Section 317 of the Corporations Code) become a bit more complicated if the director is seeking indemnification for judgments, fines, or settlements, or if she loses the suit. In the very rare eventuality that you face this sort of situation, you should consult an attorney.

Note: California has enacted special director immunity and indemnification rules which help insulate directors from personal liability for a breach of duty to the corporation and its shareholders. See the box below for a short discussion of these rules.

Reality Note: Of course, if you are forming your own professional corporation, much of the discussion in this and the subsequent sections regarding formal corporate director, officer and shareholder procedures will not apply to you. For example, formal director's meetings will probably be held infrequently (the tear-out Bylaws in this book provide for an annual meeting of the Board of Directors). Further, professional corporations do not need to be as concerned with the various legal provisions which seek to protect the interests of minority or outside-investor shareholders: in the professional corporation, only licensed professionals may hold shares in the corporation.

3. Officers

Officers (president, vice president, secretary, treasurer) are in charge of carrying out the day-to-day business of the corporation. Their powers, duties and responsibilities are set out by the Articles, Bylaws or board of directors. Like directors, officers owe a fiduciary duty to the corporation and are subject to the same requirement of acting honestly and in the best interests of the corporation. Although not specified by statute, this day-to-day authority of officers should not include authority to enter into certain major business transactions which are generally understood to remain within the sole province of the board of directors, e.g., the mortgage or resale of corporate property. Special authority should be delegated to the officers by the board for these, and other, major transactions.

Officers are considered agents of the corporation and can subject the corporation to liability for their negligent or intentional acts which cause damage to people or property if such acts were performed within the course and scope of their employment. The corporation, moreover, is bound by the contracts and obligations entered into or incurred by the corporate officers if they had *legal* authority to transact the business. This authority can be actual authority (a Bylaw provision or resolution by the board of directors), implied authority (a necessary but unspecified part of duties set out in the Bylaws or board resolution) or apparent authority (a third party reasonably thinks the officer has certain authority).

Apparent authority is a tricky concept. What does it mean? The California Corporations Code defines the far-reaching nature of this apparent authority. Section 313 of the Code allows any third party to rely on the signature of the president, vice president, secretary or assistant secretary, chief financial officer, or assistant treasurer on any written instrument, whether or not this officer had any [actual or implied] authority to sign the instrument on the part of the corporation, as long as the third party did not actually know that the corporate officer didn't have the authority to sign it.

Note: Of course, any act performed by an officer without the legal authority discussed above binds the corporation if the corporation accepts the benefits of the transaction, or the board of directors ratifies it after the fact.

Corporate officers may be compensated for their services to the corporation. The compensation must be reasonable and given for services actually performed for the corporation.

EXAMPLE: Jason Horner and Elmore Johnson form their professional corporation. Jason is the President and Elmore is the Treasurer of the corporation. Jason and Elmore are not paid as officers of the corporation. Rather, each is paid as a salaried professional practitioner working for the corporation. The point here is that the title of the person being paid is not critical (officer title versus an employee title). What does matter is the nature and extent of the work for which the person is being compensated.

The same rules as to loans and guarantees discussed in the section on directors are also applicable to officers. Officers, like directors, can be insured or indemnified against personal liability under the same rules discussed in the last section (additional nonstatutory indemnification may also be authorized for officers by including special language in the Articles of Incorporation—see the sibebar below entitled "Special California Director Immunity and Indemnification Provisions").

Again, when reading this material, remember our earlier reality note: Professional corporations do not have outside shareholders (all shareholders must be licensed professionals) and much of the following discussion will not directly apply to you. Also realize that the directors of professional corporations are not likely to wish to pay themselves dividends, preferring instead to compensate themselves directly as employees by way of deductible salaries and bonuses.

SPECIAL CALIFORNIA DIRECTOR IMMUNITY AND INDEMNIFICATION PROVISIONS

Provisions of the General Corporation Law (Corp. Code. Secs. 204(a)(10) and (11) and 204.5) allow California corporations to include language in their Articles limiting or eliminating the personal liability of directors, as directors, for monetary damages, in suits brought by or in the right of the corporation for breach of a director's duties to the corporation and its shareholders. Similarly, California corporations can include language in their Articles authorizing the corporation to indemnify (pay back) directors for legal expenses, fines, judgments and other amounts beyond the limits contain in California's corporate indemnification statute (Corp. Code §317). Note that these special statutes list specific situations in which immunity and indemnification cannot be provided (e.g., in cases of intentional misconduct or a knowing violation of law). These director immunity and indemnification provisions are usually of less concern to professional corporations which do not have outside shareholders and do not engage in business beyond the scope of the professional practice (of course, professionals can always be held personally liable for their own malpractice and for the malpractice of others under their supervision and control). If you wish to explore these special immunity and indemnification provisions, please consult a lawyer.

4. Shareholders

Shareholders are generally not considered fiduciaries of the corporation and therefore have no responsibility to the corporation beyond paying the corporation the full value of the shares they purchase. In some cases, however, courts have treated *majority* stockholders as fiduciaries of the corporation with a duty of full disclosure and fairness to the corporation in the transfer of their majority interests to outsiders.

Shareholders vote for the board of directors and do, therefore, have an indirect voice in the management of the corporation. In addition, the Corporations Code requires shareholder approval of certain corporate acts, including, with some exceptions:

- The amendment of the Articles of Incorporation after the issuance of stock;
- The sale, option or lease or other disposition of all or substantially all of the corporate assets other than in the usual and regular course of its business, except for mortgages and the like given to secure corporate obligations;
- A decision with respect to certain mergers of the corporation with another, or other, reorganizations.

Shareholder approval must, in some cases, or may, in others, be sought with respect to loans, guarantees or indemnifications given by the corporation in favor of an officer or director. Shareholders also have the power to act independently of the board of directors in certain limited situations, the most important, aside from electing directors, being a unilateral shareholder decision to:

- Amend the bylaws of the corporation;
- Remove directors from the Board;
- Dissolve the corporation.

In the absence of provisions to the contrary contained in the Articles or Bylaws, shareholders are given one vote per share, with a majority vote usually necessary to decide an issue subject to shareholder approval. Shareholders whose names appear on the record books of the corporation as of a certain date specified by the board of directors are entitled to vote on the matter in question. This record date must be no more than 60, nor less than 10, days prior to the shareholder meeting.

Aside from the limited participation in corporate affairs discussed above, shareholders' rights primarily include the right to participate in the profits of the corporation through dividends and the right to participate, after the creditors are paid, in the liquidation proceeds of a dissolved corporation.

A shareholder, like any other person, can sue the corporation for personal wrongs and damages suffered on account of corporate action. If, however, the shareholder is damaged in his or her capacity as a shareholder (wasting of corporate assets by the officers or directors, which devalues stock), the law says that the real injury is to the corporation. An injured shareholder, in this case, must ask the board of directors to bring suit or take the appropriate action. Of course, where the damage was caused by the mismanagement, negligence or fraud of the officers or directors, the shareholder is, in effect, asking them to take action against themselves and, as you might guess, this doesn't always bring immediate results.

If the shareholder can't get the officers or directors to bring suit, as in the situation described above, or if an attempt to get them to do this through intra-corporate channels would be futile, the shareholder can bring suit in his or her own name. This legal action is called a shareholder's derivative suit since, as the theory goes, the shareholder derives the right to sue from, and on behalf of, the corporation which is considered to be the party sustaining the injury. The corporation, somewhat inconsistently, is required to be named as a defendant along with the officers and directors who are responsible for the alleged damage. The court does, however, treat the corporation as the co-plaintiff of the shareholder for whose benefit the suit is brought. If, after initiation of the suit by the shareholder, the officers or directors decide to bring the action themselves, against those who are responsible for the injury, the court will dismiss the shareholder's derivative suit and litigate the case in this second action. ■

Chapter 2

THE PROFESSIONAL CORPORATION

A. Introduction

Many professionals have incorporated their businesses. Many more are considering whether it is wise to do so. If you are reading this book, you are probably one of this group. The first thing you need to know is that only the members of certain professions (listed in Section B below) *need* to incorporate under the California Moscone-Knox Professional Corporation Act as a professional corporation. If you are a member of any other profession and you wish to incorporate, you should do so as a regular business corporation under the California General Corporation Law. (See *How to Form Your Own California Corporation,* by Anthony Mancuso (Nolo)—order information is included at the back of this book.)

B. Professions Required to Incorporate as Professional Corporations

- Accountants
- Acupuncturists
- Architects*
- Attorneys (Law)
- (Licensed) Clinical Social Workers
- Chiropractors
- Dentists
- Doctors (Medical Doctors including Surgeons)
- Marriage, Family and Child Counselors
- Nurses
- Optometrists
- Osteopaths
- Pharmacists
- Physical Therapists
- Physicians' Assistants
- Podiatrists
- Psychologists
- Shorthand Reporters
- Speech Pathologists and Audiologists
- Veterinarians*

Note: Architects and veterinarians have the option to incorporate as either regular business corporations or as professional corporations (when we called the State Board of Architectural Examiners, a taped message referred us to the Secretary of State for information on forming a professional architectural corporation—see Appendix 4 for further information). Also, recent legislation allows architects to convert an architectural general partnership into a registered limited liability partnership (by making a simple filing with the Secretary of State—call the Architectural Board of Examiners in Sacramento for further information). To avoid extra formalities associated with the formation of a professional corporation, architects and veterinarians often choose to incorporate as regular business corporations (not as professional corporations).

C. Why Become a Professional Corporation?

Most readers of this book are currently doing business as either a sole proprietorship or a partnership. You have probably heard that the corporate form provides advantages. Often it does, but it depends to a significant degree on who you are, what your business is like, how much you earn, etc., and it's impossible to provide any simple formula as to exactly what corporate status will do for you. Here are some of the considerations that many professionals who have incorporated point to when asked why they decided to change the way their businesses were organized. We will discuss these in more detail later in Chapters 3 and 4:

- Limited liability for business claims and for malpractice claims against other professionals in the practice (though professionals do not have limited liability for their own malpractice—see Chapter 3, Section A1);
- Fringe benefits are, for the most part, deductible from the corporation's income;
- Corporate retirement plans which are more liberal in some respects than IRAs and Keoghs;
- Establish order in your business;
- Tax flexibility [control over how much individual income (salary) each professional will earn and report on federal and state tax returns; for some professionals, profits kept in the practice may be taxed at lower corporate rates];
- Perpetual corporate existence.

D. How Will Your Corporation Be Set Up?

A professional corporation can be any size. Thus, even a sole practitioner can incorporate—and in fact, many self-employed professionals do. If you are a professional partnership, the partnership itself can incorporate (providing all the partners are qualified licensed professionals —see Chapter 4). There is also the possibility of some, or even all, of the members of a partnership individually incorporating. The partnership will then become a partnership made up of both professional corporations and unincorporated professionals. For example, we know of a pediatrics partnership consisting of five pediatricians. Two of the pediatricians have incorporated themselves as professional corporations while the other three pediatricians have remained as unincorporated members of the partnership. (Notice that pediatricians are medical doctors and thus fall within the Professional Corporation Law.)

No matter how your professional corporation is set up, it will generally render service in a single profession (Corporations Code Section 13401). There are some exceptions whereby persons licensed in specified related professions may also be shareholders, directors, and/or officers of certain professional corporations (see Chapter 4, Sections D and E) and perform their own professional services (Corporations Code Section 13401.5).

E. California Law Covering Professional Corporations

California has a set of statutes called the General Corporation Law (GCL), a portion of the California Corporations Code relating to regular profit corporations. Anyone who wishes to incorporate must comply with these laws. However, members of certain professions must also comply with the Moscone-Knox Professional Corporation Act—another part of the Corporations Code, the Business and Professions Code, and with various administrative regulations issued by the agencies governing these professions (see Chapter 4 and Appendix 4).

F. What Agency Supervises Your Profession?

As you are no doubt aware, your profession is regulated by a California agency. The agency, its address and phone number and, where available, the website, are included in Appendix 4 to this book. BE SURE TO CONTACT THE AGENCY BEFORE YOU FILE YOUR ARTICLES OF INCORPORATION. The agency will provide some information, though you will find that some agencies are more helpful than others. The agency will provide an application form if you need a certificate of registration (see Chapter 4), and possibly keep you up to date on the latest changes in the law. Except for the State Bar (whose office is in San Francisco), the main offices of these agencies are in Sacramento. If you are seriously thinking about incorporating, you should contact the agency now.

G. Specific Requirements Covering the Incorporation of Your Profession

Though California law establishes general requirements which professionals must meet to incorporate, the agencies supervising the professions issue regulations defining additional requirements for each profession. Appendix 4 to this book sets out some of these basic rules (such as whether you need liability insurance, what names you can use, and who can own shares in the corporation) with citations to the law and regulations which apply. Be sure to refer to Appendix 4 before you begin incorporating. For a general discussion of the requirements, see Chapter 4. ■

ADVANTAGES, DISADVANTAGES, AND OTHER CONSIDERATIONS

A. Advantages

In Chapter 1, Section A, we compared the basic characteristics of unincorporated and incorporated businesses. Let's look a little more closely at some of the advantages of incorporating as a professional corporation.

1. Limited Liability

No doubt you have heard that the chief reason many people incorporate their business is to limit their liability. What this means is that the owners (i.e., the people who own shares in the corporation) cannot lose more of their personal assets than the amount they contributed to the corporation in exchange for their shares. This is unlike the situation in a partnership or sole proprietorship, where a creditor can go after the partner's or sole proprietor's personal assets, such as his or her home, car or savings account. Of course, now that regular businesses can form a limited liability company, which, like a corporation, protects all owners from personal liability for business debts and claims, this corporate characteristic has lost its uniqueness. But since professionals cannot currently form a California LLC (again, watch for changes in the law), the professional corporation still provides the only way for most professionals to limit their personal liability for business claims (lawyers, accountants and architects also have the option to change their general partnership to a registered limited liability partnership—see Chapter 1).

There are important exceptions to this rule of corporate (and LLC or RLLP) limited liability. For example, when a bank or other financial institution lends money to a small corporation, it may require that the people who own the corporation (the shareholders) independently pledge their personal assets as security for the debt. Be aware that if you do this you have waived the shield of limited liability as far as this particular debt is concerned.

Another common situation where limited liability may not protect corporate officers or directors is when the corporation has failed to pay income, payroll or other taxes. The IRS and the state Franchise Tax Board do not recognize the concept of limited liability in this instance and attempt to recover unpaid taxes from "responsible" employees (those charged explicitly or implicitly with reporting and paying corporate tax amounts) if they can't collect these taxes from the corporation. In other words, make sure to withhold, deposit, report and pay corporate income and employment taxes on time. Further information on ongoing corporate taxes is provided in Chapter 7.

Moreover, the limited liability advantage doesn't fully apply to professionals who incorporate as professional corporations. Since, traditionally, professionals have been held to a very high degree of responsibility for their own negligence, the law will not protect a professional from being personally liable for her malpractice or those of others under her supervision or control. Thus, a doctor who is organized as a professional corporation and who loses a malpractice suit can be required to pay the judgment out of her personal assets, as well as corporate assets. Of course, many practitioners have malpractice insurance to cover themselves. But in case they don't, the law will hold them personally liable.

A professional can also be personally liable for the malpractice of another professional shareholder in the corporation. But here, the non-culpable professional is protected if the corporation carries the minimum insurance required by that profession's laws and regulations. (Not all professions are required to carry adequate security—see Chapter 4, Section G. Law and accounting corporations require a written agreement guaranteeing payment, though insurance can cover it.) Then, should the judgment award be for more than the amount of the insurance policy, only the professionals who committed or participated in the malpractice act are personally liable.

Indirect Participation in Malpractice Acts: A professional may participate in a malpractice act indirectly. For example, a professional who is responsible for reviewing the work of another professional, or who consults with the other professional on the matter, may be found to have participated in the act and therefore to be responsible for any malpractice of the other professional.

Partnerships of Incorporated Professionals: Questions have been raised as to whether a professional who incorporates and enters into a partnership with other incorporated professionals can avoid responsibility for the malpractice of one of the other professionals in the partnership, even up to the required minimum amounts. The argument is that since the corporation is the partner, only it is liable and the individual professional shareholder (who really is only an employee of the corporation) is not. Since corporate assets in professional corporations can sometimes be minimal, a professional in this situation can possibly even further limit his/her liability. We suggest you obtain personal advice from an attorney if you are interested in pursuing this rather devious practice.

The corporate structure, however, will protect the professional from personal liability for non-malpractice incidents, business claims and other corporate debts. For example, if someone slips on the floor of an incorporated professional's office, limited liability rules would apply and the professional's personal assets should be protected.

Note: Accountants, lawyers and architects can get the same type of legal protection plus the benefit of partnership taxation by registering their partnership as an RLLP. See Chapter 1.

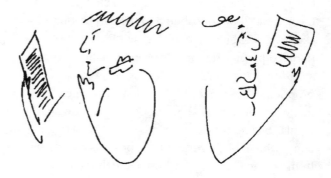

2. Taxation

In this section, we examine some of the important tax issues you'll need to consider before you incorporate.

a. Income Taxation

Federal Corporate Income Tax: The federal government taxes the first $50,000 of taxable corporate income at 15%, the next $25,000 at 25%, and the remainder of taxable income over $75,000 at 35%. To make larger corporations pay back the benefits of these lower graduated tax rates, corporate taxable incomes between $100,000 and $335,000 are subject to an additional 5% tax (and highly profitable corporations with taxable incomes over $10 million pay a 35% rate). We have included a comparison of corporate and individual tax rates as they apply to owners of small corporations in Subsection b, below.

Maximum Corporate Tax Rate on Certain Personal Service Corporations: Under recent provisions of the Internal Revenue Code, the taxable income of certain personal service corporations is taxed at a flat corporate tax rate of 35% (the lower 15% and 25% federal corporate tax brackets do not apply to these corporations). Specifically, this flat maximum federal corporate tax rate is applied to corporations (1) where substantially all the stock of the corporation is held by the employees performing professional services for the corporation and (2) where substantially all the activities of the corporation involve the performance of services in one of the following professions or activities:

- health
- law
- engineering
- architecture
- accounting
- actuarial science
- performing arts
- consulting

For a further explanation of the types of corporations that are subject to this 35% tax rate, see the boxed discussion below.

It's important to realize that even if this flat tax provision applies to you (because you are forming a professional—or even a regular business—corporation engaged in one of the above fields and all of your corporation's stock will be owned by the professionals), this doesn't mean that you will be paying 35% of your income to the IRS each year—this tax only applies to any taxable income left in the corporation at the end of the corporate tax year. If, like many professionals, you have no need to accumulate money in your corporation and prefer to pass corporate profits to yourself each year in the form of a deductible salary, fringe benefits, a substantial contribution to your pension plan, etc., then this tax provision will have little, if any, impact on your corporation's tax liability. Further, if you do end your corporate tax year with income left in the corporation and wish to avoid the imposition of this tax, electing federal S corporation tax status will pass corporate profits to you automatically each year and avoid corporate level taxes altogether (however, this election will limit your ability to pay yourself deductible fringe benefits—see Section 3, below).

Note that this special flat tax provision applies to the same professions and activities to which the lower federal corporate accumulated earnings credit of $150,000 applies (see Section C5, below).

Federal Individual Income Tax: The federal government taxes corporate profits when distributed to shareholders as dividends or salaries. The shareholders must pay individual income tax on the amounts received. As we've mentioned earlier, however, since the payment of dividends results in double taxation (the income is taxed to both the corporation and the shareholder), owners of small corporations normally use one of several methods to get money out of the corporation without being subject to double taxation. When the owner works for the corporation, the simplest is to pay out corporate profits in the form of deductible salaries, bonuses and benefits rather than in dividends. As long as salaries aren't unreasonable and the benefits are paid in accordance with IRS guidelines, the IRS should have no objection. Of course, money paid in salaries and bonuses and qualified corporate fringe benefits can be deducted by the corporation and thus is not taxed to the corporation, only to the individual.

California Corporate Franchise Tax: A California profit corporation is subject to an annual corporate franchise tax. This is an annual fee which is paid to the state for the privilege of doing business as a corporation. The tax is computed each year on the basis of your corporation's previous year's net income derived from business activity in California (and sometimes, outside California). The California franchise tax rate is 8.84% of the corporation's taxable income, with a minimum yearly payment required regardless of the amount of annual income or profits. A newly formed corporation is exempt from paying the minimum

$800 franchise tax for its first and second tax years, but it must pay the minimum amount starting with its third tax year.

California Personal Income Tax: California does, of course, impose a personal income tax. As with the federal tax scheme, double taxation at the California level is unlikely to occur since professional corporations pay their owners deductible salaries and fringe benefits, not nondeductible dividends.

California S Corporation Tax Election: California corporations that are qualified for, and have elected, federal S corporation tax status are eligible for S corporation tax treatment in California (but if you have formed more than one corporation and have to file a combined state tax report for your corporations, you may not be eligible for California S corporation tax status). This state tax election parallels the federal S corporation tax election and allows the corporation to avoid the full California corporate franchise tax rate (8.84%) on state corporate net taxable income, passing the corporation's taxable California income through to the individual state tax returns of the corporation's shareholders. We explain the advantages and disadvantages of the S corporation tax election in detail in Section C7, below. For now let's note a few special requirements of the California S corporation tax election:

CORPORATIONS SUBJECT TO FLAT 35% TAX RATE

Treasury Regulation §1.448-1T(e)(4) contains definitions and examples of the types of "qualified personal service corporations" engaged in health, consulting and the performing arts fields which are subject to a flat corporate tax rate of 35%. Let's look at a few of the rules contained in this regulation:

Health Services. This means the providing of services by physicians, nurses, dentists and other similar heath care professionals. This category does not include the performance of services unrelated to the health of the person who receives services. For example, the operation of health clubs or spas that provide physical exercise or conditioning is not included in this category.

Consulting Services. This means giving advice and counsel and does not include sales, brokerage or economically similar services. The manner in which the corporation (or other person) is compensated for services (e.g., whether the compensation is contingent on sales or some other factor) will help determine whether the services are considered consulting or sales.

The regulation includes examples of services which will or will not be considered consulting services. One example is a taxpayer (corporation) that determines a client's data processing needs after studying the client's business and focusing on the types of data and information relevant to the business and the needs of the client's employees to access this information. The taxpayer does not provide the client with computer hardware or additional computer programming services—just recommendations regarding the design and implementation of data processing systems to be purchased elsewhere. The taxpayer is considered to be engaged in consulting services (and will be subject to a flat corporate tax rate of 35%).

This regulation contains definitions and clarifications of other terms used in Section 448(d)(2) to determine if a corporation is subject to a 35% flat tax rate (and is subject to other provisions of the IRC). You or your accountant should consult this regulation for further information.

- As opposed to federal S corporation tax status where the S corporation does not normally pay any federal corporate income taxes, California S corporations must still pay the California Franchise Tax Board a 1.5% tax on net California corporate income and must pay the minimum corporate franchise tax each year beginning with the corporation's third tax year (the minimum annual payment is credited against the S corporation's 1.5% corporate tax liability for the year).

- If your California S corporation has out-of-state shareholders, each must file a consent with the California Franchise Tax Board agreeing to be subject to California taxes on his or her pro rata share of the corporation's income which is attributable to California sources.

- The Franchise Tax Board automatically presumes that corporations that have elected federal S corporation tax treatment have also elected S corporation status in California unless they specifically elect not to be treated as an S corporation in California (by filing FTB form 3560).

Is California S corporation tax status worthwhile? For most professional corporations, the answer is "no" since S corporations are restricted in paying deductible fringe benefits to the shareholder-employees of the corporation (see Section 3, below). Also, if a California S corporation has taxable earnings, then it will be subject to double taxation: the corporation will pay a 1.5% tax on its taxable income; the shareholders will pay California personal taxes on this same income when it is passed through to them. Of course, if your intention when electing California S corporate status is to pass corporate losses (rather than profits) through to your shareholders (where the losses can be deducted personally by the shareholders), then California S corporate status makes sense. However, most personal service corporations will not generate losses to pass through to shareholders, even in the beginning years of corporate life. We suggest you check with your accountant if you are considering making a state (or federal) S corporation tax election.

b. Tax Planning and Financial Flexibility

In this section, we take a preliminary look at some of the tax aspects of incorporating which can provide a significant amount of financial flexibility to the owners of an incorporated professional practice.

Splitting Personal and Business Income. Incorporating a business you actively participate in allows you to split business income between two tax entities, the corporation and yourself, as an employee-shareholder, in order to obtain the most favorable (smallest) tax rate on this income. You can pay salaries to yourself and other employees which will be taxed at individual tax rates while retaining earnings in the corporation which

will be taxed at the potentially lower corporate tax rates of 15% or 25% (provided, of course, that your corporation is not subject to the flat 35% tax that applies to certain personal service corporations as discussed earlier).

This feature of income splitting is no longer unique to the corporate way of life—limited liability companies, registered limited liability partnerships, partnerships and sole proprietorships also have the ability to elect corporate tax treatment with the IRS by filing IRS Form 8832, "Entity Classification Election." However, most unincorporated businesses do not make this election since doing so involves keeping corporate-like books and filing corporate tax returns—formalities these businesses are not accustomed to following. With the corporate form, this tax status (and tax complexity) is built in.

If you anticipate, or find, that net corporate taxable income (corporate income remaining after subtracting all deductions including business expenses, salaries, bonuses, depreciation, etc.) is significant and will be subject to more taxes at the corporate level than if taxed to you and the other shareholders personally, your corporation may wish to elect S corporation tax status—as explained in Section C7, below, this election passes corporate income through to your shareholders where it is reported and taxed on their individual tax returns only (S corporation tax status, however, does limit the availability of corporate fringe benefits to the shareholders-employees of the corporation).

A Comparison of Individual and Corporate Tax Rates and Payments for Owners of Certain Professional Corporations. If your professional corporation is not subject to a flat 35% corporate tax rate (as discussed in subsection a, above), you may find that your corporation pays less taxes on business income than you would pay as an individual or as a partner. There are two basic reasons for this corporate advantage:

- Regular corporate tax rates on taxable incomes of $75,000 or less are 15% on the first $50,000, and 25% on the next 25,000, as opposed to the 15%, 28% and 31% individual rates for similar income levels; and

- More importantly, while individual rates jump to 28% and higher at modest levels of taxable income (individual tax rates increase to 36% and 39.6%, and even higher due to the phase out of exemptions and deductions for higher-income individuals), the lower regular corporate rates stay in effect for the first $75,000 of taxable income.

Taking all this into consideration (and again ignoring personal service corporations subject to the 35% flat corporate tax rate), the result is that a fairly high level of corporate taxable income must be reached before it makes sense for a corporation to choose to have all corporate income taxed at individual rates (by normal income splitting techniques or by electing S corporation tax status) rather than the standard corporate rates. Remem-

ber, since salaries, employee fringes and other expenses of doing business are deducted by the corporation before computing taxable income, it is customary for many smaller corporations to report lower than $150,000 in taxable income.

S Corporation Tax Note: These special corporate fringe benefits are not available to 2% or greater shareholders in S corporations. (See the discussion below and Section C7 of this chapter.)

S Corporation Tax Election. An added tax flexibility allowed to many corporations is the ability to have profits and losses pass through the corporation directly to the shareholders and reported on their individual federal tax returns (in effect, to be taxed as a partnership) by electing S corporation tax status. This election may be appropriate if the owners of the business find that corporate taxes on income left in the business are greater than individual taxes on the same income. By electing S corporation status, they can avail themselves of the lower federal individual income tax rates while retaining the legal and other financial benefits of the corporation.

Further, S corporation tax status can be revoked in later years when the corporate owners decide that this tax election is no longer in their best interests. There are other incidental, and often substantial, benefits of electing S corporation tax status. For example, S corporation profits which are not paid out as salaries to the owners are automatically passed through to the owners and are not subject to Social Security tax withholding. Again, see Section C7 for further information on federal S corporations.

Other Benefits and Considerations. There are several other unique tax advantages of the corporate form. Foremost for professionals is the ability to set up a corporate retirement plan. Another benefit is the ability, in some cases, to establish a tax year for the corporation which is different from the individual tax years of the professionals in the practice. Each of these benefits is discussed further below.

The corporate form is also advantageous in that it "lends" itself to a number of arrangements for the borrowing of funds for business operations. Lending institutions are familiar with the various types of debt instruments which have been developed through the years to provide corporations with funds and the risk-conscious corporate lender with special preferences. Examples include corporate bonds (secured promissory notes) and debentures (unsecured notes) which can confer voting or management rights on the lender or can be convertible by the lender into shares which carry special dividend, liquidation or other rights.

There is one technical tax rule that may make it disadvantageous to incorporate under some circumstances. At the risk of totally confusing you with legal gobbledygook, this is called the repeal of the General Utilities doctrine and it affects who pays taxes on gains from business liquidation.

Simply put, this doctrine may mean that both the corporation and its shareholders may have to pay taxes when the corporation is sold or dissolved.

While this sounds bad (why incorporate if you're going to get taxed twice if you wind up a profitable practice?), there are a number of reasons why this does not normally produce this unhappy result for smaller corporations. Here are two: First, this corporate tax rule only applies toward appreciated assets held by the corporation. Many corporations (particularly those that provide professional services) do not hold significant assets which have appreciated during the life of the corporation (often the fair market value of assets will decrease rather than increase) and will not be subject to this corporate level tax even if they do liquidate. Second, if a corporation anticipates that its assets (such as real estate) will appreciate, it may elect federal S corporation tax treatment prior to any substantial appreciation and avoid this corporate tax since appreciation occurring while the corporation maintains its S corporation tax status is generally not taxable under this rule. Please check with your accountant for further information on this technical area of corporate taxation.

Summing Up. Of course, these are just some of the tax provisions which apply to professional corporations. The relative importance of these special provisions will vary from one business to another and, although there are several "rules of thumb" concerning the best time to incorporate a business (which change in step with constantly changing tax rates), we feel that the only sound advice we can give you is to sit down with your accountant or financial planner and determine if the corporate form will really be advantageous from a tax and financial viewpoint, based upon a careful examination of your own unique situation, taking into account such factors as:

- Your corporate tax rates (graduated rates or a flat 35%);
- The specific sources and amount of income and expenses associated with your particular business;
- The amount of money you will wish to continue to receive individually (as a corporate salary);
- The nature and extent of deductible fringe benefits (including a corporate retirement plan) you wish to provide for yourself;
- The amount of money you wish to keep in the corporation to meet the future needs of your business (or simply to shelter from individual taxation).

The taxable bottom line for each professional corporation (and each incorporator) will, of course, vary according to the specific circumstances of each business and each incorporator. Moreover, tax considerations are just one factor in arriving at your decision to incorporate. Typically, the corporate advantages of limited liability (at least until the LLC or RLLP form is available to all professions in California), the availability of a corporate retirement plan and special corporate fringe benefits to the owner-employees of the corporation, and the certainty and formality of the corporate form as a means of acquiring and disposing of ownership interests in the incorporated business through stock ownership are often of equal or greater importance in arriving at the decision to incorporate.

3. Fringe Benefits

By incorporating, you are considered an employee of your corporation. This gives you distinct advantages. The corporation can provide you (as employee) with hefty fringe benefits and deduct their cost from the corporation's income as a business expense. These include:

a. Retirement Plans

Many professionals used to incorporate just to take advantage of the opportunity to increase the amount they are allowed to contribute to their retirement plans. Although corporate pension and profit sharing plans are now, for the most part, similar in terms of their advantages to noncorporate Keogh plans, corporate plans still provide the added advantage of allowing plan participants to borrow as much as $50,000 of the funds contributed to the plan without penalty. Also, corporate defined benefit plans allow a significantly larger level of contributions to be made to the plan by participants than those permitted to Keogh participants (see Chapter 5).

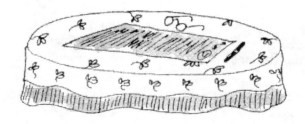

b. Other Benefits

The shareholder-employees of a corporation are eligible for certain deductible fringe benefits not available to (deductible by) noncorporate business owners. Deductible fringe benefits include health, life and disability insurance, sick pay and a qualified group legal services plan. (On group term life insurance, only premiums providing coverage of $50,000 or less per employee are deductible and must be part of a group plan. Also, the plan may not discriminate in favor of key employees.) The corporation can also deduct a death benefit payment to your beneficiary (up to $5,000 of which is also deductible by the beneficiary). In fact, the corporation may even go further and reimburse an employee for any deductible she had to pay personally on health insurance and for any services not covered under the policy—whether applicable to the employee, her spouse or dependents. These benefits are deductible by the corporation and are generally tax-free to the shareholder-employees (they do not have to report these benefits as income on their individual federal tax returns).

Special Rules: These special corporate fringe benefits are not available to shareholders who own 2% or more of the stock in S corporations. Also note that unincorporated business owners (and S corporation shareholders) are allowed to deduct a portion of the premiums paid for themselves and their spouses for health insurance. Check IRS publications and ask your tax advisor for the latest deductibility rules for health insurance premiums.

4. Establishing Order in Your Business

Many professionals incorporate because the corporate form provides a more businesslike environment. As you certainly know, being an excellent doctor, acupuncturist, child counselor, or any other professional, and running a business require two very different skills. Perhaps you have accounted for this and have hired someone to keep your books for you. But possibly you feel the need to do more to regularize your business affairs.

The corporation will pay you a regular employee wage and withhold the appropriate taxes. You may not have to worry about filing those quarterly estimated tax returns anymore (though your corporate bookkeeper will have to file corporate estimated taxes). And you will almost certainly find it easier to keep a more watchful eye on your corporation's income and expenses than you have to date. You'll probably find yourself with a smoother, more regular cash flow. We know too many sole practitioner professionals who make a good income, but because of their own financial disorganization, see very little of it.

5. Formality

A more subtle, but very real, reason many people choose to incorporate is the sense of business respectability that goes with being a corporation. While this benefit is obviously intangible, many proprietorships and partnerships feel (often justifiably) that their operations are seen by the business or financial community as too informal. Incorporating is one way for business people to put others on notice that theirs is an established business whose operations are carefully planned and routinely reviewed. In other words, although placing an "Inc." after your name will not directly increase profits, it forces you to pay serious attention to the structure and organization of your business, something that is likely to improve all aspects of your practice.

6. Perpetual Existence

A corporation is, in some senses, immortal. Unlike a sole proprietorship or partnership which terminates upon the death or withdrawal of the owner or owners, a corporation has an independent existence. A corporation can continue despite changeovers in management or ownership (see Chapter 4, Section F, on transferring professional corporation shares). Of course, like any business, it can be terminated by the mutual consent of the owners for personal or economic reasons and, in some cases, involuntarily, as in a bankruptcy proceeding. Nonetheless, the fact that a corporation does not depend for its existence on the life or continual ownership interests of particular individuals, does influence creditors and employees to participate in the operations of the business. This is particularly true as the business grows.

The perpetual existence characteristic of a professional corporation does have some limitations, however. This is because the legal restrictions on who can own shares can affect the continuation of the corporation. Shares of stock are only permitted to be owned by persons licensed to practice in that (or in some cases in a related) profession. Thus, when the professional corporation is controlled by just one, or perhaps even two, shareholders, it is possible that when the shareholders die, the corporation will terminate.

7. New Tax Year

Some professional corporations may be able to adopt a non-calendar tax year (a fiscal year which ends on the last day of a month other than December (see note below). By doing this (1) the owners of a preexisting unincorporated professional practice may be able to defer paying taxes on income earned just prior to incorporating and (2) each year the corporation can declare or pay deductible bonuses, salary increases, etc., to the employee-shareholders who will defer paying individual taxes on these amounts until the end of (or at least later in) the calendar year. The IRS is, of course, aware of this technique of using a new corporate tax year to obtain the advantage of a one-time deferral of income tax upon incorporation. Consequently, it may claim that a large amount of money received by a corporation which was earned by the former partnership or sole proprietorship should be taxed as income to the owners of the prior business (even if the business reported income on a cash basis).

Deferral techniques of this sort are beyond the scope of this book. However, if you are interested in electing a new non-calendar tax year for your corporation to defer paying taxes on income, you may be able to do so—see Section C8, below, and check with your accountant for further information.

Professional Corporation Tax Year Rules: As a general rule, personal service corporations (defined in the Internal Revenue Code as those whose principal activity is the performance of personal services substantially performed by the employee-shareholders of the corporation) are required to choose a calendar tax year for the corporation. However, exceptions to these calendar year rules do exist. For example, one automatic IRS criterion for allowing a non-calendar tax year is if the corporation derives 25% or more of its gross receipts during the last two months of a non-calendar tax year. There are other exceptions which allow these corporations to elect a non-calendar (fiscal) tax year–see Section C8 for more information.

B. Disadvantages

While incorporating your business certainly has some advantages, there are a few disadvantages you should be aware of before you create a corporation.

1. Paperwork

To incorporate you will have to comply with the California corporation laws, other special laws and regulations written specifically for your profession. You will also have to draft or have various plans and benefit programs drafted for you. This book is designed to guide you in setting up your corporation, and hopefully you won't be intimidated by the administrative process. Nevertheless, setting up and maintaining a corporation does require a good bit of paperwork.

2. Costs

You must pay a $100 filing fee to incorporate. Starting with your third tax year, you must pay a minimum of $800 to incorporate in franchise taxes. Your corporation will also have to make unemployment insurance and workers' compensation insurance payments. Your corporation's Social Security tax will be higher than what you paid before, but the part paid by the corporation is deductible. Several of the professions require you to file a certificate of registration, costing $100–$200, and annual reports, varying in cost from $10 to $150.

Setting up a corporate retirement plan that will be accepted (i.e., "qualified") by the IRS can some-times get expensive, and there are also continuing costs for administering the plan. Since you must also include nonprofessional employees in your retirement plan (though you may be able to delay their participation for a while—see Chapter 5), the more you put in for yourself, the more you may eventually have to invest for them, depending on how long they stay and how well they are paid.

You also need to consider whether your spendable income will still be high enough to allow you to live the way you would like to after you make the contributions to your new corporate plans. Sure, the costs are deductible, but setting up a plan can be expensive. Are you sure your income will be sufficient each year, so you can continually contribute to the retirement plans in the amount you agreed to initially?

Similarly, though to a lesser extent, you need to figure out whether you can afford to pay yourself greater fringe benefits. Again, tax savings do not always compensate.

The corporate form can result in increased accounting and bookkeeping fees, particularly if you have not already set up a double entry bookkeeping system and a system to generate accurate financial statements. Such double entry accounting journals and a general ledger are usually considered to be a necessity if you plan to operate as a corporation. Frankly, because there are many excellent reasons to establish good financial controls anyway, this item should probably be treated as an advantage, not an extra corporate cost.

Corporate tax rates may not save you tax dollars. We've already looked at the basic tax issues earlier in this chapter. Make sure you sit down and calculate the net effect of incorporating on your total tax situation, both personal and business. Again, many people decide to incorporate for non-tax reasons (e.g., to obtain limited liability for business debts or to formalize their practice and split up ownership interests into shares of stock). If the payment of corporate taxes on money left in the corporation results in an increased tax bill, you can decide to elect S corporation tax status to pass corporate income through to the shareholders to be taxed at their individual tax rates only.

Another disadvantage of incorporating has traditionally been the $2,000 (or often more) that you could expect to pay an attorney. This book, together with a little effort on your part, effectively eliminates, or at least minimizes, this cost.

Note: You may fear that the corporate form may prove too difficult to administer, subjecting you to a constant barrage of costly and time-consuming, record-keeping details. This fear is largely groundless. Routine ongoing corporate formalities are mostly limited to annual meetings documented with standard minute forms (see *The Corporate Minutes Book: The Legal Guide to Taking Care of Your Corporation,* by Anthony Mancuso (Nolo), for corporate minutes forms with resolutions to handle all types of ongoing corporate legal, tax and business transactions). Even if you don't incorporate, you will probably conclude that you need to prepare similar types or amounts of paperwork to make sense of your business.

C. Other Incorporation Considerations

Before you decide to incorporate, you should read through this section. The points made here aren't necessarily disadvantages of incorporating, but you do need to understand them to give yourself a fair perspective on what it means to be a professional corporation.

1. Capitalization

A professional corporation needs people and money to get started. In the common sense definition of the term, the money or dollar value of assets used to set up the corporation is called "capital" and the process of raising the money or other assets is called "capitalizing" the corporation. There are no minimum capitalization requirements for corporations in California—theoretically, you could start a corporation with next to no money, property or other assets. There must be some consideration—e.g., money—given for shares, even if it's only a one-person corporation, but there are no statutory requirements as to how much is necessary.

In a practical sense, however, starting a professional corporation without assets is not very professional. Profit corporations are in business to make money and if you don't have at least minimum assets to start with, it's unlikely that you're going to be much of a success. In a legal sense, too, an undercapitalized corporation is risky. Even though California doesn't require that a corporation have any minimum amount of assets, the courts look at "thin" (undercapitalized) corporations with a leery eye and have, in the past, subjected the shareholders of such corporations to personal liability for corporate debts (see Section 2, below). To give yourself the best chance of making a success of your professional corporation and to protect yourself from any potential court action, you should pay into the corporation enough money and other assets to commence operations and cover at least foreseeable, short-range expenses and the liabilities that might occur in the particular profession in which you plan to engage.

There are several ways to get the assets necessary to capitalize the corporation. Often this is no problem at all, as the incorporators are simply formalizing the operations of an existing professional business (partnership or proprietorship). The assets of the existing professional business are transferred to the new professional corporation in return for shares of stock.

In most other situations, a corporation is capitalized with money, property, or past services contributed to the corporation in return for shares of stock, or with money loaned to the corporation.

It should be realized that the term capitalization refers loosely to the amount of assets that a corporation starts out with and, as we've said, there should be enough to guarantee a good start. In bookkeeping terms, however, capitalization has a specific meaning and refers to the way the organizational assets are carried on the corporate books—either as equity or debt. Equity capital is the amount of money or dollar value of property or services transferred to the corporation in return for shares of stock. Debt is, quite logically, money borrowed by the corporation in return for promissory notes or other debt instruments which usually specify a maturity date and a given rate of interest.

It is often true that the nature of the capitalization of assets will, in and of itself, determine whether they will be carried on the books as equity or debt. In many cases, however, particularly in small professional corporations, the incorporators can choose whether their contribution to the corporation will be treated as equity or debt. For example, they can loan money to the corporation or contribute it in return for shares of stock. Since there are significant practical, legal and tax differences between equity and debt capital, it's important to seek the advice of an experienced accountant or other financial advisor before opting for a particular capitalization method. We'll take a brief look at these differences to give you a general idea of some of the considerations relevant to your decision.

In practical terms, a contribution of equity capital to a corporation in return for shares of stock is a "risk" investment. The shareholder will receive a return on this investment if, and only if, the corporation makes a profit and is able to distribute dividends to shareholders or, upon its dissolution, has assets left after payment of the corporate creditors to distribute to the shareholders. When equity contributions are made to a new business which hasn't operated previously in noncorporate form, this is indeed a "high risk" investment. A debt transaction is a bit safer, with the contributor relying on the terms of the loan agreement as to date of repayment and rate of return (interest) and, as we've already mentioned, often demanding that the personal assets of the incorporators be pledged for security. A standard note, however, unlike a stock certificate, doesn't carry with it the attractive possibility of providing the contributor with a percentage of the profits or liquidation assets of a successful enterprise.

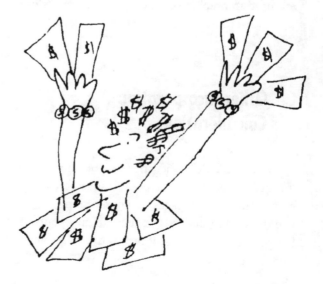

For tax purposes, an equity contribution may result in the recognition of taxable income by the shareholders: dividends paid to shareholders are taxed to them as income at their own personal income tax rates. In addition, payment of dividends to shareholders is a distribution of profits and the corporation is not allowed a business expense deduction for these payments. Debt capital, on the other hand, provides certain tax advantages to the corporation and to the note holder. Interest payments, like dividends, are taxed to the recipient as income, but the payment of principal is simply a return of capital giving rise to no tax liability. The corporation, moreover, is allowed to deduct interest payments as a business expense on its tax return.

Warning: Debt to Equity Ratios Should Be Reasonable. Your corporation should begin with a reasonable amount of equity in its capital account. One reason for this is that the courts and the IRS have often been suspicious of corporations with a high ratio of debt to equity, feeling that creditors were inadequately protected and that the corporation was a sham designed to insulate incorporators from personal liability and to grant them undeserved tax benefits. For instance, if a disproportionate amount of money is "loaned" to the corporation by the incorporators rather than paid in for stock, and the repayment terms are unduly permissive or generous, the IRS or a court might decide that the contribution was, in essence, an equity transaction contrived as debt to obtain favorable tax treatment. In this situation, the interest payments are subject to being treated as dividends, with the corporation unable to deduct these payments as a business expense and the lender-shareholder having to report repayment of the principal of the loan as income rather than a return of capital.

Another practical reason for watching your debt to equity ratio is that banks are unlikely to loan money to your corporation if this ratio is particularly lopsided (too much debt/not enough equity).

A rule of thumb (which is subject to loads of exceptions depending on specific circumstances) is that a 3 to 1 debt to equity ratio (e.g., $30,000 of debt, $10,000 of equity) is considered to be relatively safe, while higher debt to equity ratios are considered to be progressively more risky, particularly those which exceed 10 to 1. Obviously, rules of thumb really provide very little guidance, so ask your accountant or other tax advisor for her opinion before deciding on a particular level of debt when capitalizing your corporation with loans.

The courts have listed a number of criteria which they will consider when attempting to determine if a purported debt arrangement should be treated as a real debt obligation or whether it should be reclassified to the less favorable status of an equity contribution. Briefly stated, the courts have indicated that the debt instrument should be drawn up as a regular promissory note with a fixed maturity date and a specified rate of interest, and the corporation should have the right to enforce the terms of the note. The corporation should not arbitrarily grant the person making the loan any special preferences over other lenders or allow this person to postpone payments on the note. If the corporation is "thinly" capitalized (has a high ratio of debt to equity), can obtain loan funds from outside lenders, or uses the loan proceeds to acquire capital assets, these factors will make disallowance of the loan more likely.

LOANS AND THE CALIFORNIA SECURITIES LAW

As you'll see in Chapter 4, Section I, shares of stock issued by a professional corporation are exempt from registration as securities under a specific provision of California law. Notes issued by a corporation to lenders (shareholders, investors, etc.) are also considered securities and must be qualified by the Commissioner of Corporations — usually by a somewhat complicated and costly procedure requiring the assistance of an attorney —unless the notes or note transactions themselves are exempt under a special rule from qualification. Many small corporations do not substantially capitalize their corporation with loans and should not be overly concerned with these issue. Nonetheless, because of the technicalities involved with this area of law and since our focus in this book must, as a practical matter, be limited primarily to the issuance of shares, we think it would be wise to obtain the opinion of a lawyer regarding compliance with state and federal securities laws if you substantially capitalize your corporation with loan proceeds.

2. Piercing the Corporate Veil (if you want to be treated like a corporation, it's best to act like one)

After you've set up a corporation, you must act like one if you want to be sure to qualify for the legal protections and tax advantages the corporate form offers. Filing your Articles of Incorporation with the Secretary of State brings the corporation into existence and transforms it into a legal entity.

You should be aware, however, that this is not enough to ensure that a court or the IRS will treat you as a corporation.

Courts occasionally do scrutinize the organization and operations of corporations, particularly closely held corporations where the shareholders also manage, supervise and work for the corporation as directors, officers and employees. If a corporation is inadequately capitalized, doesn't issue stock, diverts funds for the personal use of the shareholders, doesn't keep adequate corporate records (e.g., minutes of annual or special meetings), or, generally, doesn't pay much attention to the theory and practice of corporate life, a court may disregard the corporate entity and hold the shareholders liable for the debts of the corporation. Using the same criteria, the IRS has been known to treat corporate profits as the individual income of the shareholders. In legalese this is called "piercing the corporate veil."

Please Note: Piercing the corporate veil is the exception, not the rule. If you follow the basic precautions mentioned below, you should never face this problem.

To avoid problems, your corporation should be adequately capitalized; issue its stock; keep accurate records of who owns its shares; keep corporate funds separate from the personal funds of the shareholders, officers and directors; and keep accurate records of all votes and decisions which occur at formal meetings of the board of directors and the shareholders. These formal meetings should be held at least annually and whenever you wish to document a change in the legal or tax affairs of your corporation (such as an amendment of your bylaws, board approval of an important tax election, etc.) or an important business transaction (purchase of corporate real estate, authorization of a bank loan, etc.).

Reality Note: Of course, many corporations, regardless of their size, hold frequent meetings of directors, shareholders, staff, department heads, committees, etc. Here, we are talking about more formal legal or tax-related meetings documented by formal minutes. For one-person or other small corporations, these formal meetings will often be held on paper, not in person, to document corporate actions or formalities which have already been agreed to ahead of time by all the parties.

For a thorough treatment of how to prepare ongoing corporate minutes, with tear-out minute forms and corporate resolutions to handle most basic corporate formalities, see *The Corporate Minutes Book: The Legal Guide to Taking Care of Your Corporation,* by Anthony Mancuso (Nolo).

3. Reallocation of Income

Sometimes, the IRS will maintain that the corporation is not really the entity which has earned the income and that, in fact, certain income was really only the professional's. This can happen when you don't transfer all the income you earn to the corporation after you've incorporated. For example, an accountant who works for both a firm and privately for herself may decide to only transfer her income from her private practice to the professional corporation she is setting up. The IRS may then treat not only her income from the firm, but possibly also her other private income, as regular (rather than corporate) income and tax it accordingly.

If you cannot transfer your income from all sources to your professional corporation, you should include a statement to this effect in your Bylaws or corporate minutes. Be sure to note that the outside activity will not interfere with your

services to the corporation. An employment contract drawn up between you and the corporation which specifies your duties and wages could help. See your accountant for more details.

SECTION 269A RESTRICTIONS

Under Section 269A of the Internal Revenue Code, a personal service corporation such as a professional corporation may have its corporate status disregarded, resulting in its income being reallocated to the owner-employees, under certain conditions. The two main conditions are:

- the corporation performs substantially all of its services for or on behalf of another corporation, partnership or other entity, and

- the principal purpose for forming or using the corporation is the avoidance of federal income tax by reducing the income of, or securing the benefit of any expense, deduction, credit, exclusion for, any employee-owner which would not otherwise be available.

Under these rules, a physician who incorporates and works solely for a hospital could be subject to IRS allocation treatment. However, if the physician also provided substantial services to other clients, she could escape from the law's application. Similarly, a physician who is a member of a partnership and who incorporates may also be subject to IRC Section 269A if the physician substitutes her professional corporation for herself in the partnership. We suggest that you talk with your tax advisor if you think you might fall within Section 269A restrictions and have him review the IRS regulations under Section 269A.

4. Paying Yourself Too Much Salary

A corporation may deduct amounts paid to employees as salaries for corporate income tax purposes. To be deductible, salaries must be reasonable and paid for services actually performed by the employee. You should pay particular attention to salaries paid to shareholder-employees. These payments are often scrutinized by the IRS since they can, and often are, used as a means of paying disguised dividends to shareholders. If the IRS determines that the salary was not related to services actually performed by a shareholder-employee, or was paid in an unreasonable amount, it will treat the excess amount as a dividend. This won't have much of an effect on the shareholder-employee's tax liability since he's got to include the money on his individual tax return either way. It will, however, prevent the corporation from deducting the payment as a business expense. So, a bit of advice—try to avoid the payment of large, discretionary bonuses and keep any increase in salaries tied to increased corporate productivity, or the going rate of pay for similar professionals. Distributing large, lump-sum bonuses at the end of the year is particularly likely to draw the attention of the IRS.

Here, too, you might want to consider drawing up an employment contract and corporate resolutions detailing your abilities, qualifications, and responsibilities, showing why you are entitled to the wages the corporation is paying you (for such a resolution, see *The Corporate Minutes Book: The Legal Guide to Taking Care of Your Corporation,* by Anthony Mancuso (Nolo)).

5. Accumulated Earnings Credit

The decision to incorporate is often based upon the desire of profitable business owners to shelter themselves from large annual individual income tax payments based upon their share of profits. The Internal Revenue Code helps corporations do this by allowing them an automatic accumulated earnings credit. For professional corporations in the fields of health, law, accounting or architecture, or for those which perform consultation services, this automatic credit is $150,000 (Internal Revenue Code Section 535(c)(2)(B)). For all other professional corporations, the credit is $250,000. What this means is that the IRS will allow you to retain this amount of earnings in your corporation without challenging you for not paying this money out to the shareholders as dividends, salaries, or other amounts which would be taxable to them on their individual tax returns. Note that federal S corporations do not need the benefit of this credit since the undistributed earnings of the corporation pass through to the shareholders of S corporations each year (see Section 7, below). This accumulated earnings

credit is, in fact, one of the advantages of doing business as a corporation—sole proprietorships and partnerships do not enjoy this type of tax flexibility.

Most small corporations will not need (or be able) to accumulate earnings beyond this $150,000/$250,000 credit since salaries, bills and other expenses will reduce earnings below this amount. If, however, you do need to accumulate income in the corporation above this limit, you may do so, as long as these excess accumulations are held for the reasonably anticipated needs of the business (not just to shelter income).

Important! If the IRS determines that corporate earnings have been unreasonably accumulated above the automatic credit amount, it will assess a whopping 39.6% penalty on the excess accumulations. You will want to stay well clear of this hefty tax penalty.

6. Personal Holding Company Penalty

In this section we briefly discuss provisions of the federal tax law (Internal Revenue Code Sections 541 through 547), which some professional corporations will need to be aware of: the personal holding company penalty tax.

This tax is a 39.6% corporate surtax, in addition to regular corporate taxes, on the income of certain types of corporations which receive a significant portion of their adjusted gross income from "passive" sources or from services performed under contract. With a few simple precautions, this tax should not pose a problem for these corporations—the only real danger is inadvertently becoming subject to this tax due to a lack of knowledge of these provisions.

Without discussing all of the technical definitions and exceptions of this federal tax law, the personal holding company tax may apply to a corporation if five or fewer of its shareholders own 50% or more of the corporation's stock and if 60% or more of the corporation's gross income (minus several technical adjustments) for the tax year is from certain types of passive sources such as dividends, interest, rents or royalties, or is derived from personal service contracts. For most professional corporations, the usual focus here is whether the corporation provides contracted services, and, if so, whether this income is subject to being classified as personal service contract income.

Under Section 543(a)(7) of the Internal Revenue Code, personal service contract income means, generally, "amounts received under a contract under which the corporation is to furnish personal services, if some person other than the corporation has the right to designate (by name or description) the individual who is to perform the services, or if the individual who is to perform the services is designated (by name or description) in the contract." In addition, the individual who is to perform the services, or who may be so designated, must be at least a 25% shareholder.

What does all of this mean? Simply stated, if your corporation is planning to provide services under the terms of a contract, you will want to make sure that the corporation has the right to designate the individual who will perform the contracted services (not the person or business for whom the services will be performed) and that the name of the individual who is to perform the services does not appear in the contract. By doing this you should be able to stay clear of this personal holding company penalty.

Note When Incorporating a Preexisting Business: If you are incorporating a personal service business, such as your own unincorporated practice, you will not want to assign your individual personal service contracts to your new corporation without checking first with your tax advisor—this could trigger a penalty.

It should be of some comfort to note that the Internal Revenue Code anticipates that corporations will be subject to this penalty tax usually due to an oversight or poor planning and, consequently, allows them to avoid the imposition of this tax, in many cases, by the payout of what is known as a "deficiency dividend." Even under this procedure, however, the corporation is subject to interest and other penalty payments. We suggest that all professionals check with their tax consultant prior to incorporating to be sure that they will not inadvertently run afoul of this penalty tax provision.

7. Federal S Corporation Tax Status

One thing you'll need to assess is whether you want to be taxed as an S corporation, which provides pass-through taxation to its shareholders.

In this Section we discuss some of the issues associated with electing federal S corporation tax status.

a. Advantages and Disadvantages

A corporation which has 75 or fewer shareholders and which meets other basic requirements may elect to fall under special federal tax provisions contained in Subchapter S of the Internal Revenue Code. Corporations which make this election are known as S corporations. Generally, a corporation which elects to become an S corporation has its profits and losses passed through the corporation to its shareholders. This means, with exceptions, that profits and losses are not taxed to, or deducted by, the corporation, but by the individual shareholders in proportion to their stockholdings. The corporation sidesteps taxation on its profits and its shareholders (like partners) get the tax benefit of the losses, credits, deductions, etc., of the corporation. Profits of the S corporation pass through to shareholders on a per-share, per-day basis, whether or not such profits are actually distributed to them. Consequently, S corporation tax status can be a very flexible planning tool, providing corporations with the ability to live in two different worlds, enjoying a corporate legal life (including limited liability status for its owners) and partnership-like tax status.

For More Information: This discussion is intended to treat the general aspects of S corporation tax status. For more detailed information and an explanation of special S corporation rules, see IRS Publication 589, *Tax Information on S Corporations.*

This pass-through of corporate income and losses to the shareholders can be advantageous to some newly formed or existing corporations. For example, corporate profits that are automatically passed through to shareholders are not subject to self-employment (Social Security) taxes. The IRS may object, of course, if an active sole shareholder attempts to avoid all employment taxes by having all profits pass to him as undistributed S corporation earnings without recognizing any of the profits as taxable wages of the sole employee-shareholder. We suggest you check with your accountant if you want to use an S corporation as a way to whittle down your self-employment tax bill.

Here are a few typical situations where electing S corporation tax status can save tax dollars:

1. In start-up businesses that expect initial losses before the business begins to show a profit, S corporation tax status can pass these initial losses to the individual tax returns of the shareholders who actively participate in the business. This allows them to offset income from other sources with the losses of the corporation (see the sidebar below entitled "What Constitutes Material Participation?" for further information).

    EXAMPLE: Janet and Bruno decide to form a part-time physical therapy practice and incorporate it. They'll continue to work during the week at their salaried jobs until their new business gets off the ground. They know that the first year or two of corporate life will generate losses. Rather than take these losses at the corporate level and carry them forward into future profitable years of the corporation, they decide they would be better off electing S corporation tax status and deducting these losses immediately against their individual full-time salary income on their individual tax returns.

    Note: Janet and Bruno do not plan to provide themselves with corporate fringe benefits, at least not right away (S corporations are limited in the benefits which they can provide to employee-shareholders—see below).

2. If the professional corporation is subject to a flat 35% corporate rate (or if the corporation is subject to regular corporate tax rates and corporate taxable income is substantial), S corporation tax status can be a handy way of taking advantage of the lower individual rates: S corporation profits are passed through and taxed at the shareholders' individual rates.

    EXAMPLE: Tomas and Gerald incorporate a successful preexisting professional practice (which will be taxed at the regular tiered corporate tax rates). They anticipate a first-year profit of $2 million and, after deducting all salaries, fringe benefits, contributions to a corporate pension plan, business expenses, depreciation, etc., a corporate taxable income that will put them in the 35% tax corporate tax bracket for all corporate income (they will lose the advantage of the lower, graduated tax brackets for the lower amounts of corporate income). They decide to form an S corporation to have this income passed through to them individually where it will be taxed to each of them at a lower individual tax rate.

3. As discussed in Section A2b, above, regular corporations with appreciated assets are subject to a corporate level tax when the corporation dissolves. S corporations are generally not subject to this tax. For some corporations, this can be a decisive factor in electing S corporation tax status.

    Exception: S corporations are subject to a "built-in gains" tax for any appreciation which occurred prior to the S corporation election (if these assets are disposed of within ten years after the effective date of the S corporation tax election). Please consult your tax advisor for information on these technical provisions.

    EXAMPLE: Sam and his partners incorporate a preexisting practice. It is expected that the corporation will hold title to real property. To avoid a corporate-level tax on appreciation associated with this property when the corporation is dissolved and the property sold, they decide to elect S corporation status prior to the purchase of any property by their corporation.

The point of these examples is simple. In some businesses, at least some of the time, it is better for business owners to be taxed as if the business was a partnership. With some technical exceptions (see the "Partnership Differences" sidebar, below), electing S corporation status allows you to do this. If you later decide that S corporation tax status no longer makes sense—for example, because you wish to split business income between yourself and your corporation—you can revoke or terminate this tax status.

Important: Always check with your tax advisor before deciding whether to elect S corporation status. You must be sure this tax election is appropriate for your business and that you will meet initial and ongoing requirements for this tax election.

Here now are some potential disadvantages of S corporation tax status:

- S corporations, like partnerships, cannot provide tax-deductible fringe benefits to owners (i.e., shareholder-employees owning more than 2% of the S corporation's stock) such as:
  1. Qualified accident and health plans (but S corporation shareholders are entitled to the same tax deduction for premiums paid for health insurance as are sole proprietors and partners—see Section A3b above);
  2. Medical expense reimbursement plans;
  3. $50,000 of group term life insurance;
  4. $5,000 death benefit;
  5. Free meals and lodgings furnished for the convenience of the corporation (e.g., furnished on company premises).

- The amount of losses that may be passed through to the business owners (shareholders) and the ability to allocate these losses in different proportions to different individuals are restricted by various technical provisions of the Internal Revenue Code and Treasury Regulations. Generally, you can only deduct losses in an S corporation up to the "basis" (tax value) of your stock plus amounts loaned by you to your corporation. Simply stated, you start out with a basis in your shares equal to the price you paid for them (or the value of the property contributed for your shares). If losses cannot be deducted by you in a given year, they can be carried forward to and deducted in future tax years if you then qualify to deduct the losses.

Material Participation Requirement: In order to use S corporation losses to offset the active individual income of a shareholder, the shareholder must materially participate in the business of the S corporation. See the accompanying sidebar for a summary of the federal material participation Treasury Regulations.

The important point is this: If you plan to elect S corporation status to pass corporate losses through to you on your individual tax return, make sure you will have sufficient basis in your stock plus enough qualified indebtedness to allow you to deduct these losses at the individual level. An experienced corporate tax advisor should be intimately familiar with this issue and able to help you make sure you can deduct S corporation losses on future individual tax returns.

WHAT CONSTITUTES MATERIAL PARTICIPATION?

In order for an S corporation shareholder to deduct corporate losses against active income, such as salary or wages, on his individual tax return, the shareholder must materially participate in the business of the S corporation. As mentioned in Chapter 1, Section A2, this material participation rule also applies to limited partners.

Here are some of the ways in which an S corporation shareholder, limited partner or other person can satisfy the IRS that he materially participates in a business activity during a taxable year:

- The person participates in the business for more than 500 hours during the year;
- The person participates in the business for more than 100 hours during the year, and that participation is not less than any other individual's participation in the business;
- The person participates in the business for more than 100 hours during the year and participates in other activities for more than 100 hours each, for a total of more than 500 hours during the year;
- The person's participation in the business for the year constitutes substantially all the participation in the business of all individuals for that year;
- The person materially participated in the business for any five of the last ten taxable years;
- The business involves the performance of personal services in the fields of health, law, engineering, architecture, accounting, actuarial science, performing arts or consulting, and the person materially participated in the business for any three preceding taxable years; or
- The person can show, based upon all facts and circumstances, that she participates in the business on a regular, continuous and substantial basis during the year.

Note: For more information, see Temp. Reg. §§ 1.469-1T, -2T, -3T, -5T and -11T and related regulations issued under Section 469 of the Internal Revenue Code.

- Like personal service corporations, S corporations must generally choose a calendar year as their corporate tax year. Exceptions exist under IRS Revenue Procedures which allow S corporations to elect a non-calendar tax year in certain circumstances, including (1) if the S corporation can show a valid business purpose for the non-calendar year or (2) if the non-calendar year results in a deferral of income for 3 months or less and other requirements are met.

  Please see subsection 8, below, for additional information on choosing a corporate tax year.
- S corporations cannot adopt an employee stock ownership plan (although they are permitted to adopt a stock bonus plan).
- In the past, some incorporators avoided electing S corporation status since this would place restrictions on contributions to their corporate pension and profit-sharing plans. However, these additional restrictions to S corporation retirement plans have, for the most part, been eliminated with S corporations and regular corporations (referred to as "C" corporations in the Internal Revenue Code) now being placed on a relatively equal footing with respect to most corporate plan provisions (however, S corporation plans are still prohibited from lending money to a participant owning more than 5% of the corporation's stock). See Chapter 5 for information on corporate and noncorporate retirement plans.

b. Qualifying for S Corporation Tax Status

In order for a corporation to qualify for S corporation tax status, it must be a "small business corporation" under Subchapter S of the Internal Revenue Code. To so qualify, the corporation must meet the following requirements [under Internal Revenue Code Section 1361(b)]:

1. It must be a domestic (U.S.) corporation;
2. Shareholders must be U.S. citizens or residents;
3. There must be only one class of stock (all shares have equal rights, e.g., dividend, liquidation rights). However, differences as to voting rights are permitted (see Treasury Regulation § 1.1361-1);
4. All shareholders must be individuals, estates, certain qualified trusts or tax-exempt organizations (includes tax-exempt charities and pension funds);
5. There must be no more than 75 shareholders. Shares which are jointly owned by a husband and wife are considered to be owned by one person.

c. Electing Federal S Corporation Tax Status

If a corporation wishes to become an S corporation and meets the foregoing requirements, it must make an election by filing Form 2553 with the IRS indicating the consent of all shareholders. The election must be made on or before the 15th day of the third month of the corporation's tax year for which the S status is to be effective, or any time during the preceding tax year. For newly formed corporations which wish to start off as an S corporation, this means making the election before the 15th day of the third month after the date the corporation's first tax year begins.

For purposes of the S corporation election, the corporation's first tax year begins when it issues stock to shareholders, acquires assets or begins doing business, whichever occurs first. Generally, your first tax year will begin on the date you file your Articles of Incorporation. Since your S corporation election will be invalid if made at the wrong time, please check with your tax advisor to ensure that you fully understand these election rules and make your election on time.

The S corporation election must be consented to by all persons who are shareholders at the time it is made, as well as by all persons who were shareholders during the taxable year before the election is made. Their consents should be indicated on the election form when it is mailed to the IRS. If the shares are held jointly (e.g., in joint tenancy) or are the community property of spouses (or if any income from the stock is the community property of spouses), each co-owner and each spouse must sign the consent form.

d. Revocation or Termination of Federal S Corporation Tax Status

Once your corporation elects to become an S corporation, it continues to be treated as one through later tax years until the status is revoked or terminated. A revocation is made by filing shareholder consents to the revocation. The consent of shareholders who collectively own at least a majority of the stock in the corporation is required to effect a revocation.

S corporation status will be terminated, however, at any time, if the corporation fails to continue to meet all the small business corporation requirements discussed above (e.g., if the corporation issues a second class of shares, issues stock to a non-U.S.. citizen, etc.). Such a termination will be effective as of the date on which the terminating event occurs (not retroactively to the beginning of the tax year).

PARTNERSHIP DIFFERENCES

Partnership tax status (available to partnerships, LLCs and RLLPs) is still more flexible than S corporation tax status in some areas. For example:

- Partnerships can admit any person or entity as a partner. S corporation shareholders must be individuals, estates or certain types of trusts or nonprofit organizations.

- Partnerships can divide profits and losses among partners as they see fit. S corporations generally must allocate dividends, liquidation proceeds and corporate losses in proportion to stockholdings. To do otherwise invites an IRS attack on the grounds that the S corporation had created an impermissible second class of stock.

- Under technical tax provisions, partners may be able to personally deduct more business losses on their tax returns in a given year than corporate shareholders. The reason: In calculating the amount of partnership losses that may be deducted individually, a partner gets to count her pro-rata share of all money borrowed by the partnership. An S corporation shareholder only can count money borrowed by the corporation directly from the individual shareholder.

A termination will also occur in certain situations where the corporation has a specified level of passive investment income. This type of income generally includes royalties, rents, dividends, interest, annuities and gains from the sale or exchange of stock or securities. Many S corporations will not have to be concerned with this type of termination since it also requires that the corporation have "accumulated earnings and profits" from operating previously as a regular C (a non-S) corporation.

Once S status has been revoked or terminated, the corporation may not re-elect S corporation tax status until five years after the termination or revocation. Note that certain inadvertent terminations will be ignored, provided, among other things, that the corporation takes specified corrective action.

8. Corporate Accounting Periods and Tax Years

The accounting period of the corporation is the period for which the corporation keeps its books and will correspond to the corporation's tax year. Generally, a corporation's accounting period (and its tax year) may be the calendar year from January 1 to December 31 or it may be a fiscal year, consisting of a twelve-month period ending on the last day of any month other than December (for example, from July 1 to June 30). In special situations, a corporation may wish to choose a "52-53 week" year. This is a period which ends on a particular day closest to the end of a month (e.g., "the last Friday of March" or "the Friday nearest to the end of March"). Professional and S corporations are subject to special rules when selecting a tax year for the corporation—see "Special Calendar Year Rules for S and Personal Service Corporations" below.

For some corporations, a calendar tax year will prove easiest since it will be the same year as that used by the individual shareholders. Others, because of the particular business cycle of the corporation or simply because December is a hectic month, may wish to choose a different month to wind up their yearly affairs. Moreover, having the corporation's tax year end after that of the individual shareholders (after December 31), may allow special initial and ongoing tax advantages such as the deferral of income to the employee-shareholders of a small corporation.

You should also realize that choosing a fiscal rather than a calendar year is often in your accountant's interest since he or she is usually busy preparing and filing individual tax returns after the end of the calendar year. In fact, some accounting firms provide discounts if you choose a fiscal year which ends after the individual tax season (January to April).

Special Calendar Year Rules for S and Personal Service Corporations: If you plan to elect federal S corporation tax status (see subsection 7 just above) or if your corporation meets the definition of a "personal service corporation" (most professional corporations will meet the definition given below), generally, you must choose a calendar year for your corporate tax year (and your accounting period) unless the IRS approves the use of a fiscal year (see the discussion of exceptions to these calendar tax year rules below).

Under provisions of the Internal Revenue Code, a personal service corporation (for purposes of choosing a corporate tax year) is defined as "... a corporation the principal activity of which is the performance of personal services ... [if] such services are substantially performed by employee-owners." Also, "...an employee-owner is any employee of the corporation who owns, on any day during the taxable year, any of the outstanding stock of the personal service corporation." [See IRC §441(i) and Treas. Reg. §1.441-4T.] Note that federal S corporations will not be considered personal service corporations (however, as we have indicated, they too are required, generally, to adopt a calendar year as their tax year).

Exceptions to Special Calendar Year Rules for S and Personal Service Corporations: Your professional corporation will be subject to this calendar-year rule for personal service corporations (whether or not it elects federal S corporation tax status). However, IRS procedures provide exceptions which allow certain S corporations and personal service corporations to adopt a non-calendar (fiscal) tax year. Please see the accompanying boxed discussion for a summary of these rules.

Note: The discussion of special fiscal year rules for S corporations and personal service corporations is intended only to introduce you to some highly technical and rapidly changing tax material. If you wish to elect a non-calendar tax year for your S or personal service corporation, make sure to discuss these and other applicable rules and regulations with your tax advisor and, above all else, be sure to file the required tax year election forms with the IRS on time.

S AND PERSONAL SERVICE CORPORATION FISCAL TAX YEAR RULES

A new corporation that plans to elect S corporation tax status can apply for a fiscal year on its S corporation election form (IRS Form 2553). Personal service corporations request a non-calendar tax year by filing IRS form 1128 with the IRS within certain time limits.

25-Percent Test: IRS Revenue Procedure 87-32 allows S corporations and personal service corporations to elect a fiscal year for their corporation if they can show that the fiscal year requested represents the natural business year of the corporation. To make this showing, these corporations must meet the "25% test." Generally, this test is met if 25% or more of the corporation's gross receipts from services or sales have been recognized during the last two months of the requested fiscal year for the past consecutive three years (e.g., if a personal service corporation wishes a fiscal year ending on June 30th, then 25% or more of its receipts from services must have derived during the months of May and June during each of the previous three years). If the corporation has not been in existence for three years, then, generally, the IRS will look at the gross receipts of the preexisting unincorporated business.

Business Purpose: Even if you cannot meet the 25% test explained above, you may be able to establish another business purpose for your non-calendar tax year (e.g., if the fiscal year requested corresponds to the natural annual business cycle of the corporation)—Revenue Procedure 87-57 contains eight factual examples of valid and invalid business purposes when requesting a fiscal year for an S corporation.

Three-Month Deferral of Income: Under Section 444 of the Internal Revenue Code, S corporations and personal service corporations may be allowed to adopt a non-calendar tax year if the tax year results in a deferral on income of three months or less. Specifically, if a fiscal year ending September 30th is requested, this tax year will be allowed for the corporation (if other requirements are also met) since this results in a three-month deferral of income when compared to the otherwise required calendar year ending December 31st. Please realize that use of this three-month deferral rule comes with a price tag: S corporations using this procedure have to make a "required payment" to the IRS each year; personal service corporations utilizing this election are limited in the amount of corporate deductions which can be taken for payments made to the employee-shareholders unless certain minimum distributions are made to these shareholders before the end of the calendar year and carrybacks of net operating losses of the personal service corporation are restricted. For further information on Section 444 elections, see Treasury Regulation §1.444-1T. For further guidance in making a §444 election, see IRS Notice 88-10 (1/15/88) and Notice 88-49 (4/4/88).

9. Becoming a Close Corporation

Though we've never seen it, a professional corporation can also incorporate as a California statutory close corporation. A statutory close corporation is like any other regular for-profit corporation, but adopts some additional special provisions of the California Corporations Code. Its chief advantages are that:

- Certain attempted transfers of stock which would result in the number of shareholders exceeding a specified number as stated in the Articles of Incorporation (35 or less) are automatically void.

- Shareholders of a close corporation can enter into a shareholders' agreement providing for informal management of the corporation without risk of a state court disregarding the corporate form. The agreement can, like a partnership agreement, provide for a division of profits different from percentages of stock ownership.

However, these advantages are not that important to professional corporations. The stock of a professional corporation can only be transferred to licensed professionals in the field (or possibly in a related field—see Chapter 4). These restrictions are often sufficient for the professional, and the built-in restrictions added by becoming a close corporation aren't really necessary.

As for the second advantage, though some attorneys feel that shareholder agreements are useful, at present we cannot recommend the use of such an agreement due to the legal and tax uncertainties and complications associated with it.

A shareholders' agreement would, of course, have to be consistent with the Professional Corporation Law.

If you do intend to also become a close corporation, you will need to include additional close corporation provisions in your Articles of Incorporation, and will probably also wish to prepare a custom-tailored close corporation shareholders' agreement. Please consult a lawyer if you wish to form this special type of California corporation.

10. Sale of Stock

Corporate stock may be sold for money, labor done, services actually rendered to or for the benefit of the corporation in its formation or reorganization, debts canceled and tangible or intangible property actually received by the corporation. If shares are sold for other than money, the board of directors must state, by resolution, the fair market value of the services, property or other form of payment given for the shares. Shares cannot be issued in return for promissory notes of the purchaser unless secured by collateral other than the shares themselves, or in return for the performance of *future* services (unless as a part of an employee or director stock purchase, or option plan). As we'll see in Chapter 4, stock of a professional corporation can only be sold to other specified professionals.

11. Dividends

The Corporations Code restricts the rights of corporations to declare dividends. Before dividends can be paid to shareholders, certain tests must be met. The law, for the most part, applies "generally accepted accounting procedures" to determine the validity of dividend payments.

A dividend cannot be paid unless:

- The amount of retained earnings of the corporation, immediately prior to the payment of the dividend, equals or exceeds the amount of the proposed dividend, or
- Immediately after the dividend,
  (a) The sum of corporate assets (not including "goodwill" and certain other assets) would at least equal one and one-fourth times the liabilities of the corporation (not including certain deferred items); and
  (b) Subject to certain exceptions, the current assets of the corporation would be at least equal to its current liabilities or, in some cases, at least equal to one and one-fourth times its current liabilities.

In addition, no dividend can be paid if the corporation is, or as a result of the payment of a dividend would be, likely to be unable to meet its liabilities not otherwise provided for, as they become due. Certain other tests apply for payment of a dividend to certain classes of stock if the corporation has more than one class of stock.

For More Information: The rules for determining the validity of payment of dividends (referred to, and included in, the term "distribution to shareholders" by the Code) are contained in California Corporations Code Section 500 and following. These tests apply technical accounting standards and you should consult an accountant or lawyer before declaring and paying a dividend. If a dividend is paid which doesn't meet the appropriate tests, the directors of the corporation may be held personally liable to the creditors and shareholders of the corporation for the amount of the illegal dividend.

12. Section 1244 Stock

Many professional corporations can provide shareholders with the benefit of treating losses from the sale, exchange, or worthlessness of their stock as "ordinary" rather than "capital" losses on their individual federal tax returns, up to a maximum of $50,000 ($100,000 for a husband and wife filing a joint return) in each tax year. This is a definite advantage since, generally, ordinary losses are fully deductible against individual income, whereas capital losses are only partially deductible (for example, they can only be used to offset up to $3,000 of individual income in a given tax year). Stock issued by a corporation that qualifies for this federal ordinary loss treatment is known as Section 1244 stock.

To qualify for Section 1244 stock treatment, the following requirements must be met:

- The shares must be issued for money or property (other than corporate securities) and more than 50% of the corporation's gross receipts during the five tax years preceding the year in which the loss occurred must have been derived from sources other than royalties, dividends, interest, rents, annuities, or gains from sales or exchanges in securities or stock. If the corporation has not been in existence for the five tax years preceding the year in which the loss occurred, the five-year period is replaced by the number of tax years the corporation has been in existence prior to the loss.

- The corporation must be a small business corporation as defined in Section 1244 of the Internal Revenue Code. A corporation is a small business corporation if the total amount of money or the value of property received by the corporation for stock, as a contribution to capital and as paid-in surplus, does not exceed $1,000,000.

- At the time of loss, the shareholder must submit a timely statement to the IRS electing to take an ordinary loss pursuant to Section 1244.

Important: Ordinary loss treatment for a stock loss under section 1244 is only available to the original owner of the stock. If you transfer your shares to your children or to other persons or entities, the benefit of this tax break will be lost.

You do not have to file a special election form with the IRS or adopt a formal Section 1244 stock plan to be eligible for this special tax treatment—you simply must meet the requirements indicated above.

The tear-out Minutes included in the Appendix contain a Section 1244 stock resolution that expresses your intent that any future stock losses be eligible for Section 1244 tax treatment by your shareholders. We expect most incorporators will wish to include this resolution in their Minutes. If your corporation does not meet the Section 1244 requirements at the time of a stock loss, the loss will simply be treated as the usual capital loss

associated with regular shares of stock. Of course, if Section 1244 treatment of future stock losses is a critical factor in your incorporation, you will want to check with your tax advisor to be sure you will be eligible for this special stock loss treatment should a loss occur.

13. IRC Section 351 Tax-Free Exchange Treatment of Your Corporation

Many incorporators will wish to issue stock in return for the transfer of property to the corporation. If you plan to do this, you should realize that taxes may have to be paid by one or more of the transferors of the property unless special requirements contained in Section 351 of the Internal Revenue Code are met. If all of your shareholders will simply pay cash for their shares, you may ignore this section since an all-cash transaction of this sort is simply a purchase of shares, not a potentially taxable transfer of property to your corporation.

First, let's back up a little. As you know, anytime you sell an asset to someone (in the case of an incorporation, you are "selling" property to the corporation in return for stock), you are normally liable for the payment of taxes on the profit you make from the transaction. In tax terms, the profit is the difference between the selling price and your "adjusted basis" in the property. Without covering all the technicalities, the basic rule for business property is that your adjusted basis in the property will be the original cost of the property minus depreciation plus capital improvements.

Here's a (simplified) example: Assume that your business purchased a building at a cost of $180,000. It has taken $90,000 of depreciation on the property and made $20,000 in capital improvements to the property since the property was purchased. The adjusted basis of the property is $110,000 (cost of $180,000 - $90,000 depreciation + $20,000 improvements). If the property is sold for $210,000, the taxable gain (profit) is $100,000 ($210,000 - $110,000 adjusted basis). Note that we are ignoring, for purposes of this example, the cost, sale price and basis of the land on which the building is located (land is not depreciable).

Naturally, most incorporators will not wish to pay taxes on the sale of property to their corporation in return for shares of stock. This is particularly true if property which has increased in value (appreciated property) is being transferred to the corporation.

EXAMPLE: If a building which originally cost $60,000 and has been depreciated down to an adjusted basis of $30,000 is being transferred to the corporation for $100,000 (the current appreciated value of the building), the gain on the transfer would be $70,000 ($100,000 - $30,000 adjusted basis).

Fortunately, many small corporations will be able to transfer property to their corporation in return for stock in a tax-free exchange without recognizing any gain or loss on the transfer. Specifically, under Section 351 of the Internal Revenue Code, the transfer of property in return for shares of stock will generally be treated as a tax-free exchange if, immediately after the transfer, the transferors (shareholders) meet certain "control" tests. The tests that must be met are:
- The transferors, as a group, must own at least 80% of the total combined voting power of all classes of issued stock entitled to vote; and

- They must also own at least 80% of all other issued classes of stock of the corporation.

Most initial stock issuance transactions of corporations using this book should meet these control tests and be eligible for this tax-free exchange treatment since this is your first stock issuance involving one class of common voting shares and you don't need to establish control over previously issued stock or other classes of stock. Also note that cash and intangible types of property such as the goodwill of a business or patents are considered property for purposes of Section 351.

EXAMPLE: Harvey, Frank and Frances decide to form a corporation. The corporation will issue 500 shares of stock at a price of $100 per share. Harvey will receive 100 shares for a $10,000 cash payment; Frank and Frances will receive 200 shares apiece for their equal interests in the assets of their preexisting partnership valued at $40,000. The transaction qualifies for Section 351 tax-free exchange treatment since at least 80% (in this case, 100%) of all shares will be owned by the transferors of money and property after the transfer. (Harvey is not personally affected by this tax-free exchange treatment since he is simply purchasing shares for cash; however, Frank and Frances do not want to recognize a taxable gain on the transfer of their partnership assets.) Moreover, even without considering Harvey's permissible transfer of money to the corporation for his shares, Frank and Frances themselves will control the required 80% of the corporation's shares after the transfer of their property (400 out of 500 shares).

Of course, nothing (or next to nothing) is really free under tax statutes and regulations. A tax-free exchange simply defers the payment of taxes until your shares are sold (e.g., when you sell your shares to someone else or your corporation, itself, is sold or liquidated). Technically (and, of course, with some exceptions), the adjusted basis of the property transferred to the corporation is carried over to your shares (the adjusted basis of the shareholder's property becomes the basis of the shareholder's newly purchased shares).

> **EXAMPLE:** You transfer property with a fair market value of $20,000 and an adjusted basis of $10,000 to the corporation in a Section 351 tax-free exchange for shares worth $20,000. Your shares will then have a basis of $10,000. If you sell the shares for $30,000, your taxable gain will be $20,000 ($30,000 selling price minus their basis of $10,000). Note also, the corporation's basis in the property received in a tax-free exchange will also generally be the same as the adjusted basis of the transferred property (in this example, the corporation's basis in the property will be $10,000).

Even in a tax-free transaction, the shareholders will be taxed to the extent of any money or property they receive in addition to stock. For example, if you transfer a truck in a tax-free exchange worth $50,000 to the corporation in return for $40,000 worth of shares and a $10,000 cash payment by the corporation, you will have to report the $10,000 as taxable income.

There are, of course, added complexities which may arise in attempting to qualify an exchange of property for stock in your corporation as a Section 351 tax-free exchange. Let's look at a few of the more common situations which may trigger special rules:

- **Where shares are issued in return for the performance of services.** Although California law allows stock to be issued for past services performed for the corporation, services are not considered "property" for purposes of Section 351 (remember, stock must be issued in return for property to qualify for this tax-free exchange treatment). Consequently, you cannot normally count shares issued to shareholders for services in calculating the 80% control requirement. Moreover, even if you are able to meet the control test (not counting the stock issued for services), any shareholder who receives stock for services will have to report the value of her shares as taxable income.

EXAMPLE: Your corporation plans to issue $50,000 worth of shares upon its incorporation to you and the cofounder of your corporation, Fred. You will transfer property worth $30,000 for $30,000 in shares while Fred will receive $10,000 in shares in return for services already performed for the corporation valued at $10,000. The transfer will be taxable to both you and Fred since the basic control test of Section 351 will not have been met: You are the only person who will transfer property in return for stock and you do not meet the control requirement of Section 351 since you will only own 75% of the shares of the corporation.

If the facts in this example are changed so that you receive 80% of the stock in exchange for property (you transfer $40,000 worth of property; Fred still receives $10,000 in shares for his services), the transfer will be tax-free under Section 351, but Fred will have to report the $10,000 in shares as taxable income.

- **Where the corporation issues notes in return for the transfer of appreciated property to the corporation.** Only stock may be received for property in a tax-free § 351 exchange, not long- or short-term notes. For example, if you transfer appreciated assets (such as the assets of a business) to the corporation in return for shares of stock plus a promissory note from the corporation, you will need to report and pay taxes on the gain (technical rules are applied to determine the amount of gain that must be reported). See your accountant if you plan to incorporate an existing business or practice and wish to receive a note in addition to shares back from your corporation.

- **Where the corporation assumes (agrees to pay) liabilities associated with the transferred property.** This technicality typically arises when an existing business is being incorporated (i.e., where the owners of a prior business transfer the assets and liabilities of the prior business to the corporation in return for shares of stock). Under this exception to Section 351 tax-free exchange treatment, the prior business owners will be subject to the payment of taxes if the liabilities assumed by the corporation exceed the basis of the business assets transferred to the corporation.

For example, if you transfer business assets with a basis of $40,000 to your corporation along with $60,000 worth of liabilities, the difference of $20,000 is, as a general rule, taxable to you.

As a conclusion to this discussion, we will simply note that this federal tax statute and its associated regulations contain many rules and exceptions to rules. As a result, if you will be transferring property to your corporation in return for shares of stock (and, possibly, notes to be repaid by the corporation), you will need to check with an accountant to ensure favorable tax results under IRC § 351.

Recordkeeping Note: Federal income tax regulations require the corporation and each shareholder to file statements with their income tax returns listing specific information concerning the Section 351 tax-free exchange (Treasury Regulation Section 1.351-3). Permanent records containing the information listed in these statements must also be kept by the corporation and the shareholders.

14. Tax and Financial Considerations When Incorporating a Prior Business

In this section, we discuss a few key financial and legal tax issues involving the incorporation of an existing business. If you are simply incorporating a new business, you may wish to skip this section.

a. When Is the Best Time to Incorporate the Prior Business?

You will want to incorporate your prior business at a time which results in the most favorable tax treatment (mostly, this means the time which results in your paying the least amount of taxes).

> **EXAMPLE:** If you anticipate a loss this year and a healthy profit next year, you may wish to remain unincorporated now and take a personal loss on your individual tax return. Next year you can incorporate and split your business income between yourself and your corporation to reduce your overall tax liability.

b. Special Financial and Tax Considerations

Typically, when incorporating a preexisting business or practice, all the assets and liabilities of the prior business will be transferred to the new corporation which will then carry on the preexisting business. Further, as explained in subsection 13, above, most incorporators will want the transfer of the assets of the prior business to the corporation in return for shares of stock to qualify for tax-free exchange treatment under Section 351 of the Internal Revenue Code. In special circumstances,

however, some incorporators may not wish to transfer all assets or liabilities of the prior business to the corporation, or, for special reasons, may not wish this transfer to qualify for Section 351 tax-free exchange treatment. We discuss these special circumstances in this subsection.

i. **Do you wish to retain (not transfer) some of the assets of the prior business?** In some instances, the prior business owners may not wish to transfer some of the assets of the prior business to their new corporation. For example:

- Sufficient cash should be retained to pay liabilities not assumed by the corporation (such as payroll and other employment taxes).
- You may wish to retain ownership in some of the assets of the prior business. For example, you may wish to continue to own a building in your name and lease it to your corporation. In this way, you can continue to deduct depreciation, mortgage interest payments, and other expenses associated with the property on your individual tax return (the corporation, moreover, can deduct rent payments made under the lease).

ii. **Do you wish to have the corporation assume some, but not all, of the liabilities of the prior business?** As with the assets of your unincorporated business, you may not wish to transfer (have your corporation assume) all of the liabilities of the prior business. Two considerations relevant to this decision are given below:

- The assumption of the liabilities of the prior business may, in special situations, result in the recognition of taxable gain by the prior business owners under an exception to the tax-free exchange rule of Section 351 (as discussed in subsection 13, above).

• Payment of liabilities and expenses by the prior business owners, rather than by the corporation, will allow the owners to deduct these expenses on their individual tax returns (to reduce their individual taxable incomes).

iii. **Is a Section 351 tax-free exchange desirable?** Although not typical, a small number of incorporators may wish to have the transfer of assets of the prior business to the corporation be a taxable exchange. Since the general rule under Section 351 (discussed in subsection 13, above) is that the exchange of property for stock by individuals who will be in control of the corporation after the exchange is a tax-free transfer, oddly enough, you may need to do a little tax advance tax planning to accomplish this taxable result. Reasons why a few incorporators may wish to be taxed on the transfer of the assets of their prior business to the corporation include the following:

• Some incorporators may wish to recognize taxable gain on the transfer of business assets to increase the corporation's "basis" in these assets. For example, let's assume that you will transfer assets with a fair market value of $50,000 to your corporation. Your basis in these assets is $30,000. If you transfer these assets to the corporation for $50,000 worth of stock in a taxable exchange, you will recognize a taxable gain of $20,000. However, the corporation's basis in these assets will be your basis before the sale ($30,000) plus the amount of gain recognized by the transferor (your individual gain of $20,000). Consequently, the corporation's basis in these assets will be increased to $50,000. This allows the cor-

poration to take additional depreciation in these assets over time and will lower the gain the corporation will have to pay upon a sale of these assets (if the corporation sells the assets for $60,000, the gain will be $10,000—the difference between the corporation's basis and the selling price).

On the other hand, if these assets had been transferred to the corporation in a tax-free exchange, the corporation's basis would be the same as your pre-transfer basis in the property ($30,000) and the gain recognized by the corporation from the sale of these assets would be the higher figure of $30,000 (the difference between the corporation's $30,000 basis and the $60,000 selling price). Of course, whether the advantages of obtaining a higher corporate basis in assets is worth the gain which you, the transferor, will have to pay in a taxable exchange, will be determined by the individual facts of your incorporation (e.g., will you be able to offset this individual gain with losses or deductions on your individual tax return? etc.). As we've said, normally, you will want to transfer assets to your corporation in a tax-free exchange to avoid the recognition of gain on the transfer.

• Some incorporators may wish to recognize a loss on the transfer of assets to their corporation. If you transfer assets to your corporation under Section 351, you cannot recognize either a gain or a loss on the transfer. If the value of the assets has decreased below your basis in the property, you may wish to take a loss on the transfer. For example, if your basis in a building is $75,000, and, because of market conditions, the current value of the building is now only $60,000, you will need to transfer the building to the corporation in a taxable exchange (and meet other technical requirements) to recognize this loss of $15,000. Again, this is not a typical situation but it may be relevant to some incorporators.

c. Liability for the Debts of the Prior Business

In addition to the above considerations involving the assumption of liabilities of the prior business by your new corporation, legal rules exist concerning the liability of the prior business owners and the corporation for the debts of the prior business.

Note: These rules will have little significance for most newly formed corporations which will wish, as a matter of course and as a matter of simple good-faith business dealings, to continue to carry on the business and continue to pay all the debts and liabilities associated with the business, whether incurred before or after incorporation. However, to underscore the fact that you cannot incorporate as a means of avoiding the liabilities of the prior business, and by way of briefly mentioning other specific considerations related to this issue, we include the following points:

- Regardless of whether or not the corporation assumes the debts and liabilities of the prior business, the prior owners remain personally liable for these debts and liabilities.
- The new corporation is not liable for the debts and liabilities of the prior business unless it specifically agrees to assume them, but even if the corporation does assume them, the prior owners remain personally liable for them also unless the creditor signs a release that lets the business owners off the hook personally.

- If the transfer is fraudulent or done with the intent to frustrate or deceive creditors, the creditors of the prior business can file legal papers to seize the transferred business assets. Similarly, if the corporation does not, in fact, pay the assumed liabilities of the prior business, the creditors of the prior business may be allowed to seize the transferred assets.
- If transferred assets are subject to recorded liens (for example, a mortgage on real property), these liens will survive the transfer and the assets will continue to be subject to these liens.
- The former business owners can be personally liable for post-incorporation debts if credit is extended to the corporation by a creditor who thinks that she is still dealing with the prior business (for example, a creditor who has not been notified of the incorporation). See Chapter 7, Section A4 for the steps to take to notify creditors of the prior business of your incorporation.
- The corporation may be liable for delinquent sales, employment or other taxes owed by the unincorporated business.

Also realize that a corporation that specifically assumes all of the debts and liabilities of the unincorporated business is exempt from most of the provisions of the California Bulk Sales Law. This results in a reduction in incorporation paperwork (see Chapter 6, Step 9A).

15. Dissolution of the Corporation

We're sure the dissolution of your corporation is the last thing on your mind. Nevertheless, it might be comforting to know that you can wind up the affairs and business of your corporation with a minimum of legal formality. Here is a quick look at the basic rules which apply when voluntarily dissolving a California corporation:

For Information on Involuntary Dissolution: The rules in this section concern what is legally referred to as a "voluntary dissolution" of the corporation (where a majority of your shareholders mutually agree to dissolve the corporation). The California Corporations Code also contains involuntary dissolution procedures where a court is petitioned (by dissatisfied or deadlocked shareholders, directors or the Attorney General) to force the dissolution of a corporation. If you're interested in these special rules, see the California Corporations Code, starting with Section 12620.

Any California corporation may, on its own motion and out of court, elect to voluntarily wind up and dissolve for any reason by the vote of at least 50% of the voting power of the shareholders.

In addition, the board of directors may elect to dissolve the corporation, without shareholder approval, if any of the following conditions apply:

- The corporation has not issued any shares.
- An order for relief has been entered under Chapter 7 of the Federal Bankruptcy Law for the corporation.
- The corporation has disposed of all its assets and hasn't conducted any business for the past five years.

Voluntary dissolution, upon the request of the corporation, three or more creditors, or other interested parties, may be subject to court supervision.

In any voluntary (or involuntary) dissolution, the corporation must cease transacting business except to the extent necessary to wind up its affairs and, if desired, to preserve the goodwill or going-concern value of the corporation pending a sale of its assets. All shareholders and creditors on the books of the corporation must be notified of the dissolution. All debts and liabilities, to the extent of corporate assets, must be paid or provided for, with any remaining assets distributed to shareholders in proportion to their stockholdings and any special stock preferences. A certificate of dissolution must be filed with the Secretary of State stating that a person associated with the corporation assumes liability for any unpaid taxes owed by the corporation until a tax clearance is issued by the California Franchise Tax Board. Once the Secretary receives the tax clearance statement from the Franchise Tax Board showing that all corporate franchise taxes have been paid or provided for, the corporation is dissolved.

Corporate dissolutions subject to Superior Court supervision must include the publication of a notice to creditors at least once a week for three successive weeks in the county in which the court is located. Creditors not filing claims within a specified period (ranging from three to six months after publication) are barred from participating in any distribution of the general assets of the corporation.

For further information on the voluntary dissolution of a California corporation, together with sample forms and instructions, obtain the "Guide to Corporate Filings" from the California Secretary of State's office. Call the Secretary's office at 916-657-5448 for current ordering information or download the booklet directly from the Secretary of State's website at http://www.ss.ca.gov/business/corp-corp-stkdissinfo.htm (for profits) or http://www.ss.ca.gov/business/corp/corp-npdissinfo.htm (nonprofits).

Professional Corporation Note: The Board which oversees your profession may implement additional rules which must be followed when dissolving a professional corporation—check with your Board before initiating a dissolution of your professional corporation. ■

Chapter 4

SPECIFIC REQUIREMENTS FOR PROFESSIONALS WHO INCORPORATE

THERE ARE SPECIFIC California laws and regulations pertaining to the professions listed in Chapter 2, Section B. Professionals who incorporate must comply with provisions such as who can own shares in the corporation, who can be the directors and officers, what happens when a shareholder dies or leaves the corporation, and how much security the corporation must put up to protect itself and its shareholders from malpractice actions. The laws can be found in the Corporations Code (beginning with Section 13401) and in the Business and Professions Code of the California statutes, under the respective profession. The regulations appear in Title 16 of the California Administrative Code (except the rules for law corporations which appear in the Business and Professions Code).

We review particular provisions of each profession in Appendix 4. But it will be useful to review here the general kinds of restrictions and requirements you will need to meet if you decide to incorporate.

Important: The rules covered in this chapter and in the Appendix are subject to change. You will want to contact your board before incorporating or a copy of the latest corporate rules that apply to your profession.

A. Licensing

The professional must be licensed by the appropriate state board. Most boards come under the State Department of Consumer Affairs, namely:

- State Board of Accountancy
- State Board of Architectural Examiners*
- State Board of Behavioral Science Examiners, including
  - Licensed Clinical Social Workers
  - Marriage, Family and Child Counselors
- State Board of Court Reporters
- State Board of Dental Examiners
- State Board of Medical Quality Assurance (BMQA), including
  - Division of Licensing:
  - Medical (Doctors and Surgeons)
  - Division of Allied Health Professions:
  - Acupuncture
  - Physical Therapy
  - Physicians' Assistants
  - Podiatric
  - Psychological
  - Speech Pathology and Audiology
- State Board of Registered Nursing
- State Board of Optometry
- State Board of Pharmacy
- Board of Examiners in Veterinary Medicine

* At the time of this edition, the Board of Architectural Examiners has not implemented procedures to register or oversee professional architectural corporations (all calls to the Board regarding professional architectural corporations are referred to the Secretary of State's office). See Appendix 4 for further information.

The separate boards are:

- State Bar—Law (Attorneys)
- State Board of Osteopathic Examiners
- State Board of Chiropractic Examiners

All the boards require professional corporations to deal with their main office in Sacramento, except that law corporations deal with the State Bars San Francisco office.

B. Certificate of Registration

About one-half of these professional corporations must apply for a certificate of registration from their appropriate board after their Articles of Incorporation are approved by the Secretary of State. The Board of Medical Quality Assurance and its divisions, the State Board of Pharmacy, the Board of Examiners in Veterinary Medicine, the Board of Architectural Examiners, the Board of Registered Nursing and the Certified Shorthand Reporters Board do not require a certificate.

Each board which requires a certificate supplies its own application form. Fees vary from $100–$200.

C. Names

All professional corporations are restricted in the style of name they may use. Some of the laws and regulations specifically spell out the requirements. Provisions of other professions refer to the choice of name more generally.

In all cases, professional corporations must indicate that they are a corporation. Usually, the indication is restricted to "Professional Corporation," "Corporation," or "Incorporated," or an abbreviation of these terms. In a few instances, the professional corporation may use any other "wording or abbreviation denoting corporate existence."

The corporation may use the full name or just the surname of one or more of the shareholders. For example, "Dulac and Greenaway, Professional Corporation," or "Walter P. Crane, A Medical Corp." The names used may be the names of present, prospective or former shareholders or of persons who were associated with a predecessor person, partnership or organization (Corporations Code Section 13409). Optometric corporations require the former name be deleted within two years after the person ceases to be a shareholder.

Most permissible names for each professional corporation include a reference to the profession, e.g., "a law corporation," though some regulations do not make this a requirement.

In addition, several professions permit corporations to use a name other than that of one or more of the shareholders. In these cases, fictitious name permits are required, and must be applied for from the appropriate board. There is an initial fee, and you usually need to renew it every year or two (with a renewal fee).

The corporations which are allowed to use fictitious names are:

- (Licensed) Clinical Social Worker
- Dental
- Law*
- Medical
- Optometric
- Osteopathic
- Podiatric
- Physical Therapy
- Psychology

* Special rules apply to the use of fictitious names by law corporations. Attorneys interested in using a fictitious name should see the Law Corporation section in Appendix 4 and the "fictitious name" subsection thereunder.

In some of these (e.g., for osteopathic and optometric corporations) there is an additional requirement that if a fictitious name is used, the names and professional degrees of the shareholders must be posted at the office and used on printed matter and in advertising.

Examples of fictitious names are: "The Physical Therapy Clinic, Inc." or "The Dental Store, A Prof. Corp."

See Appendix 4 and check with your appropriate board and the Secretary of State before you file to be sure the name(s) you use will be accepted.

D. Who May Be Shareholders?

Only people licensed in the profession (or in several instances, in a specified related profession) may own shares in a professional corporation (Corporations Code Section 13406). Thus, only licensed attorneys may be shareholders of a law corporation. Medical, podiatry, psychological, speech pathology, audiology, nursing, marriage, family and child counseling, licensed clinical social workers, physicians' assistants and chiropractic corporations allow certain other persons to be shareholders so long as the sum of the shares owned by the other persons does not exceed 49% of the total number of shares of the corporation and so long as the number of these other persons does not exceed the number of professionals holding shares who are licensed by the agency regulating the designated profession (Corporations Code Section 13401.5).

For example, licensed podiatrists, psychologists, registered nurses, optometrists, licensed marriage, family and child counselors, licensed clinical social workers, licensed physicians' assistants and licensed chiropractors may own shares in a medical corporation.

See Appendix 4 for who may own shares in the other corporations.

E. Who May Be Directors and Officers

Each director and officer of a professional corporation must be licensed in the particular profession of your corporation (except that in medical, podiatric, psychological, speech pathology, audiology, nursing, marriage, family and child counseling, licensed clinical social worker and physicians' assistants corporations, the directors and officers may be other specific licensed persons (see the discussion in the shareholder section, above)). Also see the exceptions for unlicensed officers in a one-shareholder corporation and for unlicensed assistant officers in certain professions as discussed below.

1. Directors

If your corporation has three or more shareholders, it must have at least three directors (Corporations Code Section 212(a)). However, a professional corporation with one shareholder may have only one director who must be the sole shareholder (Corporations Code Section 13403). Similarly, a professional corporation with two shareholders may have two directors who must be the two shareholders (Corporations Code Section 13403).

2. Officers

Under the language of Section 13403 of the Professional Corporation Act, a professional corporation should fill four officer positions: President, Vice-President, Secretary and Treasurer (also referred to as the Chief Financial Officer).

We assume that most professional corporations will not mind complying with the technicality of electing a Vice-President (and have allowed for the election of this officer in the tear-out Bylaws and Minutes in the Appendices of this book). However, under the provisions of Section 312(a) of the General Corporation Law, only the three offices of President, Secretary and Chief Financial Officer (Treasurer) are required.

Since it appears that most boards follow this more liberal rule and only require these latter three officer positions to be filled, your corporation may be able to simply provide for and fill the three officer positions of President, Secretary and Treasurer. If you wish to do this, please check with your board first.

One-Shareholder Rule: If your professional corporation has only one shareholder, this shareholder must serve as President and Treasurer of your corporation. The other officer positions (Vice-President and Secretary) may be filled by unlicensed persons.

Again note that Section 312(a) of the General Corporation Law allows one person to fill all the officer positions in the corporation and the various professional boards seem to follow this one-person rule in one-shareholder situations. However, since the language of Section 13403 is again unclear on this point, check with your board if you wish to fill all the officer positions in your one-shareholder corporation. It may be just as simple to follow the apparent intent of Section 13403 here and have an unlicensed person (such as your spouse) fill the other officer position(s) in your one-shareholder corporation.

Pharmacy Corporations Note: Section 4124 of the Pharmacy Corporation Law says that each officer other than an assistant secretary and assistant treasurer *must* be licensed. Unlike the laws for the other professional corporations, the Pharmacy Law makes no reference to Section 13403 of the Corporations Code. This could have been an oversight since the Pharmacy Law was passed in 1981 and no regulations have yet been issued under it. However, we suggest you note this uncertainty and check with the State Board of Pharmacy if you intend to incorporate as a pharmacy corporation.

Two-Shareholder Rule: If your professional corporation has only two shareholders, between them these two shareholders must fill the offices of President, Vice-President, Secretary, and Treasurer (for example, with one serving as President and Secretary and the other as Vice-President and Treasurer (Corporations Code Section 13403). Again, under Section 312(a) of the General Corporation Law, your two shareholders may only need to fill the three offices of President, Secretary and Treasurer.

Assistant Officers: Although not required, if you wish to provide for assistant officer positions, an assistant secretary and assistant treasurer need not be licensed in medical, chiropractic, psychological, physical therapy, speech pathology and audiology, acupuncture, osteopathic, podiatric, nursing, physicians' assistants, and pharmacy corporations.

F. Transferring Shares

Since only licensed persons may own shares in a professional corporation (Corporations Code

Section 13406), obviously there are restrictions on the sale or transfer of the shares. If someone leaves the corporation, her shares must be sold to either another licensed professional permitted to own shares in the corporation, or back to the corporation. (See Corporations Code Section 13407 and specific board regulations.) There are also laws and regulations providing for the sale or transfer of shares of a shareholder who dies or becomes disqualified to hold shares (perhaps because she lost her license). For example, under Corp. Code Section 13407, a transfer of shares must be within 90 days following disqualification or six months following the death of a shareholder. These ownership and transfer restrictions must be set out in the Articles of Incorporation or in the Bylaws.

Also, on each share of stock, a notation (or "legend") must appear which informs the person that there are specific restrictions on the transfer of that profession's stock (see Appendix 4).

Technical Question for One-Person Incorporated Practices: A question arises when the sole shareholder of a professional corporation dies. If no other licensed professional permitted to own the shares obtains the shares, would the professional corporation then become a general corporation? We think so, but since the general corporation cannot legally provide professional services, its only purpose would presumably be to wind up the business and be dissolved.

G. Security for Malpractice

All of the state boards are empowered to formulate and enforce requirements that the corporation provide security for claims against it arising out of its professional services. However, only about one-half have actually drawn up rules. There are presently no guidelines for acupuncturists, architects, licensed clinical social workers, marriage, family and child counselors, shorthand reporters, psychologists, physical therapists, pharmacists, speech pathologists, audiologists, nurses, physicians' assistants and veterinarians. The absence of any provision regarding security may mean that the other professionals in the corporation (not just the professional(s) who committed the malpractice) are still fully personally liable. However, one could also interpret this absence of provisions to indicate that only the professional(s) who committed the malpractice are personally liable. In actuality, sufficient insurance should be provided so the problem will not arise.

The rules governing the other shareholders vary somewhat, but most require that professional corporations provide insurance up to specified limits, or the shareholders will be "jointly and severally" (meaning together and individually) liable up to these limits. Thus, if the corporation has no insurance (or possibly other security—see medical and podiatric corporations in Appendix 4, which also allow bonds and certificates of deposit), a shareholder can be liable for another shareholder's malpractice up to a certain amount. (See the discussion under limited liability in Chapter 3, Section A1.) Law and accounting corporations are required to furnish their boards with written agreements by the shareholders, guaranteeing payment for claims against them, though insurance can cover these amounts.

The stated minimum and maximum amounts of coverage vary from $50,000 upward (check Appendix 4 for specific provisions for each profession).

Awards in excess of the stated limits are only borne by those parties who committed or participated in the malpractice. (See Chapter 3, Section A1.)

H. Reports

Approximately one-half of the professions must file annual reports with their boards. These are:
- Accounting
- Dental
- Law
- Licensed Clinical Social Workers
- Marriage, Family, and Child Counselors
- Optometric
- Osteopathic
- Shorthand Reporters

Fees vary between $10 and $150 per year.

Special reports referring to such things as changes in share ownership, share transfers, and new certificates of registration are also required of some corporations. These reports must be filed within 30 days, usually on forms provided by the appropriate board. Fees vary from $5 to $150.

Change of address reports may also be required.

I.   The Professional Corporation Stock Qualification Exemption

An important attribute of the professional corporation, and one of its many major advantages, is that, unlike the large, private shareholder corporations or those which offer their shares to the public, it is exempt from "qualifying" the issuance of its shares with the Commissioner of Corporations. This requires a little explanation.

Issued shares are simply those which are sold to a shareholder by a corporation. Sale of stock has traditionally been subject to abuse. For instance, promoters have sold their property to a corporation which they helped organize for more than the fair market value. In return, they received a certain percentage of the share of the corporation whose book value reflected the inflated purchase price of the property. This dilutes the value of the stock belonging to the other shareholders, as the honest value of the corporate assets backing up their stock is now less than before the promoters made their dishonest deal.

In order to protect the public and other outside shareholders from this kind of "watered stock" as well as from other unfair or fraudulent stock issuance transactions, both the California and federal governments have enacted security regulation laws. In California, these provide that a corporation must "qualify" the stock with the Commissioner of Corporations before it is issued (Corporations Code Sections 25110-25122). This qualification or approval process involves the submission of financial data, takes time, and can be expensive (accounting, attorney and filing fees, etc.).

Fortunately, the Commissioner of Corporations has exempted professional corporations from this qualification requirement under 10 Cal. Code of Regs. Section 260.105.6. (If you intend to transfer shares from one professional to another or back to the corporation, contact a lawyer to insure compliance with state and federal securities laws.)

J.   Federal Securities Law

Federal securities law also applies to the offering of shares by a corporation. You must register your initial offering of stock with the Securities and Exchange Commission (SEC) unless you fall under a specific exemption from registration. Registration with the SEC is very expensive. According to figures released by the SEC, the average amount paid by "small" corporations for registering is $100,000, $40,000 of which is paid to the lawyer involved with the registration. There are several exemptions available, and most professional corporations should not need to register with the SEC.

Here's a very brief description of the more obvious choices available to issuers in order to effect an unregistered private offering of securities under the federal Securities Act of 1933 and exemption rules promulgated under this Act.

Traditionally, most small corporations wishing to privately issue their initial shares to a limited number of people have been able to rely on the SEC intrastate offering or nonpublic offering exemptions. One of these exemptions will still probably be your most obvious choice in seeking an exemption from registration or notification of your initial stock offering with the SEC.

The intrastate offering exemption is contained in Section 3(a)(11) of the Act and exempts certain intrastate offers and sales of stock. Generally it applies to the issuance of shares offered and sold only to persons resident within a single state if the issuer (the corporation) is resident and doing business within the state. This is, perhaps, the most popular exemption relied on by small corporations when issuing their initial shares. SEC Rule l47 defines more precisely the technical language used in this statute and provides a set of guidelines and procedures to follow to make reliance on this exemption a bit safer. For instance, limitations should be placed on resales of shares, precautions should be taken against later interstate offers and sales, and purchasers should make written representations as to their residency within the state.

The nonpublic offering exemption is a one-line exemption contained in Section 4(2) of the Securities Act. The courts have discussed the basic elements which should be present when relying on this exemption [a leading case on this exemption is *SEC* v. *Ralston Purina Co.,* 346 U.S. 119 (1953)]:

- the offerees and purchasers are able to fend for themselves due to their previous financial/ business experience, relationship to the issuer (the corporation, its directors, officers), and/or significant personal net worth;
- the transaction is truly a nonpublic offering involving no general advertising or solicitation;
- the shares are purchased by the shareholders for their own account and not for resale;
- the offerees and purchasers are limited in number;
- the offerees and purchasers must have access to or are given information relevant to the stock transactions in order to evaluate the pros and cons of the investment (the same type of information supplied on an SEC registration statement).

More recently, the SEC adopted a number of "500 series" rules as part of Regulation D, a series of provisions "...designed to simplify and clarify previous exemptions, to expand their availability, and to achieve uniformity between federal and state exemptions in order to facilitate capital formation consistent with the protection of investors." For the most part, these rules, together with Section 4(6) of the Act, allow corporations to privately sell a limited amount of securities to no more than 35 investors and to an unlimited num-

ber of accredited investors (those meeting certain sophisticated investor standards related to personal net worth, annual individual income, position of responsibility within the corporation, etc.). Generally, these rules also require the disclosure of information to prospective purchasers, prohibit general solicitation or advertising and impose limitations on resale of the securities (they can't be resold without being registered or being eligible for an exemption from registration). Use of these Regulation rules or of Section 4(6) requires a Notice of Sales of Securities form to be filed with the SEC. For more information on Regulation D, you may wish to obtain a copy of SEC Release No. 33-6389, or a summary of Regulation D available at http://www.sec.gov/smbus/forms/formssb.htm.

Most lawyers will probably feel that your professional corporation's initial stock issuance will not require registration with, or notification to, the SEC. Nonetheless, this is a complex area with more than a few ambiguities and pitfalls and we advise you to check with a lawyer to ensure that you are in fact eligible for an SEC exemption. Note that whether or not you have to register or provide notification to the SEC of your stock offering, the antifraud provisions of the Securities Law always apply, so DISCLOSE, DISCLOSE, DISCLOSE!

For more information about Regulation D requirements, go to www.sec.gov. This is the SEC website that contains publications and information about private offerings and other federal securities exemptions.

Finally, if your offering of securities involves a state outside of California (e.g., if your offer is made outside of California or if a purchaser is not a California resident), you should consult an attorney to see if the securities laws of that state apply to your offering. ■

Chapter 5

RETIREMENT PLANS

A. Introduction

Federal tax legislation has largely succeeded in eliminating the distinctions between qualified pension plans offered by corporations and those available under Keogh (H.R. 10) plans for self-employed persons. However, there are still some advantages in corporate plans. The clearest is that members of corporate plans may borrow from the plan while loans to Keogh members are not permitted; see Sections C and F, below. There are also certain fringe benefits available to corporate employees, such as health and disability insurance, group-term life insurance and medical reimbursement, which are generally not permitted to unincorporated individuals or partners; see Chapter 3, Section A3. Also, incorporated professionals will generally not be liable for the malpractice of other professionals in the corporation (as would be the case for an unincorporated practice), provided that certain professional liability insurance coverage standards are met—see Chapter 4, Section G.

Another important consideration in assessing various retirement plans is the various restrictions placed on "top-heavy" corporate and Keogh plans (top-heavy plans are those which benefit "key" employees—see Section H, below). Additional restraints have also been imposed on certain kinds of professional corporations—see Chapter 3, Section C3, *Section 269A Restrictions*.

Tax reform has obviously brought about a variety of significant changes to retirement program planning. A large number of these changes are very technical and complex. In the interest of clarity, and in keeping with this chapter's goal of presenting only a helpful overview of retirement planning, many of the more intricate changes resulting from the Tax Reform Act have been omitted. Also note that this highly technical tax material is constantly changing as tax and other legal provisions are amended. *So please check with your tax or retirement plan advisor for the latest rules on each of the plans discussed below.*

For further information on corporate plans and comparable or contrasting provisions for non-corporate plans, see the following IRS publications:

334:    *Tax Guide For Small Business*

560:    *Self-Employed Retirement Plans*

575:    *Pension and Annuity Income*

590:    *Individual Retirement Arrangements*

1048: *Filing Requirements for Employee Benefit Plans*

Also see *Creating Your Own Retirement Plan: IRAs and Keoghs for the Self-Employed*, by Twila Slesnick (Nolo), which contains detailed information and tips on creating retirement plans.

Generally, retirement plans offer substantial tax breaks. The amounts you contribute are deductible. You don't pay any taxes on your contributions nor on the interest and earnings the money makes while invested until you withdraw it at retirement (when presumably your tax bracket will be lower). Thus, in most cases, it follows that the more you can invest in your plan, the more you can take advantage of a lucrative tax shelter. Let's look at the various types of plans available to the professional practitioner.

B. Individual Retirement Arrangement (IRA)

This is the most basic type of plan. Qualified individuals, whether working as an employee or self-employed, can contribute up to $2,000 yearly to a traditional IRA and deduct the contribution from their income taxes, or make nondeductible contributions to a Roth IRA. With Roth IRAs, your contributions are not deductible, but your qualified distributions are tax-free. However, if your adjusted gross income exceeds a certain amount ($95,000 for single filers, $150,000 for joint filers), your contribution amount is reduced, and the availability of Roth IRAs is phased out completely for taxpayers whose adjusted gross income exceeds $110,000 (single filers) and $160,000 (joint filers). Special rules apply to contributions made on behalf of working and nonworking spouses. Given the restrictions on the deductibility of traditional IRA contributions and the phase-outs for Roth IRAs, the attractiveness of IRAs is questionable for incorporated professionals wishing to set up a corporate retirement program. However, if you can incorporate and still work

within the IRA restrictions, such a plan may be desirable due to its relative simplicity. For further information on IRAs, see IRS Publication 590, *Individual Retirement Arrangements*.

SIMPLE RETIREMENT PLANS

Corporations with 100 or fewer employees can adopt a so-called "SIMPLE" retirement plan. The plan can take the form of an IRA established for each participant or a cash or deferred (401k) arrangement. The advantage of SIMPLE plans is that they are easier to set up and operate (less paperwork and filing formalities, and simpler rules) than other qualified retirement plans, and allow top professional to receive a greater level of contributions (than those allowed under the nondiscrimination rules that apply to standard retirement plans). Potential disadvantages of SIMPLE plans are (1) the corporation cannot maintain another retirement plan for employees, (2) elective contributions—the amount the employee elects to have deducted from salary and contributed to his account in the SIMPLE plan—are limited to $6,000 annually, and (3) the corporation must normally make a minimum matching contribution each year of at least 3% of the employee's elective contribution (as little as 1% may be matched by the corporation two out of every five years if it elects to do so).

C. Keogh

The Keogh Plan is designed for people who are self-employed (i.e., sole proprietorships and partnerships) and their employees. As with corporate plans, there are two types of Keogh plans: *defined contribution* and *defined benefit* plans. The overall limits on contributions are generally the same as the limits applicable to corresponding corporate plans: for defined contribution Keoghs the limit is the smaller of $30,000 or 25% of the participant's compensation; for defined benefit Keoghs, the limit is $130,000 or 100% of the participant's average compensation for her highest three years (both dollar figures are subject to annual cost-of-living increases). The retirement benefit provisions in Keoghs are the same as corporate plans: unless the participant elects otherwise, benefits must commence by the latest of (1) age 65; (2) the 10th anniversary of the date the participant came under the plan; or (3) the year a person retires. Top-heavy plan rules apply to Keoghs as well as corporate plans (see Section H below).

For the most part, provisions under the former tax laws that made corporate retirement plans more attractive to professionals than Keoghs have been eliminated. The result, as we see it, is that the tax shelter advantages of corporate plans over Keoghs have been negated for the most part.

However, there are still some differences. The main advantage to corporate plan members is that they can borrow from their plan, while a member of a Keogh plan generally cannot; see Section F. Also, rules governing certain lump-sum distributions before age 59 1/2, certain carryovers and certain rollover contributions favor corporate plan members. We suggest you speak to your tax advisor about some of the finer distinctions between the two types of plans. (And don't forget the fringe benefits such as health insurance, group-life insurance and medical reimbursement also benefiting corporations; see Chapter 3, Section A3.) Also see IRS publication 560, *Self-Employed Retirement Plans*.

D. SEP (Simplified Employee Pension Plans)

Employers, whether incorporated or not, may contribute to their employees' IRAs. Deductible contributions are limited to $30,000 or 15% of the employee's annual compensation, whichever is less. The employee maintains the account.

The employer's contributions are tax deductible as a business expense. They are also deductible from the employee's taxable income (until withdrawal at retirement). As discussed in Section B, above, a qualified employee can personally contribute up to $2,000 to the IRA and deduct that too.

It is possible for individuals involved in small SEP plans to elect to have their employers make contributions directly to their SEPs or to receive cash instead under a special type of salary reduction SEP. Check with your accountant for more details on applicable procedures and restrictions.

E. Corporate Retirement Plans

Here is an outline of several of the different kinds of corporate retirement plans. By reviewing this before you discuss the subject with your pension consultant, you'll have a better understanding of the various alternatives. Remember, only a well-informed financial advisor can truly tell you which plan is best suited for you.

Where the professionals in your business have different ideas on what is best, or on how to manage the fund, you may consider offering more than one plan. Or you may provide that each professional will individually decide how to invest his or her portion (by permitting each professional employee this discretion, you will probably also have to allow each lay employee the same right).

Professionals who individually incorporate and then form a partnership (see the example noted in Chapter 2, Section D) will have even more flexibility in tailoring their own plans to meet their personal and financial needs and still be associated with other members of the profession. However, such incorporated partnerships may face special problems—see Chapter 3, Section C3, Section 269A *Restrictions*.

As we noted in the discussion on Keogh plans above (see Section C), restrictions on Keogh plans, which formerly resulted in Keogh plans being less attractive than corporate plans to the high-earning professional, have been largely eliminated. But a few still remain, such as borrowing from a corporate plan (see Section F). The professional must also now be concerned with top-heavy plans whether setting up a corporate or Keogh plan (see Section H, below).

1. Defined Benefit (Pension) Plan— Fixed Plan

This plan defines or fixes the amount of money you will receive upon your retirement. The maximum is 100% of your average income for the three highest consecutive years (salary up to $160,000 per year is counted) or $130,000. (This dollar amount limitation is adjusted periodically to the cost of living). The business must contribute a required amount each year, actuarially determined (i.e., what age you are now and what age you plan to retire), taking into account the interest earnings on the contributions so that the plan will provide the guaranteed benefit at retirement. Excess interest earnings cannot be used to increase the benefits, and the business will be required to reduce its contribution accordingly. Similarly, if interest earn-

ings are below what was expected, the business must make up the difference.

The defined benefit plan is often the choice of older professionals. They will be able to make larger contributions under this plan and accumulate the necessary funds in a shorter time to reach the desired pension benefit.

For example, if you are earning $70,000 a year, under a defined benefit plan you can contribute enough money each year so that at the year you plan to retire, you will have an annual benefit of $70,000. How much you actually contribute yearly is actuarially determined and will fluctuate if the plan earns less or more than anticipated.

2. Defined Contribution (or Money-Purchase Pension) Plan

Under this plan, the business contributes a fixed percentage of your earnings. The annual amount contributed will thus fluctuate with your annual earnings.

The risk with defined contribution plans is obvious. There is no guarantee on how much you will receive at retirement. Should the business not obtain a favorable return on the money it invests in the pension plan, it is not required to make up the difference (as it would in a defined benefit plan).

The maximum contribution is $30,000 or 25% of your earnings, whichever is less. (The $30,000 limitation on contributions is subject to adjustment for cost of living increases.)

For example, if your annual income is $80,000, you can contribute up to $20,000 (25%).

3. Targeted Benefit Pension Plans

This plan combines features of the defined benefit and contribution plans. The targeted benefit is based on a percentage of your earnings at retirement. The amounts contributed to the plan are the actual amounts necessary to fund the benefit (as in a defined benefit plan). However, the contributions cannot exceed the limitations of a defined contribution plan, i.e., $30,000 or 25% of earnings, whichever is less.

Thus, though you set up the account with a targeted benefit, the actual amount is unknown until retirement, since it is contingent on how well (or poorly) the funds do while invested. Unlike the defined benefit plan, the business does not have to decrease (or increase) its contribution if earnings of the fund are not in line with expectations.

For example, if you wish to have a targeted benefit of $60,000 yearly, you will contribute a certain amount each year (as actuarially determined) so that if the earnings of the plan were constant, you would reach that target. (Note that contributions are limited to $30,000, adjusted annually, or 25% of earnings.) However, you may end up with a yearly retirement benefit of more or less than $60,000 since the plan is dependent on how the earnings of the fund actually do.

4. Profit Sharing Plans

Profit sharing plans, as the term indicates, receive their contributions from the profits of the business. The maximum deductible contribution is 15% of covered compensation. The business need not apply a fixed formula in determining how much to contribute each year. In fact, the business is not even required to make any contributions, if the directors choose not to.

Professional businesses often combine a profit-sharing plan with another plan. However, in doing so you won't be able to take the maximum benefits under each plan, but rather will have to combine them. Nevertheless, profit sharing plans are very attractive to professionals because they have discretion on how much to invest each year.

F. Borrowing Under a Corporate Plan

As mentioned earlier one of the advantages of a corporate retirement plan over a Keogh is the ability to borrow from the corporate plan. Generally, an individual can obtain a loan from a plan which will not be considered taxable income if the loan does not exceed $50,000 (or 1/2 the amount invested) and if the loan is repaid within five years. (An exception to the five-year repayment period is made if the loan is used to acquire a home that will be a principal residence within a reasonable amount of time after the loan is made.)

Note, however, the $50,000 limit for loans is reduced by a formula utilizing the highest outstanding balance of the loan during the 12-month period before any new loan is made. Furthermore, all loans must be amortized with level payments made at least quarterly.

With careful planning, plan loans can be made in a manner that puts the participants of a corporate plan at an advantage over a Keogh participant (remember, loans to Keogh plan members are usually not permitted, but see the note just below).

Approval of Keogh Loans: The Labor Department has established criteria for approving exemptions to the no-loan rule for Keoghs. If no more than 25% of plan assets are lent to owners, funds are lent at market rates, plan balance isn't used as security for the loan and an independent fiduciary approves the loan first, the Department of Labor may approve the loan transaction. For further information on applying for a loan exemption for a Keogh plan, call the Department of Labor Exemption Division in Washington, D.C.

G. The Retirement Plan and Employees

A big consideration in setting up a retirement plan will very likely involve whether you have employees. The more you have, the more costly it can get. There are strict rules for retirement plans relating to who must be covered, when benefits must vest (when a participant must receive a non-forfeitable right to benefits) and when benefits must be paid. Although the rules do permit a degree of flexibility (such as the ability to integrate the plan with social security or to use different vesting schedules), be prepared to set up a plan for all professionals *and* lay employees in your practice. Also note that even less flexibility is permitted to top-heavy plans (see the next section).

H. Top-Heavy Plans

A top-heavy plan is a plan which primarily benefits key employees to a substantially greater extent than the other employees. The plan may either be a corporate or a Keogh plan. Key employees generally include (1) certain officers, (2) the 10 employees who had the largest ownership interests in the company, (3) employees who own more than 5% of the company and (4) employees

who own more than 1% of the company and whose income exceeds $150,000. Note that sole proprietors, partners and shareholder/practitioners are considered "employees" of the company.

A variety of top-heavy plan restrictions deal with (1) quicker vesting guidelines for non-key employees, (2) minimum contributions or benefits for non-key employees and (3) limits on contributions and benefits for key employees.

Since many, if not most, retirement plans for professionals are likely to be top-heavy, you and your tax advisor will need to consider the effect a top-heavy plan will have on key and non-key employees included in your plan.

I. Cafeteria Plans and 401(k) Plans

Your tax advisor should also be able to instruct you on whether your corporation can set up a "cafeteria" style plan (under Section 125 of the Internal Revenue Code) allowing employees to pick and choose their own package of qualified fringe benefits. Cafeteria plans presently have no limits on the amounts of income that can be put into the plan or on the amount of benefits available (they must not, however, discriminate in favor of key employees or highly compensated participants).

Another option is a 401(k) plan which is a qualified cash or deferral arrangement under which employees may elect to have the employer pay them cash benefits or have these amounts deferred (paid into a trust) under the plan. The employees receive, and pay taxes on, the deferred amounts upon retirement.

Employee deferrals under 401(k) plans are limited to $9,500 per calendar year (indexed to the Consumer Price Index). Nondiscrimination rules limit the amount of deferrals that can be elected by highly paid employees.

J. Where Do You Go for a Pension Plan? (Whether IRA, Keogh, SEP or Corporate)

Though you will want a plan tailored to your specific requirements, it doesn't mean you have to go to an accountant or tax attorney. In fact, there are specialized pension consulting firms, some of whom are excellent (and some, however, are not). Check carefully.

Note that there is a difference between Custodial Plans and Trustee Plans. Custodians such as banks and insurance companies often do not have as much flexibility as trustees (who are usually private corporations) in the kinds of investments available to the plan and in the investment deci-

sions you can make. Thus, though a plan offered by a bank or insurance company is often sufficient and usually inexpensive, be sure to make certain that it allows you to change investments at any time, make loans, make voluntary contributions, and obtain pre-retirement death benefits, as well as anything else you feel is important. If you are using a plan offered by an insurance company, look out for a requirement that you purchase unnecessary, expensive life insurance.

All pension and retirement plans have to be "qualified" (approved) by the IRS. To actually submit a plan to the IRS for qualification takes a long time. So what most financial advisors do is fit you into a master or prototype plan which has already been accepted by the IRS and then offer you options within it. Sometimes the advisor may lead you to believe that you are getting an individually designed customized plan, but customized plans, which are actually developed from the ground up, are expensive and take a long time to become qualified. Few self-employed professionals or small professional corporations think it's worth all the extra time and money for such a personally tailored plan. ■

Chapter 6

STEPS TO FORM A PROFESSIONAL CORPORATION

THIS CHAPTER SHOWS you how to prepare and file Articles of Incorporation, prepare Bylaws and take other steps necessary to form your own California professional corporation. We recommend that before you file your Articles of Incorporation, you have them and your Bylaws reviewed by a lawyer and accountant (see Chapter 8 for specifics). This is not required by law and some incorporators may not feel that this is necessary in their situation. Just the same, we think it makes excellent sense to consult people who have more experience in the often complicated questions that surround incorporation than you do. An experienced lawyer and accountant are very likely to make helpful suggestions, some of which may save you much time and aggravation later. A consultation with a lawyer and accountant to review these forms and other organizational aspects of your incorporation *before* you file your articles and officially become a corporation is a far cry from having them do it all for you. Their job is to answer your specific, informed questions and review your papers at an hourly fee agreed upon in advance, not to do all the routine paperwork.

Important: Although we've noted fees which are scheduled or likely to increase, all fees (and the addresses of the Secretary of State offices) mentioned in this chapter are subject to change at any time (filing fees often change on the first day of the year; franchise tax amounts can change at any time). To be doubly sure that the fee amounts (and addresses) given in this chapter are current at the time of your incorporation, call the nearest office of the Secretary of State (located in Fresno, Los Angeles, Sacramento, San Diego and San Francisco) just prior to filing your documents. The Secretary of State office addresses and phone numbers are listed at the beginning of Appendix 1 at the back of the book.

COMPANION DISK FOR COMPUTER USERS

Included at the back of this book is a CD-ROM containing files with word processing (rich text format or RTF) and text-only versions of all tear-out forms included in Appendix 1 through 3. For specific instructions for using the forms on the disk, see How to Use the Forms Disk, Appendix 5.

A. Choose a Name

The first step in organizing your corporation is selecting a name which pleases you and meets the requirements of state law. Please begin by reviewing Chapter 4, Section C, on appropriate names for professional corporations. Then check Appendix 4 for the particular rules applying to your profession, and follow up with a phone call to the agency regulating your profession to find out whether there have been any recent changes. Note that not all professions are permitted to use fictitious names.

Corporations Code Section 13409 says that the name should not be substantially the same as that of another corporation. However, the Secretary of State will allow you to file a similar name if your corporation's name is restricted to the name or the last name of one or more of the present, prospective or former shareholders or of persons who were associated with a predecessor person, partnership or other organization, or whose name appeared in such predecessor organization. Thus, there can be a "Robert Van Gulik, Prof. Corp." and a "Robert Van Gulik, Inc." as long as a Robert Van Gulik is connected with each.

The name of the corporation must be included in the Articles of Incorporation and is usually first submitted for approval by the California Secretary of State when the Articles are filed with this office. It is often advisable, however, to check the availability of your name ahead of time. You can check the availability of up to three corporate names by mail by sending a note to the Secretary of State at 1500 11th Street, Sacramento, California, 95814. We have provided a tear-out name availability request letter in Appendix 1 that you can use for this purpose.

The computer disk file name for this form is NAMECHEK. For further instructions, see Appendix 5.

The Secretary will respond to your written request within one week or two. A simpler and easier way to check name availability while reserving a name for your use with the Secretary of State is explained below.

To Check Name Availability by Telephone: You can check available names by phone if you establish a prepaid account. Call the Secretary of State at 916-654-9889 for information.

For a small fee, you can check the availability of up to three names at once and reserve the first available name by mail with the Sacramento office of the Secretary of State. We think it makes sense to do this rather than simply checking to see if your name is available since this ensures that your name will be available for your use when you file your Articles.

If your name is available, it will be reserved exclusively for your use for a period of sixty days. If you cannot file your Articles within this period, you can re-reserve the name by preparing a new reservation letter and paying another fee. Note that a second reservation letter must be received by the Secretary of State at least one day after the first certificate expires (the law does not allow two consecutive reservations of corporate name—therefore the requests must be separated by at least one day).

The fee to reserve a corporate name for 60 days is $10. Simply use the tear-out form in Appendix 1 as you follow the instructions and sample form below.

Check your proposed corporate name online. The Secretary of State's website (see Appendix 1 for the URL) allows you to search the names of existing corporations, LLCs and limited partnerships already registered with the Secretary of State. If your proposed name is the same as an active corporation, LLC or limited partnership, it is not available for your use. If it is similar to a registered name, you may or may not be able to use it depending on how similar your proposed name is to the registered name. To find out, send a name availability letter or name reservation letter listing your proposed name as explained above (or simply choose another name that does not appear in similar form on the list of active names registered with the Secretary of State).

The computer disk file name for this form is NAMERES. For further instructions, see Appendix 5.

Warning: Fees are subject to change. If you want to be doubly sure that this fee amount is current at the time of your incorporation, call the nearest office of the Secretary of State.

RESERVATION OF CORPORATE NAME REQUEST

Secretary of State
Corporate Filing and Services Division
1500 11th Street
Sacramento, CA 95814

Secretary of State:
Please reserve the first available corporate name from the list below for my use.
My proposed corporate names, listed in order of preference, are as follows:
(list up to four proposed corporate names—the Secretary will use the first available name from this list for your corporation)
I enclose a check or money order for the required reservation fee, payable to the Secretary of State.
Very truly yours,

_____

(your signature)

Name: _____

Address: _____

_____

Telephone: _____

Make sure one of the persons who will sign your Articles of Incorporation (one of your initial directors—see Section B below) prepares and signs your reservation request letter since your corporate name will be reserved for use by the individual who signs this letter.

You can also reserve a corporate name in person at any one of the offices of the Secretary of State. The Secretary of State office addresses and phone numbers are listed at the beginning of Appendix 1 at the back of the book.

The fee for reserving a name in person is $20. The clerk will ask for *two* $10 checks. If your proposed name is not available, the clerk will only return one $10 check to you.

You should be aware that approval by the Secretary of State's office of your corporate name (when you file your Articles) doesn't necessarily mean that you have the legal right to use this name (particularly a fictitious name)—it may violate another person's or business' prior rights to the name as a trademark, service mark or trade name (a trade name is simply a name used in connection with a business). Generally, whoever first adopts and uses a name has the right to it. Some incorporators may wish to consult a lawyer and conduct a state and federal trademark, service mark, or trade name search and register their proposed corporate name as a trade or service mark in order to feel a little more comfortable about their right to use it. The California Secretary of State does not check to see that your proposed corporate name is different from trademarks or service marks registered with the Secretary of State's office—they simply check to make sure that your proposed name is different from other corporations listed with the Secretary's office.

Typical Name Selection by a Professional Corporation: Most professional corporation names are not fictitious or fanciful and often simply include the surnames of the professionals,

followed by the word "Incorporated" or the abbreviation "Inc." (or other corporate designator approved by the board that regulates your profession). If you do use a fictitious business name for your corporation, however, you may want to call the Secretary of State's trademark division, check the local county clerk's fictitious business name list and check the federal Trademark Register to make sure your proposed fictitious business name is not similar to one already in use. Trademark search companies and trademark lawyers routinely perform searches of this sort—if you're interested in performing one or more searches, call around and compare fees. You may now search the federal Trademark Register yourself for free by pointing your Internet browser at the Patent and Trademark Office's Website at http://www.uspto.gov.

B. Prepare Articles of Incorporation

The next step in organizing your corporation is preparing and filing the Articles of Incorporation with the Secretary of State.

Filing is a formality. The Secretary must file your papers if they conform to law and the proper fees are paid. You will find ready-to-use, tear-out Articles at the back of this book in Appendix 1.

● The computer disk file name for this form is ARTICLES. For further instructions, see Appendix 5.

You simply fill in the blanks following the directions included as part of the sample Articles which immediately follow. A circled number in the sample Articles indicates that you should refer to the special instructions that apply to that sec-tion. The special instructions immediately follow the sample Articles.

There is nothing difficult about preparing these forms. Relax, take your time and read the instructions carefully and you will be surprised at how easy it is. You will probably want to tear the blank Articles out of the back of the book now so that you can have them in front of you as you go through the sample.

SAMPLE ARTICLES OF INCORPORATION

OF

_____ **(name of corporation)** _____

ONE: The name of this corporation is ___(name of corporation)___ . ❶
[Remember: The circled numbers refer to Special Instructions which immediately follow these sample Articles.]
TWO: The purpose of the corporation is to engage in the profession of
_____❷ and any other lawful activities (other than the banking or trust company business) not prohibited to a corporation engaging in such profes-sion by applicable laws and regulations.
THREE: The corporation is a professional corporation within the meaning of Part 4 of Divisions of Title 1 of the California Corporations Code.
FOUR: The name and address in this state of the corporation's initial agent for service of process is:
_____(name and address of agent)_____ ❸
_____
_____

FIVE: This corporation is authorized to issue only one class of shares of stock which shall be designated common stock. The total number of shares it is autho-rized to issue is ___(number of shares)___ ❹ shares.

SIX: The names and addresses of the persons who are appointed to act as the initial directors of this corporation are:
NAME   ADDRESS

_____

_____

_____

(full name and business or residence address for each director)❺

IN WITNESS WHEREOF, the undersigned, being all the persons named above as the initial directors, have executed these Articles of Incorporation.
Dated: ___(date of signing)___ ❻ _____(sign names as shown above)_____
                        (print or type names below signature line)

_____

_____

The undersigned, being all the persons named above as the initial directors, declare that they are the persons who executed the foregoing Articles of Incorporation, which execution is their act and deed.
Dated: ___(same as above)___ _____(same as above)_____

_____

_____

SPECIAL INSTRUCTIONS

❶ Indicate the name of the corporation, remembering the requirements given in Step 1 of this chapter. If you've reserved a name, indicate the number of the reservation certificate in your cover letter to the Secretary of State (see Section C 3, below).

❷ Indicate the profession(s) your corporation intends to engage in. Note that some professional corporations may engage in more than one related profession (see Chapter 4, Section D, and Appendix 4). (However, if your corporation plans to engage in more than one profession, you will not be able to use the stock certificates included as part of the corporate kits advertised at the back of this book—see Section E, below.)

❸ Indicate the name and business or residence address of a person you wish to authorize to receive legal documents in connection with any future lawsuits against the corporation (your agent for service of process). This person must be a resident of California. Normally, the name of one of the directors and the principal office of the corporation will be given. You can't use a P.O. box.

❹ Indicate the number of authorized shares of the corporation. Authorized shares are simply those which the corporation can later sell to shareholders, at which time they are referred to as issued shares. The number of authorized shares must be sufficient to provide for your initial stock issuance.

❺ Indicate here the full names and business or residence addresses of your initial directors. We discuss the requirements for the number and qualification of directors in Chapter 4, Section E. To summarize that section: California corporations are generally required to have at least three directors. However, a professional corporation with one shareholder need have only one director who must be the sole shareholder. Similarly, a professional corporation with two shareholders need have only two directors who must be the two shareholders.

❻ Have all of the persons named as initial directors date and sign the Articles in both places shown. Make sure that their signed and typed names correspond exactly to their names as given in Article Six. Use a black ink pen when signing your Articles—the Secretary of State must be able to microfilm your signatures.

Important Note: This book does not get into the problems involved in transferring shares to another professional. As we mentioned in Chapter 4, Section D, shares can only be owned by certain professionals. But if and when shares are transferred, perhaps because of death, disability or withdrawal of a shareholder, what method of valuation for the shares will you use? You may want to consider "buy-out" provisions in your

Articles now—before the event occurs and possibly disrupts the continuity of the corporation.

For more information on creating a buy-sell agreement, see *How to Create a Buy-Sell Agreement and Control the Destiny of Your Small Business*, by Anthony Mancuso and Bethany K. Laurence (Nolo).

C. File Your Articles of Incorporation

There are three steps you must follow in order to properly file your Articles of Incorpation. Let's look at them in detail below.

1. Make Copies

After you've completed filling out and signing the Articles, make photocopies, which will be certified by the Secretary of State and returned to you. Two copies should be enough for your immediate purposes—one for inclusion in the Minutes of the First Board Meeting and one as an extra copy. These two copies will be certified for free. All copies should be legible with good contrast. Do not use rivet-type fasteners in putting your Articles together. If you retype your Articles, use letter-size paper, type on one side of the paper only and leave a 3-inch-square space in the upper right-hand corner of the first page for the Secretary of State's file stamp.

2. Pay Fees

You'll have to pay a $100 filing fee when filing the Articles of Incorporation. Make your check or money order payable to the "Secretary of State."

There is an extra fee for more than two certified copies. The Secretary will compare and certify two copies of the Articles for free. If you include more than two copies, they will be certified at an extra cost of $8 each (and you will have to modify the sample cover letter accordingly).

Secretary of State
Corporate Filing and Services Division
1500 11th Street
Sacramento, CA 95814

RE: _____(name of corporation)_____

Secretary of State:
I enclose an original and ___(number)___ copies of the proposed Articles of Incorporation of _____(name of corporation)_____.
[This corporate name was reserved with your office pursuant to Certificate of Registration #_____.]
Also enclosed is a check/money order in payment of the filing fees:
Please file the original Articles and return the certified copies to me.

_____

Incorporator

Name: _____

Address: _____

_____

Telephone: _____

Delaying the Filing of Your Articles: California law (California Corporations Code § 110) allows you to request a delayed filing date for your Articles as long as this date is no more than 90 days from the date of receipt of your Articles. If you wish to do this, add a conspicuous sentence to your cover letter asking that your Articles be filed on a specific future date (the delayed date may be a weekend day or a holiday but your Articles must be received at least one business day before the requested future filing date).

3. Send in Articles and Fees

Prepare the tear-out cover letter in Appendix 1 following the sample form.

The computer disk file name for this form is COVERLET. For further instructions, see Appendix 5.

Mail the letter along with the original Articles, the photocopies of the Articles, and your check or money order made payable to the Secretary of State, at the address given in the cover letter. If you have already reserved a corporate name, as explained in Section A, include the optional bracketed sentence shown in the sample to indicate your reservation certificate number. Make sure to insert your incorporator's printed name, address and telephone number at the bottom of the letter.

Filing Your Articles in Person: You may file your Articles in person at the Sacramento, Fresno, Los Angeles, San Diego or San Francisco offices of the Secretary of State if you wish. The Secretary of State office addresses and phone numbers are listed at the beginning of Appendix 1 at the back of the book.

There is an additional $15.00 special handling fee for filing your Articles in person. This fee is retained by the clerk if your Articles are rejected. You must provide Fresno, Los Angeles, San Diego or San Francisco office of the Secretary of State with an extra signed copy of your Articles (this copy is in addition to the two copies indicated above). This additional copy will be forwarded by the local office to the Sacramento office of the Secretary of State.

Expect to wait. The California economy, including the formation of dot.com corporations, has been booming. A side-effect of this glut of corporate formations is the increased amount of time you can expect to wait before your Articles are filed and returned to you. Currently, you can expect to wait up to one month before your Articles are filed by mail and returned to you. To eliminate this delay, you may want to trek over to the nearest local office of the Secretary of State to file your Articles in person, as explained above. Although it's yet another possible pricey workaround, the Secretary of State expects to allow expedited filing services in October 2000. These services should include four-hour and 24-hour filing, but the expected extra fees for these services are planned to range from $250 to $1,000! Check the Secretary of State website to find out if these services have been implemented and the fees for any services provided.

D. Order Corporate Seal and Set Up a Corporate Records Book

A corporation is not legally required to have or use a corporate seal, but many find it handy to do so and we recommend that you obtain one. A corporate seal is a formal way of indicating that a given document is the duly authorized act of the corporation. It isn't normally used on everyday business papers (invoices, purchase orders, etc.) but is commonly employed for more formal documents such as leases, stock certificates, deeds of trust, bank loans and the like. A good quality, reasonably priced pocket seal is available as part of the corporate kits advertised at the back of this book. Either embossed or stamped seals are also available through legal stationers for about $25–$40. Most are circular in form and contain the name of the corporation and the state and date of incorporation. When ordering a separate seal, make sure to give the stationer or stamp maker the proper date of incorporation. This is the date the copies were "endorsed filed" by the Secretary of State, not the date of certification on the facing page of each certified copy.

You will also need a corporate records book to keep all your papers in an orderly fashion. Setting up a neat, well-organized records book is one of your most important tasks. Some legal stationers sell fancy-looking loose-leaf notebooks at inflated prices. You will do as well with any three-ring binder or by ordering a reasonably priced corporate kit which includes a binder with separators (see Section E, below).

For more information on preparing corporate minutes, see the *The Corporate Minutes Book: The Legal Guide to Taking Care of Your Corporation*, by Anthony Mancuso (Nolo).

E. Order Stock Certificates or a Corporate Kit

This book provides all the forms you'll need to set up a corporation except for stock certificates. Since the language (known as a legend) required on the stock certificate (see Chapter 4) will vary with each profession, we couldn't duplicate them all here. Instead, you can order them from a legal stationer, providing you are sure of the proper legend to apply. Check Appendix 4, and then with the board regulating your profession. You should also have an attorney review it. You may

prefer, however, to order one of the corporate kits advertised at the back of this book which will provide you with twenty preprinted stock certificates containing the legend appropriate to your profession. However, since the law and regulations do change frequently, you should also have a lawyer review these or check with your board on their acceptability. Also, as noted in Section B, special instruction 2, above, if your corporation plans to engage in more than one profession, you will not be able to use the stock certificates used in the corporate kits described at the back of this book. Be sure to order your certificates immediately after you receive the certified copies of the Articles from the Secretary of State.

Note: As of this edition, stock legend regulations have not been issued for architectural corporations, pharmacy corporations, nursing corporations, physicians' assistants corporations, and veterinary corporations. Consequently, the legends on the Nolo corporate kit stock certificates for these corporations are adapted from other professional corporation regulations and the statutes.

F. Prepare the Bylaws

After you've received the certified copies of the Articles from the Secretary of State, you should prepare the Bylaws. The Bylaws are basic and we've included a set in Appendix 2.

⊙ The computer disk file name for this form is BYLAWS. For further instructions, see Appendix 5.

However, you will have to fill in a few blanks and, more importantly, add some specific provisions from the regulations applicable to your profession, as explained in the instructions to Article II below and as set out in Appendix 4 of this book. The provisions relate to who can own shares in the corporation, the transfer of the shares (with the appropriate legend on the stock certificates—see Section E, above), and what to do when a shareholder dies or is disqualified. You may also be required to include a statement guaranteeing payment on claims against the corporation up to a certain amount (check the "security" section of Appendix 4 listing the specific concerns of professional corporations and be sure to contact your board). Law corporations will also need to add two additional provisions relating to share legends and income to a disqualified shareholder (see Appendix 4). Medical corporations will also need to indicate that a director's term of office may not exceed three years (a partial exception is available if the corporation has more than 200 shareholders—see Appendix 4). An accountancy corporation which uses Certified Public Accountant or CPA in its name will need to include a provision limiting the ownership and transfer of shares to CPAs (see Accountancy Corporations, Appendix 4).

Read the Bylaws carefully to understand their purpose and effect. Many provisions have already been discussed in the earlier chapters. These Bylaws have been carefully drafted and compiled to serve a few important purposes. First, they reflect specific information central to the organization and operation of a professional corporation (i.e., number of directors, dates of meetings, location of principal executive office). Second, they restate the most significant provisions of the laws which apply to the organization and operation of the professional corporation. Third, they provide a practical, yet formal, set of rules for the operation of the corporation.

It should be noted that several alternative models were considered before deciding on provisions relating to the operating formalities of the corporation. For example, formalities such as annual director and shareholder meetings, duties and responsibilities of directors and officers, notice of meetings, etc. were included because of the need for the corporation to be able to rely on and refer to a set of rules to resolve disputes, to provide certainty regarding procedures, and to insure at least minimum control over corporate operations. You may want to modify these Bylaws. You should have an attorney review any modifications you make to the tear-out form.

Technical Note on Indemnification of Directors and Officers: Article VIII of the tear-out Bylaws simply authorizes indemnification of corporate directors, officers and other agents "to the fullest extent permissible by the provisions of Section 317 of the California Corporations Code." As mentioned in Chapter 1, Section D, you may wish to go further and indemnify directors and officers beyond the limits specified in this section of the Corporations Code. If so, you will need to consult a lawyer to modify this section of your Bylaws and add special indemnification language to your Articles.

To prepare the Bylaws, fill in the blanks, as follows:

Article I, Section 1: Indicate the city and county of the corporation's principal executive office. Legally, this doesn't necessarily mean the principal *place of business* of the corporation. It is the legal address of the corporation and, generally, fixes the county where legal action must be brought against the corporation.

Article II: You must include in this article the proper provisions relating to share ownership and transfer, disqualified and deceased shareholders, and possibly the security guarantee. Begin by looking up these provisions in the Appendix 4 section applicable to your profession. Follow up by checking with your professional board on whether any changes have been made and/or whether they require any additional provisions (law corporations, for example, need to add some extra paragraphs). Then copy the required provisions from the Appendix 4 section for your profession (with any appropriate changes) into this Article. Note that the regulations in Appendix 4 will state which subsections must be included in the Articles or Bylaws. (By including these provisions in the Bylaws rather than in the Articles, you will have an easier time amending them should they ever need to be changed.) You may wish to have a lawyer check your completed Article II.

Article III, Section 2: Indicate the date on which the annual shareholders' meeting is to be held. This will be the same date as the regular directors' meeting (see Article IV, Section 7), and is commonly set shortly before or after the close of the corporation's tax year so that the prior year's business can be reviewed and the coming year's business discussed and planned. It's usually best to designate a specific date (e.g., the second Monday of June) to avoid having the meeting fall on a weekend.

Article IV, Section 2: Indicate the authorized number of directors. This should be the same as the number of initial directors named in the Articles (Section B, above).

Article IV, Section 8: Indicate the number of directors who must be present at a directors' meeting to constitute a quorum so that business can be conducted. Although the usual practice is to provide for a majority, the Bylaws may provide that a quorum be as little as 1/3 the number of authorized directors or two, *whichever is larger*. A one-person corporation, however, may (and will) provide for a one-director quorum.

For example, a four-director corporation, under the above minimum rules, may provide for a quorum of two, rather than a majority of three. Applying these rules to a three-director corporation, however, results in a majority quorum of two.

Whatever you decide, you should realize that this section of the Bylaws concerns a quorum, not a vote requirement. Action can be taken by a majority of directors at a meeting at which a quorum is present. For example, if a six-director corporation requires a majority quorum and a meeting is held at which a minimum quorum (4) is present, action can be taken by the vote of three directors, a majority of those present at the meeting.

If you wish to change the majority vote rule for directors (Article IV, Section 8 of the Bylaws) or the majority quorum or vote rules for shareholders (Article III, Section 8 of the Bylaws), you will have to add provisions to your Articles of Incorporation and should consult an attorney.

Note that the Waiver of Annual Report in Article VII, Section 4 applies only to corporations with less than 100 shareholders [Corporations Code Section 1501(a)].

G. Hold the First Meeting of the Board of Directors

The next step, now that you've filed the Articles and prepared the Bylaws, is to hold the first meeting of the board of directors. The purpose of this meeting is to formally adopt the Bylaws, to make and authorize business and tax elections, to elect officers and to authorize the corporate officers to take action necessary to complete the organization of the corporation.

Aside from its formal significance, this meeting gives the directors a chance to review and discuss the Articles and Bylaws of the corporation and to transact the initial business of the corporation as a group.

H. Prepare the Minutes of the Meeting

Some of the resolutions contained in the minutes of the first meeting which you will find in the back of the book (see Appendix 3) should be used by all corporations; others are optional and will be used only if they apply to your corporation. Tear the minutes out of the book.

The computer disk file name for this form is MINUTES. For further instructions, see Appendix 5.

There is nothing hard here, but there are a number of details that require attention.

1. Fill in Waiver of Notice and Consent to Holding of First Meeting

This form is necessary in order to dispense with formal notice requirements which apply to special meetings. Fill in this form as provided, giving the time, date and place of the meeting. Have all the directors sign the form. It may be signed and dated before the actual meeting of the board.

2. Fill in the First Page of the Minutes of the First Meeting of the Board of Directors

Fill in the blanks on this page, indicating the names of the directors present and absent from the meeting (a quorum of the board must be in attendance). Name one of the directors temporary chairperson, and another temporary secretary of the meeting. Corporations with one director will, of course, show his or her name in both of these blanks.

3. Fill in Pages 2 and 3 of the Minutes of the First Meeting

Articles Resolution: Indicate the date the Articles were filed by the Secretary of State (the endorsed filed date which appears in the upper right corner of the first page of your certified copies).

Bylaws Resolution: This resolution should be included in your minutes to show acceptance of the Bylaws by the directors.

Election of Officers Resolution: Indicate the names of the officers (see Chapter 4, Section E, and Appendix 4 regarding restrictions on who may fill officer positions).

Corporate Seal Resolution: Stamp or impress the corporate seal in the space provided. If you have decided not to order one, line out the provisions of this resolution.

4. Fill Out Pages 4–6 of the Minutes of the First Meeting

Stock Certificate Resolution: Include this resolution to show acceptance of the form of stock certificate you will use (see Section E).

Accounting Period Resolution: This resolution allows you to specify the accounting period of your corporation. You should normally select this period with the help of your corporate tax advisor (see Chapter 3, Section C8, for a discussion of the rules which apply to selecting a corporate accounting period and tax year).

Indicate the date (month and day) of the end of your corporation's accounting period in the blank in this resolution. For example, if you choose a calendar year accounting period for your corporation, type the ending date as "December 31."

You should realize that the California Franchise Tax Board and the IRS will look to your initial tax returns to determine the ending date of your corporate accounting period and tax year: If your first corporate tax returns are submitted for a period ending on July 30th, this date will be taken as the end date of your corporate tax year. In other words, you are not bound by this initial minute resolution.

After you file your initial returns, you will usually need the consent of the IRS and the California Franchise Tax Board to change your corporate tax year.

Principal Executive Office Resolution: Indicate the street address and city where the principal executive office of the corporation is located (this address should be within the city and county designated in Article I, Section 1, of your Bylaws—see Section F, above). Do not use a post office box here.

Bank Account Resolution: Indicate the bank and branch office where the corporation will maintain accounts. In paragraph 5, indicate how many people must sign the checks, giving the names of the appropriate individuals. They should be the officers or other employees of the corporation who are charged by the Bylaws with carrying out the day-to-day business of the corporation.

5. Fill Out Last Page of Minutes

Exempt Sale of Common Stock Under 10 California Administrative Code, Section 260.105.6 (here you must jump to the last page of the minutes): See Chapter 4, Section I. Include this resolution as the *last page of the minutes*. Have the secretary sign your Minutes at the bottom of the page.

6. Fill Out Pages 7–13 of the Minutes of the First Meeting

Sale and Issuance of Capital Stock Resolution: Indicate the total number of shares authorized by Article Five of your Articles of Incorporation.

Use one or more of the following resolution(s) included with the Minutes to authorize the sale of stock. Note that these resolutions do not result in the issuance of shares, they simply authorize the officers to do so.

Resolution (a): Sale and Issuance of Capital Stock for Cash. If you are issuing stock for cash, fill out the blanks in this resolution and show the total amounts sold, the price per share, and the number of shares transferred to and the amount of money to be paid by each shareholder. Remember, all shares should be sold for the same price per share.

Resolution (b): Sale and Issuance of Capital Stock for Property Actually Received. Use this resolution if your corporation is receiving property other than that comprising the assets of a business being bought out by your corporation. [In the case of a buy-out of an existing business, use Resolution (f) below.] Show the number of shares issued and the price per share (which should be the same as the price for shares purchased for cash). In addition, the number of shares transferred to each shareholder and a description of the property actually received must be included. The description should state the nature of the property and its fair market value. Finally, the overall market value of the property should be given.

Resolution (c): Sale and Issuance of Capital Stock for Indebtedness Canceled. Use this resolution, if appropriate, showing the number of shares issued and the price per share (which should be the same as the price for other shares). In addition, the number of shares transferred to each shareholder and a description of the indebtedness canceled must be included. The description should state the nature of the indebtedness—in most cases it will be a loan made by an incorporator to meet organizational costs. The fair market value of the indebtedness also should be given. Remember, when loan transactions are involved in your incorporation (this includes issuing shares in cancellation of loans), you should consult a lawyer.

Choosing Between the Following Two Resolutions: Though Corporations Code Section 409 refers separately to labor done and services

rendered, we don't believe there is much, if any, real distinction between these two types of consideration for shares. Our guess is that "labor done" is meant to apply to contracting-type services performed for the corporation (construction of a building and the like) as opposed to organizational or administrative services. In any case, this distinction is not very important—feel free to use either of the following two resolutions to authorize the issuance of shares in return for work performed for your corporation.

Resolution (d): Sale and Issuance of Capital Stock for Labor Done. Use this resolution, if appropriate, showing the number of shares issued and the price per share (which should be the same as the price for other shares). In addition, the number of shares transferred to each shareholder and a description of the labor done also should be given. The description should include the fair market value of the labor given by each shareholder. Finally, the overall fair market value of the labor done should be given.

REVIEW NOTES

Here's a quick review of a few points mentioned in preceding chapters and steps regarding the issuance of your shares:

Make sure that the total number of shares to be issued to all shareholders is not greater than the number of shares authorized to be issued in Article Five of your Articles of Incorporation—Article Five places an upper limit on the number of shares which you can actually issue.

Under California law, you may issue shares for any legal consideration which includes:

- Cash
- Tangible or intangible property actually received by the corporation
- Debts canceled (the cancellation of a note reflecting money owed by the corporation to the shareholder)
- Labor done or services actually rendered to the corporation, or for its benefit, or in its formation

You *cannot* issue shares in return for the performance of future services by a shareholder nor can you issue shares in return for promissory notes (a promise by the shareholder to pay for the shares later) unless certain conditions related to adequate security for the notes are met (see Chapter 3, Section C10). We assume you will check with a lawyer or accountant before issuing shares in return for such notes. Furthermore, most small corporations will not be in a position to issue shares for labor done or services rendered since they are just getting started.

As a matter of common sense, and to avoid unfairness or fraud, issue your shares for the same price per share to all initial shareholders. Make sure to place a fair value on the assets or other property or services being given in return for the shares. If you are transferring the assets of an existing business to your corporation in return for shares (if you are incorporating a prior business), we suggest that you have an accountant or other qualified appraiser make a written determination of the value of these assets. You may also wish to have a balance sheet prepared for the prior business, showing the assets and liabilities being transferred to your corporation (you can attach this balance sheet to the Bill of Sale which you can prepare as part of Section I, below, to document this type of transfer). Be realistic in your determination of fair value of all noncash payments for shares, particularly if you will be issuing shares in return for speculative or intangible property such as the goodwill of a business, copyrights, patents, etc. You don't want to "shortchange" other shareholders who have put up cash or tangible property of determinative value.

Resolution (e): Sale and Issuance of Capital Stock for Services Actually Rendered to the Corporation or for Its Benefit or in Its Formation. Use this resolution, if appropriate, showing the number of shares issued and the price per share (which should be the same as the price for shares purchased for cash). Be sure to include the number of shares transferred to each shareholder and a description of the services rendered. The description should include the fair market value of the services rendered by each shareholder and the overall fair market value of the services rendered.

Resolution (f): Sale and Issuance of Capital Stock for Assets of Business. Include this resolution in the minutes of your meeting if stock is being transferred in return for assets of a going business. Indicate the total number of shares to be issued to the owners of the prior business, the price per share amount and the name of the prior business in the body of the beginning resolution. In the columns below the first resolution, show the name of each share purchaser (prior business owner), the number of shares to be sold to each and the percentage of each owner's interest in the particular business being transferred (show this under the Description of Property column). Finally, indicate in the last blank the fair (most commonly, the book) value of the business (the price per share times the number of shares sold to each prior business owner should equal this figure)—an accountant can help you determine this figure.

EXAMPLE: If two business owners will be incorporating their preexisting partnership, "Kelsey & Chesley," the following simple description in the Description of Property column would be appropriate for each shareholder (each prior business owner):

"One-half interest in assets of the partnership 'Kelsey & Chesley,' as more fully described in a Bill of Sale to be prepared and attached to these minutes."

This Bill of Sale can be prepared as part of Section I4, below. A few additional points regarding this resolution: Shares should be issued in the same proportion as the percentage of ownership figures in the preexisting business just prior to incorporating. This resolution does not result in the transfer of the business. It simply authorizes the officers to execute the documents necessary to effect a transfer—this will be accomplished by the execution of a Bill of Sale and any other necessary papers—see Section I4, below. This resolution also authorizes the officers to take any steps necessary to comply with the Bulk Sales Law. These provisions apply only to the transfer of certain types of businesses (see Section I, below). Of course, the price per share amount shown in this resolution will be the same as the price-per-share amount given in all other stock issuance resolutions you have prepared.

7. Include Pages 14-16 of the Minutes of the First Meeting

Federal S Corporation Tax Treatment Resolution: If you plan to elect S corporation tax status (see Chapter 3, Section C7), include this resolution in your minutes.

Compensation for Officers Resolution: If you wish to provide for officers' salaries (see Chapter 3, Section C4), indicate the salaries to be paid in the blanks provided. Most incorporators will leave all officer salary lines blank (or will show $0 for each officer's salary) since professional practitioners are usually paid as professional employees of their corporation, not as officers.

Payment and Deduction of Organization Expenses Resolution: This resolution is optional, but many incorporators will wish to include it in their minutes to allow the corporation to reimburse the incorporators for, and have the corporation pay and deduct over a period of time, the expenses incurred in organizing the corporation under Section 248 of the Internal Revenue Code (without a specific election to deduct these expenses over a specified period of time, such a deduction is normally not possible). Note that you must implement this federal tax election by attaching a statement to your first federal corporate income tax return indicating that you are choosing to amortize organization expenses, providing a description of the expenses together with other required details. Check with your accountant for help in deciding whether to use this resolution (and for help in preparing the statement to send to the IRS).

8. Include Page 17 of the Minutes of the First Meeting

Section 1244 Stock Resolution: If, after reading Chapter 3, Section C12, and consulting your accountant, you decide that you wish to have your stock treated as Section 1244 stock (most incorporators will), include this resolution in your Minutes. Note the necessity of keeping ongoing records to insure that you will be able to meet the requirements of Section 1244—your accountant can help you with the records.

Important: You are now done with the minutes. It wasn't so hard, was it? But don't forget to keep your records properly. After you've prepared the minutes, put them in your corporate records book. It's best to separate the book into three sections: (1) Corporate Documents, (2) Minutes of Meetings and (3) Stock Certificates.

Have the secretary sign the last page of the Minutes and Bylaws. Place the Waiver of Notice and Consent to the Holding of the First Meeting in the minutes section of your corporate records book, followed by the prepared Minutes, a certified copy of the Articles, a copy of the Bylaws (certified by the corporate secretary), and a

sample copy of the corporation's stock certificates (mark it prominently across its face as a "SAMPLE"). Depending upon the type of stock transaction (i.e., whether cash, labor done, services rendered, property actually received, indebtedness canceled, or assets of a business), you may need or wish to prepare additional documentation to attach to your minutes as explained above (e.g., a Bill of Sale may be prepared if stock will be issued in return for the transfer of assets of a business).

Place all extra copies of the Articles and Bylaws and your stock certificates and stubs in your corporate records book. You should keep the corporate records book at the corporation's principal executive office at all times. Copies of future corporate documents should be retained and placed in your corporate records book.

I: Issue Shares of Stock

After the first meeting of the board of directors, stock certificates should be issued in return for cash, cancellation of indebtedness, labor done, property actually received, services rendered or the assets of a going business. Before explaining the process of issuing your shares, we need to mention two technicalities related to your share issuance: California's Bulk Sales provisions and the method of taking title to your shares.

1. If Applicable, Comply With California's Bulk Sales Law

The California Bulk Sales Law (Division 6 of the California Commercial Code, starting with Section

6101) generally applies if you are incorporating an existing business or practice and if:

- You are transferring more than half the value of the inventory and equipment of an unincorporated business located in California to your new corporation (if you are incorporating an existing sole proprietorship or partnership);
- The value of the business assets being transferred is $10,000 or more; *and*
- The business being incorporated is a restaurant or is engaged in the principal business of selling inventory from stock (such as a retail or wholesale business including a business that manufactures what it sells).

Exemption: Even if the Bulk Sales Law applies to your incorporation of an existing professional practice, an exemption from its provisions applies if the value of the assets being transferred is more than $5 million.

We don't expect this act to apply to most professional corporations, but professions like optometrists, and any other profession which might, as a primary function, sell a product, should ask their lawyer whether the California Bulk Sales Law may apply to their incorporation. If it does, you must publish a notice of bulk sales in a local newspaper and file this form with the county recorder's and tax collector's offices. A local legal newspaper can help you meet these standard publication and filing requirements for a small fee.

2. Taking Title to Stock

Taking title to stock means no more than putting your name on the ownership line on your stock certificates. If you are the sole owner of shares, you simply show your name on the ownership line of your stock certificate—that's all there is to it.

Married shareholders often take title to their shares jointly (in co-ownership) with their spouses. However, since a fundamental rule of professional corporations is that only licensed professionals in a given field (or, in some cases, in a related field) may hold shares in a professional corporation, even married professionals should take title to their shares as sole owners (not jointly with their spouse). Of course, if both spouses are licensed professionals in the incorporated practice, they are permitted to take title jointly to their shares (it's also likely, in this situation, that each spouse will wish to be issued separate, sole-owner stock certificates).

Community Property Note: Even if a married shareholder takes title to shares as the sole owner, the shares will generally be considered community property if purchased with community property funds or property. Generally funds or property acquired during marriage are considered the community property of both spouses. Each spouse is given a one-half interest in the community property. Please consult your tax advisor for further information on the legal, tax and other financial aspects of community property.

3. Filling Out the Stock Certificate

Issue stock by filling out the blank certificates and stubs that you ordered separately or as part of a corporate kit (see Section E, above) and have them signed by the president and the secretary or treasurer (depending on the form of stock certificate you order). Simply follow the directions on the Sample Certificate and the special instructions below, where appropriate. Each stock certificate can represent more than one share of stock.

SPECIAL INSTRUCTIONS

These instructions assume you are using the certificates included with one of the corporate kits at the back of the book. If you are using other certificates, follow their instructions instead.

1. Put in the name of the professional shareholder.

2. Fill in the other spaces on the certificate as indicated on the sample.

3. Fill out each separate stub page as indicated in the kit.

4. The transfer sections (both on the separate stub pages and the back of the printed stock certificate) should be left blank. They are to be used only if and when the stock certificates are transferred to someone else by the original shareholders—with the aid of an attorney.

5. Leave the completed stub pages in the stock certificates section of your corporate records book. The corporate kits contain a separate "stock transfer ledger." Simply fill out one line on the left side of each page (the right side is used for transfers of the original shares) for each shareholder in the appropriate alphabetical box. If you have stock certificates left over after filling out the certificates for your initial stock issuance, it's best to tear them up and throw them away. This way you won't be tempted to use them later in a transference or later issuance transaction. Future stock issuances or transfers may require a permit from the California Commissioner of Corporations (or the filing of a notice with the Department of Corporations if the stock issuance is exempt from registration) and you will need to consult a lawyer to ensure compliance with state (and federal) securities laws.

4. Distributing the Stock Certificates

Have the president and secretary of the corporation sign the stock certificates, and give each shareholder a completed share certificate in return for:
- Cash; or
- Labor done; or
- Services rendered; or
- Property actually received by the corporation, which includes but is not limited to:
  - Assets of a going business;
  - Property other than the assets of a going business.

Tear-Out Receipts: Tear-out versions of each sample receipt/acknowledgment/bill of sale form below is contained in Appendix 3 (in the Receipts section just after the tear-out Minutes).

A disk version of each sample receipt/acknowledgment/bill of sale form shown below is contained in the RECEIPTS file. For further instructions, see Appendix 5.

a. Issuance of Stock for Cash or Cancellation of Indebtedness

If shares are issued for either cash or for cancellation of indebtedness or any combination of the two, the treasurer of the corporation should fill out and sign a receipt following one of the forms shown in the samples and special instructions given below.

SAMPLE RECEIPT FOR CASH PAYMENT FOR SHARES

Receipt of $_____, paid by check No._____, from
_____(name of shareholder)_____, representing payment in full for _____(number
of shares)_____ shares of common stock of this corporation, evidenced by Certificate No. _____(number of stock certificate issued to a shareholder in return for
cash payment)_____, is hereby acknowledged.

Date: _____
_____(name of corporation)_____
By _____(signature)_____, Treasurer

SAMPLE ACKNOWLEDGMENT OF CANCELLATION OF INDEBTEDNESS

This issuance of _____(number of shares)_____ shares of this corporation to
_____(name of shareholder)_____ for the cancellation by _____(name of shareholder)_____ of a current loan outstanding to this corporation, dated _____,
19__, with a remaining unpaid principal amount and unpaid accrued interest, if
any, totaling $_____, is hereby acknowledged.

Date: _____
_____(name of corporation)_____
By _____(signature)_____, Treasurer

SPECIAL INSTRUCTIONS

Cash should be paid to the corporation by personal check—a canceled check is the best (and easiest to obtain) proof of payment. When the money or canceled notes are received and share certificates have been prepared and distributed (all at the same time), do the following:

- Make two photocopies of each receipt and acknowledgment.
- Make two copies of the front and back of each endorsed check or canceled note and attach them to the appropriate receipt or acknowledgment.
- Place one copy of each receipt or acknowledgment and attachments in the share certificates section of the corporate records book, give one

to the shareholder, and save the other to show the attorney who will review your incorporation (see Chapter 8).

b. Issuance of Stock for Assets of a Business

If shares are issued in return for the assets of a going business, you may wish to prepare a Bill of Sale form, following the sample form and special instructions below. As indicated in the form, attach to the Bill of Sale an inventory of the assets of the prior business which will be transferred to the corporation. If you have any questions, your tax advisor can help you with the preparation of this inventory and in deciding on the options offered in this form.

SAMPLE BILL OF SALE FOR ASSETS OF A BUSINESS

This is an agreement between:

  (name of prior business owner) ❶

  (name of prior business owner) ❶

herein called "transferor(s)," and   (name of corporation) ,❷ a California professional corporation, herein called "the corporation."

In return for the issuance of   (number of shares) ❸ shares of stock of the corporation, transferor(s) hereby sell(s), assign(s), and transfer(s) to the corporation all rights, title, and interest in the following property:

All the tangible assets listed on the inventory attached to this Bill of Sale and all stock in trade, goodwill, leasehold interests, trade names, and other intangible assets [except   (show any nontransferred assets shown here) ❹] of   (name of prior business) ❺, located at   (address of prior business) ❻.

In return for the transfer of the above property to it, the corporation hereby agrees to assume, pay, and discharge all debts, duties, and obligations that appear on the date of this agreement, on the books and owed on account of said business [except   (any unassumed liabilities shown here) ❼]. The corporation agrees to indemnify and hold the transferor(s) of said business and their property free from any liability for any such debt, duty, or obligation and from any suits, actions, or legal proceedings brought to enforce or collect any such debt, duty, or obligation. ❽ The transferor(s) hereby appoint(s) the corporation as representative to demand, receive, and collect for itself any and all debts and obligations now owing to said business and hereby assumed by the corporation. The transferor(s) further authorize(s) the corporation to do all things allowed by law to recover and collect any such debts and obligations and to use the transferor's(s') name(s) in such manner as it considers necessary for the collection and recovery of such debts and obligations, provided, however, without cost, expense, or damage to the transferor(s).

Date: _____ ❾   (signature of business owner)   ❾
                     (typed name), Transferor
                     (signature of business owner)   ❾
                     (typed name), Transferor

Name of Corporation: _____ ❾
By:
                     (signature of President)   ❾
                     (typed name), President
                     (signature of Treasurer)   ❾
                     (typed name), Treasurere

SPECIAL INSTRUCTIONS

❶ Type (or print) the names of the prior business owners.

❷ Show the name of your corporation.

❸ Enter the total number of shares to be issued to all prior owners of the business in return for the transfer of the business to the corporation.

EXAMPLE: If Patricia and Kathleen will each receive 2,000 shares in return for their respective half-interests in their pre-existing professional partnership (which they are now incorporating), they would indicate 4,000 shares here.

❹ Use this line to show any assets of the prior business that are not being transferred to the corporation (e.g., you may wish to continue to personally own real property associated with your business and lease it to your new corporation). For most businesses being incorporated, all prior business assets will be transferred to the corporation and you will not use this bracketed clause.

Note: As indicated in this paragraph of the bill of sale, you should attach a current inventory showing the assets of the prior business transferred to the corporation.

❺ Indicate the name of the prior business being transferred to the corporation. For sole proprietorships and partnerships not operating under a fictitious business name, the name(s) of the prior owners may simply be given here (e.g., "Paul Solomon and Chester Treacher").

❻ Show the full address of the prior business.

❼ This paragraph indicates that your corporation will assume the liabilities of the prior business. This will be appropriate for the incorporation of most small businesses and practices. If your corporation will not assume any of the liabilities of the prior business, then omit this paragraph from your bill of sale.

In the blank in this paragraph, list any liabilities of the prior business which will not be assumed by the corporation. Normally your new corporation will assume all liabilities of the prior business and you will not need to use this bracketed clause in your bill of sale.

❽ This paragraph is included in the Bill of Sale to indicate that your corporation is appointed to collect for itself any debts and obligations (accounts receivable) owed to the prior business which are being transferred to the corporation.

❾ Date the form (in two places) and have the prior business owners (transferors) and the President and Treasurer of the corporation sign the Bill of Sale when you distribute the stock certificates to the prior business owners. Place the completed original in your corporate records book and give each transferor a copy of the original completed form.

NOTE ON THE TRANSFER OF REAL PROPERTY OR LEASES

If you are transferring real property or a lease to your corporation, you will have to prepare and execute new corporate owner-ship papers, such as deeds, leases, assign-ments of leases, etc. (the assignment of a lease will usually only occur as part of the transfer of a preexisting business to the corporation). An excellent California guide to transferring property interests and preparing new deeds (with tear-out forms) is *The Deeds Book*, by Mary Randolph (Nolo). When it comes to rental property, you should talk to the landlord about having a new lease prepared showing the corporation as the new tenant. (An alternative is to have the prior tenants assign the lease to the corpora-tion; however, read your lease carefully before trying to do this as many leases are not assignable without the landlord's permission.)

If the property being transferred is mort-gaged, then you will most likely need the permission of the lender to transfer the property. If your real property note agree-ment contains a "due on sale or transfer" clause, you may even be required to refinance your deed of trust (mortgage) if rates have gone up substantially since the existing deed of trust was executed. This, of course, may be so undesirable that you decide not to transfer the real property to the corporation, preferring to keep it in the name of the original owner and lease it to the corporation. Also, don't forget that the transfer of real property to your corporation may trigger a Proposition 13 reassessment of the property; check with your tax advisor before completing a real property transfer to your corporation.

Prepare and execute these new ownership papers, lease documents, etc., before you distribute shares to the prior owners of the property.

c. Issuance of Stock for Items of Property

If shares are issued in return for property actually received other than the assets of a going business, complete a Bill of Sale for items of property (as shown in the sample below) and execute it by dating the form, having the transferor of the prop-erty and president and treasurer of the corpora-tion sign on the appropriate lines, showing the name of the corporation. Make copies of the Bill of Sale. Give one copy to the person making the transfer, and place the original in the share certifi-cate section of the corporate records book.

SAMPLE BILL OF SALE FOR ITEMS OF PROPERTY

This is an agreement by __(name of person transferring property)__, herein called "transferor," and _____(name of corporation)_____, herein called "the corporation." In return for the issuance and delivery of __(number of shares)__ shares of stock of ___(name of corporation)___, I hereby sell, assign, and transfer to the corporation all my right, title, and interest in the following property:

(describe property)

Date: _____   _____(signature)_____
                                                (typed name), Transferor

Name of Corporation: _____
                         By: _____(signature)_____
                                                (typed name), President
                                         _____(signature)_____
                                                (typed name), Treasurer

---

d. Issuance of Stock for Labor Done or Services Rendered

If shares are issued in return for labor done or services rendered, the treasurer of the corporation should fill out an acknowledgment following the sample form and special instructions given here. Both the treasurer and the shareholder should sign the form.

SAMPLE ACKNOWLEDGMENT OF SHARE ISSUANCE FOR LABOR DONE OR SERVICES RENDERED

This issuance of _____(number of shares)_____ shares of _____(name of corpora-tion)_____, evidenced by Certificate No. _____(number of stock certificate issued to shareholder)_____ to _____(name of shareholder)_____ in exchange for payment in the form of labor done or services rendered the corporation by him or her, valued at $_____(dollar value of labor done or services rendered_____, is hereby acknowl-edged.

Date: _____   _____(shareholder's signature)_____
                                                                    (typed name)

Name of Corporation: _____(name of corporation)_____

                                      By: _____(Treasurer's signature)_____
                                                  (typed name), Treasurer

SPECIAL INSTRUCTIONS

This form should be used only after the labor or services have actually been performed. (Remember, in California, payment with future services is prohibited.) Fill in the form to show the name of the shareholder, name of the corporation, the number of shares, the number of the issued certificate, and the agreed-upon dollar value of the labor or services previously rendered to the corporation.

Then, do the following:

- Print or make one copy of the completed form.
- After the shareholder and treasurer sign both forms, place the copy of the form in the stock certificates section of the corporate records book, and give the original signed form to the shareholder.

Note: The value of the stock that the shareholder receives when shares are issued for services or labor done is income and is subject to income tax. Also, problems may arise in this situation with respect to Section 351 tax-free exchange treatment (see Chapter 3, Section C13).

J. File Your Certificate of Registration (if required)

As we noted in Chapter 4, Section B, about one-half of the professions require the filing of a certificate of registration before the corporation may begin practice. The form is available from the board supervising your profession, and the board is available to answer any questions you may have. The application may require such information as the name of the corporation, its principal office, the names of the directors, officers, shareholders, and the employees who will be practicing in the profession, a copy of the Articles certified by the Secretary of State, a copy of the Bylaws, and possibly a security requirement. You will also have to pay a fee.

You have now completed your last incorporation step for setting up a new corporation! There is one last point we wish to make which is central to the operation of your newly formed corporation. One of the reasons you decided to form a corporation was to limit your personal liability in business affairs. So, from now on, whenever you sign a document on behalf of the corporation, be certain to do so in the following manner:

_____(name of corporation)_____

By: ____(signature of corporate officer)_____

(name), (corporate title, e.g., President)

If you fail to sign documents this way (on behalf of the corporation in your capacity as a corporate officer or director), you may be leaving yourself open to personal liability for corporate obligations. This is but one example designed to illustrate a basic premise of corporate life: From now on, it is extremely important for you to maintain the distinction between the corporation which you've organized and yourself (and the other principals of the corporation). As we've said, the corporation is a separate legal "person" and you want to make sure that other people, businesses, the IRS and the courts respect this distinction (see Chapter 3, Section C2, for a further discussion).

Follow-Up Steps: Please read and follow the post-incorporation procedures contained in Chapter 7. ■

Chapter 7

AFTER YOUR CORPORATION IS ORGANIZED

AT THIS POINT THE organization of your corporation should be complete. As you know, operating any professional practice or business, regardless of its size, involves paying attention to paperwork. In this chapter, we show you how to take a few final necessary steps associated with organizing your corporation and how to comply with the various ongoing state and federal tax requirements which may apply to your corporation. We also discuss other formalities related to hiring employees and conducting corporate business. Due to the individual nature of each corporation and its business, it is not possible to discuss every tax for which your corporation may be liable. Rather, this discussion is intended to be a general guide to routine tax obligations that every corporation faces. Most of the tax forms we discuss below can be obtained from the IRS or California Franchise Tax Board (or your tax advisor).

A. Final Formalities After Forming Your Corporation

After you've formed your corporation, there are a few minor details you'll need to take care of which we've summarized in this section.

1. File California Annual Domestic Stock Corporation Statement

Shortly after you have filed your Articles of Incorporation, you will receive an Annual Statement of Domestic Stock Corporation from the California Secretary of State's office. This form must be filled out and sent back to the Secretary within 90 days of the date your Articles were filed together with a small filing fee. The purpose of this form is to provide the public with current information as to the corporation's principal executive office, its directors and officers, etc.

Every two years, you will receive a new Domestic Stock Corporation Statement which must be filled out and returned by the due date indicated. If the corporation fails to file the initial or annual statements within the appropriate time limits, it is subject to a fine and a possible suspension of corporate powers. In other words: Make sure to follow this simple formality.

Note that you may also have to file annual and special reports (showing similar information) with the board supervising your profession. See Chapter 4, Section H, and Appendix 4.

2. File and Publish Fictitious Business Name Statement (if appropriate)

If your corporation is to do business under a name other than the exact corporate name given in your Articles of Incorporation, you will be operating under a *fictitious business name* and you should file and publish a fictitious business name statement in the county of the corporation's principal place of business.

Important: Note that you must also comply with any fictitious business name requirements administered by your professional board—the fictitious business name statement we discuss here is in addition to any fictitious business name requirements and procedures overseen by your professional board. See Appendix 4 for additional fictitious business name requirements associated with each profession and make sure to call your board *first* to obtain approval for your fictitious business name before following the procedure discussed below.

For instance, if the name stated in your Articles is "Anthony, Aaron & Arthur Dental Group, Inc.," and you plan to do business under the acronym, "AAA Dental Group," you will be operating under a fictitious business name and you should file and publish a fictitious business name statement. If you are the first to file this statement for a particular name in a particular county and if you actually engage in business in this county under this name, you are presumed to have the exclusive right to use this name in connection with your business in this county. Although this presumption can be overcome (because another business has been using the same or a similar name first), this can be a helpful legal presumption.

The law (Section 17900, and following, of the California Business and Professions Code) requires that this statement be filed not later than 40 days from the time you start to transact business under your fictitious name. Also, you can be barred from using the courts to sue another business or person involving a transaction or contract in which you used your fictitious name until you first file and publish this statement.

FOR MORE INFORMATION

A truly excellent source of general legal information on starting a small business, is *The Legal Guide for Starting and Running a Small Business* by Fred S. Steingold (Nolo). Another excellent sourcebook of practical information, including financial ledgers and worksheets, is *Small Time Operator* by Kamaroff (Bell Springs Publishing). See back of book for ordering information.

We suggest all incorporators obtain IRS Publication 509, *Tax Calendars*, prior to the beginning of each year. This pamphlet contains tax calendars showing the dates for corporate and employer filings during the year.

Further information on withholding, depositing, reporting and paying federal employment taxes can be found in IRS Publication 15, *Circular E, Employer's Tax Guide* and the Publication 15 Supplement, as well as IRS Publication 937, *Business Reporting*. Further federal tax information can be found in IRS Publication 542, *Tax Information on Corporations* and Publication 334, *Tax Guide for Small Business*.

Helpful information on accounting methods and bookkeeping procedures is contained in IRS Publication 538, *Accounting Period and Methods* and Publication 583, *Information for Business Taxpayers*. These publications can be picked up at your local IRS office, ordered by phone at 800-TAX-FORM, or you can download the forms directly from the IRS website, http://www.irs.gov.

For information on withholding, contributing, paying and reporting California employment taxes, obtain the *California Employer's Tax Guide* (Publication DE 44) and *Employer's Guide* (Publication DE 4525—for unemployment and disability tax information) from your local California Employment Tax District Office or they may be available at the California Employment Development Department's website, http://www.ced.gov.

To file and publish your fictitious business name statement, do the following:

a. Obtain a Fictitious Business Name Statement and instructions from a legal newspaper or from your local county clerk's office. Many county clerk's offices are now on the Internet and provide information and forms over the Web. Check your county's website for more information. You should also check the county clerk's files (on microfiche display or a computer terminal, available for your use at their offices, or you can often search directly on their website) to make sure that another business is not already using your fictitious name in the county.

b. Prepare the statement, following the instructions which apply to corporations.

Note: If your fictitious business name (not your formal corporate name) includes a corporate designator such as "Incorporated," "Inc.", "Corporation," or "Corp.," you may have to provide proof that you are a corporation (by showing the county clerk a certified copy of your Articles).

c. File the original statement with the county clerk of the county in which the principal executive office of the corporation is located, paying the current filing fee. Obtain a file-endorsed copy of the statement from the county clerk.

d. Mail a copy of the statement to a qualified legal newspaper of general circulation in the county of the corporation's principal place of business for publication of your fictitious name statement and for filing of an affidavit of publication with the county clerk (including, of course, the newspaper's fee for this service). The newspaper will publish the statement once a week for four successive weeks and should file an affidavit of publication with the County Clerk for you. If you wish to make this filing yourself, follow the instructions accompanying the statement.

e. Place a copy of the endorsed-filed fictitious business name statement and endorsed-filed affi-davit of publication in your corporate records book.

f. Make a note in your corporate records book to file another statement before the last day of December, five years after your original filing (as explained in the instructions). The county clerk will not notify you of this renewal date.

g. Make similar filings (and publications of the statement), if you wish, in other counties in which you plan to use this name.

3. File Final Papers on Prior Business

If you have incorporated a preexisting practice or business (transferred the assets of a business to the corporation in return for shares), the prior business owners should file all papers needed to terminate their prior business (including final sales tax and employment tax returns, if appropriate). Of course, you should close your previous business bank accounts and open up the corporate bank accounts indicated in the bank account resolution of your minutes. In addition, if the old business holds any licenses or permits, these may need to be canceled and new licenses or permits taken out in the name of the corporation. Of course, the shareholders, directors, officers, and employees of your professional corporation who are to practice in the profession must be licensed or supervised by a licensed person. Check with the board supervising your profession for specific licensing requirements—see Appendix 4.

For More Information: The *California Professional and Business License Handbook*, published by the California Trade and Commerce Agency, is a comprehensive guide to California license requirements, as well as a thorough sourcebook on California's regulatory agencies and the red tape involved in doing business in California. Call the

Trade and Commerce Agency in Sacramento (916-445-8872) to obtain an order form for this publication, or download it from the Internet at http://commerce.ca.gov/business/small/management/pub/license/index.html.

4. Notify Creditors and Others of Dissolution of Prior Business

If you have incorporated a prior business or transferred its assets to the corporation, you should notify the creditors of the prior business and other interested parties (e.g., suppliers, others with whom you have open book accounts or lines of credit, etc.), in writing, of the termination and dissolution of the prior business and the fact that it is now a corporation.

If the prior business was a partnership, you should use the following notification procedure (non-partnership businesses can simply send out a notification letter as discussed in Paragraph d below).

a. Obtain at least two copies of a Notice of Dissolution of a Partnership form from a legal newspaper.

b. Fill out the Notice following the instructions on the form.

c. Send the completed Notice to a legal newspaper(s) circulated in the place or places at which the partnership business was regularly carried on with the request that they publish the Notice at such place(s) and file an affidavit of publication with the county clerk within 30 days after such publication. Include publication and filing fees with your request. Place copies of the notice form and the endorsed-filed affidavit of publication in your corporate records book.

d. Notify creditors (and other interested parties) by mail of the dissolution of the partnership

(or other type of business). This notice should be in letter form, addressed and sent to each creditor, and contain the same information as that included in the published Notice (you will want to modify the information in the letter to show that it is directed to a particular individual or business, rather than the general public). You will want to indicate that your prior business has been dissolved and that you are now doing business as a corporation under your new corporate name. You should, of course, indicate your new corporate address if you have changed the location of your principal place of business. Place a copy of each letter in your corporate records book.

Note: Some professionals may also wish to notify their clients of the incorporation of the professional practice. If you do, simply send a personal letter as discussed above.

B. Tax Forms—Federal

There are a few federal tax housekeeping matters you'll need to take care of after you form your corporation. Fortunately, most of the IRS forms discussed below are available at http://www.irs.gov.

1. S Corporation Tax Election

If you've decided to elect federal S corporation tax status, and have included an authorizing resolution in your minutes, you must make a timely election by filing IRS form 2553 and consents of the shareholders (see Chapter 3, Section C7). If you haven't made your election yet (and haven't consulted a tax advisor as to the timing of the election (see Chapter 8, Section B), call your accountant now and make sure the election form is sent in on time—you don't want to miss the deadline for this election.

Tax Year Reminder: Remember that S (and personal service) corporations must generally choose a calendar tax year for their corporation. Procedures are available to allow some S (and personal service) corporations to adopt a non-calendar (fiscal) tax year. Make sure to file the proper form in a timely manner if you wish to adopt a non-calendar tax year for your S (or personal service) corporation—see Chapter 3, Section C8, and check with your accountant.

2. Federal Identification Number

As soon as possible after the articles are filed, your corporation must apply for a Federal Employer Identification Number by filling out IRS Form SS-4 and sending it to the nearest IRS center. If you are incorporating a pre-existing sole proprietorship or partnership, you will need to apply for a new Employer Identification Number. This number is needed for the employment tax returns and deposits discussed below.

3. Employee's Withholding Certificates

Each employee of the corporation must fill out and furnish the corporation with an Employee's Withholding Exemption Certificate (IRS Form W-4) on or before commencing employment. Obtain the most recent version of Form W-4. This form is used in determining the amount of income taxes to be withheld from the employee's wages.

Generally, any individual who receives compensation for services rendered the corporation subject to the control of the corporation, both as to what shall be done and how it should be done, is considered an employee. All shareholders of the corporation who receive salaries or wages for services as directors, officers, or nontitled personnel are considered employees of the corporation and must furnish a W-4. Directors, with certain exceptions, aren't considered employees if they are only paid for attending board meetings. If, however, they are paid for other services or are salaried employees of the corporation, they will be considered employees whose wages are subject to the employment taxes discussed below—check with the IRS and your local state Employment Tax District Office. Be careful of trying to avoid the payment of employment taxes by classifying people as independent contractors. The law in this area is fuzzy, and the IRS is obstinate. For more information, see IRS Publication 937.

For in-depth information on hiring independent contractors, see *Hiring Independent Contractors: An Employer's Legal Guide*, by Stephen Fishman (Nolo).

4. Income and Social Security Tax Withholding

The corporation must withhold federal income tax and Social Security tax (FICA) from wages paid to each employee. These, as well as other employment taxes, are withheld and reported on a calendar-year basis, regardless of the tax year of the corporation, with returns and deposits being submitted on a quarterly or more frequent basis.

The amount of federal income tax withheld is based upon the employee's wage level, marital status and the number of allowances claimed on the employee's W-4.

Social Security taxes are withheld at a specific rate on an employee's wage base (the rate and wage-base figures change constantly). The corporation is required to make matching Social Security tax contributions for each employee.

5. Quarterly Withholding Returns and Deposits

The corporation is required to prepare and file a Withholding Return (IRS Form 941) for each quarter of the calendar year showing all income and Social Security taxes withheld from employees' wages as well as matching corporation Social Security tax contributions.

The corporation is required to deposit federal income and Social Security taxes on a monthly (or more frequent) basis in an authorized commercial or federal reserve bank. Payment for undeposited taxes owed at the end of a calendar quarter must be submitted with the quarterly return. Consult IRS Publication 15 for specifics.

⚠ Regardless of your business's structure, the IRS will hold you, the owner of the business, personally liable for unpaid payroll taxes. IRS § 6502 provides that payroll taxes are personal liabilities of business owners, so always pay your payroll taxes in full and on time.

6. Annual Wage and Tax Statement

The corporation is required to furnish two copies of the Wage and Tax Statement (IRS Form W-2) to each employee from whom income tax has been withheld or would have been withheld if the employee had claimed no more than one withholding exemption on his W-4. This form must show total wages paid and amounts deducted for income and Social Security taxes. A special six-part W-2 should be used in California to show state income tax and disability insurance contributions in addition to the required federal withholding information. W-2 forms must be furnished to employees no later than January 31 following the close of the calendar year.

The corporation must submit the original of each employee's previous year's W-2 form and an annual Transmittal of Income and Tax Statements (Form W-3) to the Social Security Administration on or before the last day of February following the close of the calendar year.

7. Federal Unemployment Tax

Your corporation is subject to paying Federal Unemployment Tax (FUTA) if, during the current or preceding calendar year, the corporation:

a. Paid wages of $1,500 or more during any calendar quarter, or

b . Had one or more employees for some portion of at least one day during each of 20 different calendar weeks. The 20 weeks don't have to be consecutive.

FUTA taxes are paid by the corporation and are not deducted from employees' wages. The FUTA tax is determined by the current rate and employee wage base and is paid by the corporation (as usual, rates and wage-base figures are subject to change). The corporation receives a credit for a percentage of this tax for California unemployment taxes paid, or for having been granted a favorable experience rating by the state.

Generally, the corporation must deposit the tax in an authorized commercial or federal reserve bank within one month following the close of the quarter. For help in computing your quarterly FUTA tax liability, see instructions in IRS Publication 15. An annual FUTA return (IRS Form 940) must be filed by the corporation with the nearest IRS center by January 31 following the close of the calendar year for which the tax is due. Any tax still due is payable with the return.

8. Corporate Income Tax Return

Corporations must file an annual Corporation Income Tax Return (IRS Form 1120) on or before the fifteenth day of the third month following the close of the tax year. A two-page Short-Form Corporation Income Tax Return (IRS Form 1120-A) is available for use by smaller corporations with gross receipts, total income and total assets of $500,000 or less. The corporation's tax year must correspond with the corporation's accounting period (the period for which corporate books are kept as specified in your Minutes) and is established by the first income tax return filed by the corporation. For a discussion of special corporate tax year require-

ments for S corporations and personal service corporations, see Chapter 3, Section C8.

Your first corporate tax year may be a short year of less than twelve months. For example, if the corporate accounting period selected in the Minutes is the calendar year, January 1 to December 31, and the corporate existence began on March 13 (the date the Articles were filed), the corporation would establish its calendar tax year and report income for its first tax year by filing its first annual return on or before March 15 of the following year.

Note that this first return would be for the short year, March 13 to December 31. If the Minutes select a fiscal tax year, say from July 1 to June 30, and the corporate existence begins on May 1, the first return would be filed on or before August 15 for the first short year of May 1 to June 30.

9. S Corporation Income Tax Return

Even though federal S corporations are, for the most part, exempt from payment of corporate income tax, such corporations must file an annual U.S. Small Business Corporation Income Tax Return (IRS Form 1120S) on or before the fifteenth day of the third month following the close of the tax year for which the S corporation tax election is effective.

10. Corporate Shareholder and Employee Returns

Corporate shareholders and employees report dividend and employment income on their annual individual income tax returns (IRS Form 1040). S corporation shareholders report their pro-rata share of undistributed corporate taxable income on Form 1040, Schedule E and may be required to pay estimated taxes during the year on these amounts—see footnote to Chapter 3, Section C7.

11. Estimated Corporate Income Tax Payments

Most corporations are required to make estimated tax payments. Estimated tax payments must be deposited in an authorized commercial or federal reserve bank. Both the due date and amount of each installment are computed by a formula based upon the corporation's income tax liability.

To determine corporate estimated tax liability and the date and amount of deposits, obtain Form 1120-W. This form is to be used for computational purposes only and should not be filed with the IRS.

C. Tax Forms—State

In addition to IRS rules, you'll need to comply with some state tax requirements after you form your corporation. Fortunately, most of these forms are available at http://www.ftb.ca.gov.

1. Corporate Estimated Tax Return

As already mentioned, a California profit corporation is required to pay an annual California franchise tax based upon its annual net taxable income, and must pay the minimum annual franchise tax each year (but there is no minimum

franchise tax charged for the corporation's first and second tax year). The corporation is required to estimate its franchise tax liability each year and make advance franchise tax payments each quarter.

Delaying the Start of Corporate Existence: To avoid having a short first tax year, you can ask the Secretary of State to file your papers on a specific day after receipt of your Articles as explained in Chapter 6, Step 2. For example, you can mail your Articles to the Secretary of State at the beginning of December and ask in your cover letter that the Articles be filed on January 1st—by doing this you avoid having a short first tax year (in this example, from the beginning of December to the end of the month).

Exception for Very Short First Tax Years: There is a second way to avoid paying franchise taxes during a short first tax year: If your corporation has a first tax year less than *one-half month* and the corporation is inactive during this period, a state corporate tax return is not required and no franchise taxes are owed during this period. For example, if a corporation selects a calendar tax year and files its Articles on December 20th, as long as the corporation is inactive during this period, it is not required to make a minimum tax payment during the December 20th–31st period. The maximum number-of-days duration of this one-half month period varies depending upon the length of the month involved—call the FTB in Sacramento for further information if you want to establish a short first tax year of less than one-half month.

The FTB Fine Print: FTB rules say that a short tax year will be ignored if, in the case of a 28-day month, the Articles were filed on the 15th of the month or later; if Articles were filed during a 29- or 30-day month, they must have been filed on the 16th or later; and for a 31-day month, on the

17th or later. Double-check these requirements with the FTB prior to filing Articles if you wish to avoid payment of franchise taxes during a short (one-half month or less) initial corporate tax year.

2. Annual Corporate Franchise Tax Return

Your corporation must submit an annual Corporate Franchise Tax Return (Form 100) on or before the 15th day of the third month following the close of its tax year. Payment must be submitted with the return for any portion of the tax due which wasn't estimated and paid during the year, as explained above.

3. Employer Registration Forms

All California corporations with employees (individuals who perform services for wages or fees) must register with the California Employment Development Department within 15 days of becoming subject to the California personal income tax withholding provisions and the California Unemployment Insurance Code (most are subject to these provisions immediately)—register right now if you haven't done so. Registration forms are available at the nearest California Employment Tax District Office or on the Employment Development Department's website, http://www.edd.ca.gov. If you are incorporating a preexisting business, you'll need to reregister with the Employment Development Department (even though you may be given the same account number). See the *Employer's Guide* mentioned in the introduction to this chapter and contact your

local Employment Tax District Office for more information.

As noted earlier, be careful about classifying people who perform services for your corporation as "independent contractors." The EDD is particularly aggressive when it comes to collecting state unemployment taxes from businesses and this office routinely investigates employee complaints and conducts field audits to monitor compliance with California's Unemployment Insurance Code provisions.

4. State Withholding Allowance Certificate

Although the corporation can use the information contained in the federal W-4 form to compute the amount of state personal income taxes to be withheld from employee wages, it is required to make a special State Withholding Allowance Certificate (DE-4) available to all employees. Use of this form by the employee is optional. If not used, the corporation withholds state personal income tax from an employee's wages in accordance with the allowances on the employee's federal W-4.

5. Personal Income Tax Withholding

The amount withheld by the corporation from employee wages for state personal income tax is based on tax tables which take into account the marital status, claimed allowances and wages of the employee. These tables automatically allow for applicable exemptions and the standard deduction.

6. California Unemployment and Disability Insurance

Unemployment insurance contributions are paid by the corporation at its employer contribution rate shown on the Quarterly Withholding Return (DE-3) discussed below. Employer contributions are payable on the current employee wage-base amount.

The employer contribution rates vary and, except for new businesses, are based upon the employer's experience rating for each year. Experience ratings can go up or down depending upon how many former employees of the corporation obtain unemployment benefits.

Disability insurance contributions are paid by the employee. Expect rate and wage-base figures to increase periodically.

Special Rules for Officers, Directors and Shareholders: While officers are employees for purposes of unemployment insurance contributions, unemployment benefits may be denied to them if they are laid off or terminated by the corporation if the corporation pays them any "fringes" while they are not working (for example profit-sharing payouts or pension benefits). Also, if the officers and directors are the only shareholders of the corporation, they won't be eligible for benefits unless the corporation is subject to paying federal unemployment taxes (see Section B7, above).

Also, a sole shareholder who is also an officer of the corporation may be able to file a disclaimer and be exempt from California disability insurance contributions. Note that the shareholder waives all corresponding benefits. Contact your California Employment Tax District Office for more information on these special rules.

7. Withholding Returns

A corporation is required in most cases to file Monthly Withholding Returns (Form DE-3M) with the state, indicating personal income tax withholding and disability and unemployment tax contributions for each employee.

The corporation must file a Quarterly Withholding Return (Form DE-3) reporting personal income tax withholding and disability and unemployment insurance contributions for the previous quarter and pay any balance not already paid with Monthly Returns. For more specific information, consult the *California Employer's Tax Guide* available from your local Employment Tax District Office as mentioned in the introduction to this chapter.

8. Annual Wage and Tax Statement

The corporation should prepare a six-part combined federal/state Annual Wage and Tax Statement (Form W-2) as discussed in Section B6 of this chapter. One copy must be filed with the state as explained below.

9. Annual Reconciliation of Income Tax Withholding Forms

The corporation must file a completed Reconciliation of Income Tax Withheld Form (Form DE-43 or DE-43A) together with one copy of each employee's W-2 and a total listing of all personal income tax withheld with the California Employment Development Department on or before February 28 following the close of each calendar year.

10. Sales Tax Forms

Subject to a few exceptions, every corporation which has gross receipts from the sale of personal property (e.g., merchandise sold to customers) in California must apply for a Seller's Permit by filing an application (Form BT-400) with the nearest office of the California Board of Equalization. These forms are available at the Board of Equalization's website, http://www.boe.ca.gov. (Since many professional corporations only provide services, they will not need to apply for a Sales Tax Permit. But those which also sell merchandise, such as pharmacy corporations, will need this permit.) This form also provides for registration as an employer with the Employment Development Department. No fee is required in applying for and obtaining the Sales Tax permit.

Some applicants may be required to post a bond or other security for payment of future sales taxes. A separate permit is required for each place of business at which transactions relating to sales tax are customarily entered into with customers. Sales tax is added to the price of certain goods and is collected from the purchaser.

Wholesalers, as well as retailers, must obtain a permit. A wholesaler, however, is not required to collect sales tax from a retailer who holds a valid Seller's Permit and who buys items for resale to customers, provided a resale certificate is completed in connection with the transaction.

Sellers must file periodic sales and use tax returns, reporting and paying sales tax collected from customers. A seller must keep complete records of all business transactions, including sales, receipts, purchases, and other expenditures, and have them available for inspection by the board at all times.

D. Workers' Compensation

With some exceptions, all employees of a corporation, whether officers or otherwise, are required to be covered by Workers' Compensation Insurance. Rates vary depending on the salary level and risk associated with an employee's job. Generally, if all of the officers are the only shareholders of the corporation, they do not have to be covered by Workers' Compensation. Also, if directors are only paid travel expenses for attending meetings, they may be exempt from coverage (although flat per meeting payments will generally make them subject to coverage). Make sure to check with your commercial insurance broker or local State Compensation Insurance Commission office for names of carriers, rates, and extent of required coverage.

E. Private Insurance Coverage

Corporations, like other businesses, should carry the usual kinds of insurance to prevent undue loss in the event of an accident, fire, theft, etc. Although the corporate form may insulate shareholders from personal loss for claims against the business, it won't prevent corporate assets from being jeopardized by such eventualities. Basic commercial coverage should be obtained and often includes coverage for autos, inventory, personal injuries on premises, etc. Additional coverage for product liability, directors' and officers' liability and other specialized types of insurance may also be appropriate (of course, these policies may be more difficult, i.e., costly, for a closely held corporation to obtain). Many smaller companies elect to have a large deductible to keep premium payments down.

Obviously, there are a number of options to consider when putting together your corporate insurance package. The best advice here is to talk to a few experienced commercial insurance brokers and compare rates and areas and extent of coverage before deciding. Look for someone who suggests ways to get essential coverage for an amount you can live with—not someone who wants to sell you a policy that will protect you from all possible risks. In the first place, this type of policy really doesn't exist. Secondly, even if it did, you probably wouldn't want to pay the price.

Of course, professionals must also comply with the special malpractice insurance requirements associated with each profession—see Appendix 4. ■

Chapter 8

LAWYERS AND ACCOUNTANTS

A. Lawyers

As we've mentioned previously, consulting an experienced attorney prior to incorporating for her review of your incorporation papers and suggestions as to any specific modifications you may need to make in view of the unique needs surrounding your incorporation is often a good idea. Reviewing your incorporation papers with an attorney is a sensible way to insure that all of your papers are up-to-date and meet your specialized needs.

A consultation with a lawyer to review the forms and organizational aspects of your incorporation is quite different than having him do, or redo, it all for you. The lawyer should have experience in small business incorporations, and should be prepared to answer your specific, informed questions and review, not rewrite (unless absolutely necessary), the forms you have prepared.

Throughout this book we have flagged areas of potential complexity where a degree of customization may be warranted. If any of these loom large to you, go over them with an experienced lawyer before filing your Articles of Incorporation. For example, you will need to consult a lawyer if you wish to add customized stock buy-out provisions to your Bylaws or prepare a special shareholders' buy/sell agreement for the repurchase of shares in your corporation—see special instructions to Chapter 6, Step 2.

The best lawyer to choose is someone whom you both personally know and trust and who has lots of experience advising small businesses. The next best is usually a small business expert whom a friend (with her own business experience) recommends. If you make some calls, you can almost always find someone via this excellent "word of mouth" approach. Far less preferable, although occasionally necessary as a last resort, is to select names from the phone book and begin calling. As part of doing this, you may also call a local bar association referral service for a recommendation. We don't advise this approach as many referral services are operated on a strict rotating basis—you'll get the name of the next lawyer who says he handles small businesses (experienced lawyers with plenty of business are rarely on these lists in the first place). Also realize that there is a growing movement to private (and highly suspect) referral services that often refer people to themselves—watch out for these.

When you call a prospective lawyer (not just her law office), you can probably get a good idea of how the person operates by paying close attention to the way your call is handled. Is the lawyer available, or is your call returned promptly? Is the lawyer willing to spend at least a few minutes talking to you to determine if she is really the best person for the job? Do you get a good personal feeling from your conversation? Oh, and one more thing: Be sure to get the hourly rate the lawyer will charge set in advance. (Rules of the State Bar require a lawyer to provide you with a written fee agreement in advance if the fee for services will exceed certain a certain amount (or in contingency fee cases.) If you are using this book, you will probably not be impressed by someone who charges $350 per hour to support an office on top of the tallest building in town.

Looking Up the Law Yourself: Many incorporators may wish to research legal information not covered in this book on their own. County law libraries are open to the public (you will not be asked to produce a bar card before being helped) and are not difficult to use once you understand how the information is categorized and stored. They are an invaluable source of corporate and general business forms, corporate tax procedures and information, etc. Research librarians will usually go out of their way to help you find the right statute, form or background reading on any corporate or tax issue. If you are interested in doing self-help legal research, an excellent source of information on how to break the code of the law libraries is *Legal Research: How to Find and Understand the Law*, by Steven Elias and Susan Levinkind (Nolo). Also, you may wish to obtain a copy of the California Corporations Code to look up code sections yourself (an edition published by West Publishing Co. is available through Nolo).

and specific corporate tax issues throughout the manual. For example:

- If you have the choice under law, would you be better served forming a registered limited liability partnership instead of a professional corporation (currently lawyers, accountants and architects have this choice)?—see Chapter 1, Section A2.
- Should you elect federal (and state) S corporation tax status?—Chapter 3, Section C7
- Do you need help in selecting and electing your corporate tax year?—Chapter 3, Section C8
- Are you eligible for Section 351 tax-free exchange treatment of your incorporation?—Chapter 3, Section C13
- Do you wish to set up a retirement plan or IRS qualified fringe benefit packages for yourself and other employees?—Chapter 3, Section A3, and Chapter 5
- Will you rely on an accountant or other professional in setting up your corporate books (double-entry journals and general ledger) and in making ongoing corporate and employment tax filings?—See the discussion below.

B. Accountants

As you already know, organizing and operating a corporation involves a significant amount of financial and tax work, and many important decisions need to be made. Again, we have flagged areas of special consideration involving financial planning

- Do you need to obtain a valuation of the assets of a prior business being transferred to your corporation in return for shares?
—Chapter 6, Section I4

Generally, although we tend to use the terms tax advisor, financial consultant and accountant interchangeably, you may prefer to refer these initial incorporation considerations to a certified public accountant with corporate experience. For general assistance and advice, a qualified financial planner may also be very helpful. Retirement plan custodians and trustees can help you adopt a pre-qualified master or prototype retirement plan—see Chapter 5, Section J.

Once your initial incorporation questions have been answered, your corporation set up and your books established, you may want to have routine tax filings and bookkeeping tasks performed by corporate personnel or independent contractors who have been trained in bookkeeping and tax matters (in many instances trained or recommended by the accountant you have previously consulted). Most corporations will have at least

their annual corporate returns handled by their accountant or other tax return preparer.

For future financial advice, you may wish to contact an officer in the corporate department of the bank where you keep your corporate account(s). Banks are an excellent source of financial advice, particularly if they will be corporate creditors—after all, they will have a stake in the success of your corporation.

Whatever your arrangement for financial or tax advice and assistance, you may wish to order the IRS publications listed in the "For More Information" box in Chapter 7 to familiarize yourself with some of the tax and bookkeeping aspects of operating a corporation.

When you select an accountant, bookkeeper, financial advisor, etc., the same considerations apply as when selecting a lawyer. Choose someone you know or whom a friend with business experience recommends. Be as specific as you can regarding the services you wish performed and find someone with experience in corporate taxation and with corporate and employee tax returns and requirements. ■

APPENDIX 1

Secretary of State Contact Information

Name Availability Request

Reservation of Corporate Name Request

Cover Letter to Secretary of State

Articles of Incorporation

CALIFORNIA SECRETARY OF STATE
CORPORATION INFORMATION
Website: http://www.ss.ca.gov

Office hours for all locations are Monday through Friday 8:00 a.m. to 5:00 p.m.

Corporations Unit

Name Availability   916-654-7960
(recorded information on how to obtain)
1500 11th Street
Sacramento, CA 95814

Document Filing Support and
Legal Review   916-653-2318
1500 11th Street
Sacramento, CA 95814

Information Retrieval and
Certification   916-653-2121
1500 11th Street
Sacramento, CA 95814

Status   916-653-7315
(recorded information on how to obtain)
1500 11th Street
Sacramento, CA 95814

Statement of Officers   916-653-1742
(filings only)
P.O. Box 944230 (94244-2300)
1500 11th Street
Sacramento, CA 95814

Substituted Service of Process   916-653-8304
(must be hand delivered)
1500 11th Street
Sacramento, CA 95814

Fresno Branch Office   209-243-2100
2497 West Shaw, Suite 101
Fresno, CA 93711

Los Angeles Branch Office   213-897-3062
300 South Spring Street,
Room 12513
Los Angeles, CA 90013-1233

San Diego Branch Office   619-525-4113
1350 Front Street, Suite 2060
San Diego, CA 92101-3690

San Francisco Branch Office   415-439-6959
1350 Front Street, Suite 2060
San Diego, CA 92101-3690

Note: When filing Articles of Incorporation in a branch office, submit duplicate original documents, plus any copies to be certified.

NAME AVAILABILITY REQUEST

Secretary of State
Corporate Filing and Services Division
1500 11th Street
Sacramento, California 95814

Secretary of State:

Please advise if any of the following names are presently available for corporate use:

1. _____

2. _____

3. _____

I enclose a stamped, self-addressed envelope for your reply.

Very truly yours,

_____

Name: _____
Address: _____
_____
Telephone: _____

RESERVATION OF CORPORATE NAME REQUEST

Secretary of State
Corporate Name Availability
1500 11th Street
Sacramento, California 95814

Secretary of State:

Please reserve the first available corporate name from the list below for my use. My proposed corporate names, listed in order of preference, are as follows:

1. _____
2. _____
3. _____

I enclose a check or money order for the required reservation fee, payable to the Secretary of State.

Very truly yours,

_____

Name: _____
Address: _____
_____
Telephone: _____

COVER LETTER TO SECRETARY OF STATE

Secretary of State
Corporate Filing and Services Division
1500 11th Street
Sacramento, CA 95814

Secretary of State:

I enclose an original and _____ copies of the proposed Articles of Incorporation
of _____.

Also enclosed is a check/money order in payment of the filing fees:

Please file the original Articles and return the certified copies to me at the above
address.

_____
Incorporator

Name: _____
Address: _____
_____
Telephone: _____

ARTICLES OF INCORPORATION

OF

_____

ONE: The name of this corporation is _____.

TWO: The purpose of this corporation is to engage in the profession of _____
_____.
and any other lawful activities (other than the banking or trust company business)
not prohibited to a corporation engaging in such profession by applicable laws
and
regulations.

THREE: The corporation is a professional corporation within the meaning of Part 4
of Division 3 of Title 1 of the California Corporations Code.

FOUR: The name and address in this state of the corporation's initial agent for
service of process is:

_____

_____

_____

_____

FIVE: This corporation is authorized to issue only one class of shares of stock which shall be designated common stock. The total number of shares it is authorized to issue is _____ shares.

SIX: The names and addresses of the persons who are appointed to act as the initial directors of this corporation are:

Name   Address

_____   _____

_____   _____

_____   _____

_____   _____

IN WITNESS WHEREOF, the undersigned, being all the persons named above as the initial directors, have executed these Articles of Incorporation.

DATED:_____   _____

                             _____

                             _____

                             _____

The undersigned, being all the persons named above as the initial directors, declare that they are the persons who executed the foregoing Articles of Incorporation, which execution is their act and deed.

DATED:_____   _____

                             _____

                             _____

                             _____

APPENDIX 2

Bylaws

In Article II of these Bylaws, you will see a heading "Special Provisions for the Professional Corporation." These special provisions relate to who can own shares in the corporation, the transfer of shares and what happens when a shareholder dies or is disqualified. You may also have to include a security guarantee provision. Certain corporations (e.g., law and accountancy corporations) may be required to add other provisions as well. To properly fill in this Article, see Chapter 6, Step 6, and Appendix 4.

BYLAWS

OF

_____

ARTICLE I

OFFICES

SECTION 1. PRINCIPAL EXECUTIVE OFFICE

The principal executive office of the corporation shall be in the City of
_____, County of _____, State of
California.

The corporation may also have offices at such other places as the Board of Directors may from time to time designate, or as the business of the corporation may require.

ARTICLE II
SPECIAL PROVISIONS FOR THE PROFESSIONAL CORPORATION

ARTICLE III
SHAREHOLDERS' MEETING

SECTION 1. PLACE OF MEETINGS

All meetings of the shareholders shall be held at the principal executive office of the corporation or at such other place as may be determined by the Board of Directors.

SECTION 2. ANNUAL MEETINGS

The annual meeting of the shareholders shall be held on the _____ of _____ in each year, if not a holiday, at _____ o'clock __.M., at which time the shareholders shall elect a Board of Directors and transact any other proper business. If this date falls on a holiday, then the meeting shall be held on the following business day at the same hour.

SECTION 3. SPECIAL MEETINGS

Special meetings of the shareholders may be called by the Board of Directors, the Chairperson of the Board of Directors, the President or by one or more shareholders holding at least 10 percent of the voting power of the corporation.

SECTION 4. NOTICE OF MEETINGS

Notices of meetings, annual or special, shall be given in writing to shareholders entitled to vote at the meeting by the Secretary or an Assistant Secretary, or, if there be no such officer, or in the case of his or her neglect or refusal, by any director or shareholder.

Such notices shall be given either personally or by first-class mail or other means of written communication, addressed to the shareholder at the address of such shareholder appearing on the books of the corporation or given by the shareholder to the corporation for the purpose of notice. Notice shall be given not less than ten (10) nor more than sixty (60) days before the date of the meeting.

Such notice shall state the place, date and hour of the meeting and (1), in the case of a special meeting, the general nature of the business to be transacted, and that no other business may be transacted, or (2), in the case of an annual meeting, those matters which the Board at the time of the mailing of the notice intends to present for action by the shareholders, but subject to the provisions of Section 6 of this Article, any proper matter may be presented at the meeting for such action. The notice of any meeting at which directors are to be elected shall include the names of the nominees which, at the time of the notice, the Board of Directors intends to present for election. Notice of any adjourned meeting need not be given unless a meeting is adjourned for forty-five (45) days or more from the date set for the original meeting.

SECTION 5. WAIVER OF NOTICE

The transactions of any meeting of shareholders, however called and noticed, and wherever held, are as valid as though had at a meeting duly held after regular call and notice, if a quorum is present, whether in person or by proxy, and if, either before or after the meeting, each of the persons entitled to vote, not present in person or by proxy, signs a written waiver of notice or a consent to the holding of the meeting or an approval of the minutes thereof. All such waivers or consents and approvals shall be filed with the corporate records or made a part of the minutes of the meeting. Neither the business to be transacted at the meeting, nor the purpose of any annual or special meeting of shareholders need be specified in any written waiver of notice, except as provided in Section 6 of this Article.

SECTION 6: SPECIAL NOTICE AND WAIVER OF NOTICE REQUIREMENT

Except as provided below, any shareholder approval at a meeting, with respect to the following proposals, shall be valid only if the general nature of the proposal so approved was stated in the notice of meeting, or in any written waiver of notice:

1. Approval of a contract or other transaction between the corporation and one or more of its directors or between the corporation and any corporation, firm or association in which one or more of the directors has a material financial interest, pursuant to Section 310 of the California Corporations Code;

2. Amendment of the Articles of Incorporation after any shares have been issued pursuant to Section 902 of the California Corporations Code;

3. Approval of the principal terms of a reorganization pursuant to Section 1201 of the California Corporations Code;

4. Election to voluntarily wind up and dissolve the corporation pursuant to Section 1900 of the California Corporations Code; and

5. Approval of a plan of distribution of shares as part of the winding up of the corporation pursuant to Section 2007 of the California Corporations Code.

Approval of the above proposals at a meeting shall be valid with or without such notice, if by the unanimous approval of those entitled to vote at the meeting.

SECTION 7. ACTION WITHOUT MEETING

Any action which may be taken at any annual or special meeting of shareholders may be taken without a meeting and without prior notice if a consent, in writing, setting forth the action so taken, shall be signed by the holders of outstanding shares having not less than the minimum number of votes that would be necessary to authorize or take such action at a meeting at which all shares entitled to vote thereon were present and voted.

Unless the consents of all shareholders entitled to vote have been solicited in writing, notice of any shareholders' approval, with respect to any one of the following proposals, without a meeting, by less than unanimous written consent shall be given at least ten (10) days before the consummation of the action authorized by such approval:

1. Approval of a contract or other transaction between the corporation and one or more of its directors or another corporation, firm or association in which one or more of its directors has a material financial interest, pursuant to Section 310 of the Corporations Code;

2. To indemnify an agent of the corporation pursuant to Section 317 of the California Corporations Code;

3. To approve the principal terms of a reorganization, pursuant to Section 1201 of the California Corporations Code; or

4. Approval of a plan of distribution as part of the winding up of the corporation pursuant to Section 2007 of the California Corporations Code.

Prompt notice shall be given of the taking of any other corporate action approved by shareholders without a meeting by less than a unanimous written consent to those shareholders entitled to vote who have not consented in writing.

Notwithstanding any of the foregoing provisions of this section, directors may not be elected by the unanimous written consent of all shares entitled to vote for the election of directors.

A written consent may be revoked by a writing received by the corporation prior to the time that written consents of the number of shares required to authorize the proposed action have been filed with the Secretary of the corporation, but may not be revoked thereafter. Such revocation is effective upon its receipt by the Secretary of the corporation.

SECTION 8. QUORUM AND SHAREHOLDER ACTION

A majority of the shares entitled to vote, represented in person or by proxy, shall constitute a quorum at a meeting of shareholders. If a quorum is present, the affirmative vote of a majority of shares represented at the meeting and entitled to vote on any matter shall be the act of the shareholders, unless the vote of a greater number is required by law and except as provided in the following provisions of this section.

The shareholders present at a duly called or held meeting at which a quorum is present may continue to transact business until adjournment notwithstanding the withdrawal of enough shareholders to leave less than a quorum, if any action is approved by at least a majority of the shares required to constitute a quorum.

In the absence of a quorum, any meeting of shareholders may be adjourned from time to time by the vote of a majority of the shares represented either in person or by proxy, but no other business may be transacted except as provided in the foregoing provisions of this section.

SECTION 9. VOTING

Only persons in whose names shares entitled to vote stand on the record date for voting purposes fixed by the Board of Directors pursuant to Article IX, Section 2 of these Bylaws, or, if there be no such date so fixed, on the record dates given below, shall be entitled to vote at such meeting.

If no record date is fixed:

1. The record date for determining shareholders entitled to notice of, or to vote at a meeting of shareholders, shall be at the close of business on the business day next preceding the day on which notice is given, or, if notice is waived, at the close of business on the business day next preceding the day on which the meeting is held.

2. The record date for determining the shareholders entitled to give consent to corporate actions in writing without a meeting, when no prior action by the Board is necessary, shall be the day on which the first written consent is given.

3. The record date for determining shareholders for any other purpose shall be at the close of business on the day on which the Board adopts the resolution relating thereto, or the 60th day prior to the date of such other action, whichever is later.

Every shareholder entitled to vote shall be entitled to one vote for each share held, except as otherwise provided by law, by the Articles of Incorporation or by other provisions of these bylaws. Except with respect to election of directors, any shareholder entitled to vote may vote part of his or her shares in favor of a proposal and refrain from voting the remaining shares or vote them against the proposal. If a shareholder fails to specify the number of shares he or she is affirmatively voting, it will be conclusively presumed that the shareholder's approving vote is with respect to all shares the shareholder is entitled to vote.

At each election of directors, shareholders shall not be entitled to cumulate votes unless the candidates' names have been placed in nomination before the commencement of the voting and a shareholder has given notice at the meeting, and before the voting has begun, of his or her intention to cumulate votes. If any shareholder has given such notice, then all shareholders entitled to vote may cumulate their votes by giving one candidate a number of votes equal to the number of directors to be elected multiplied by the number of his or her shares or by distributing such votes on the same principle among any number of candidates as he or she thinks fit. The candidates receiving the highest number of votes, up to the number of directors to be elected, shall be elected. Votes cast against a candidate or which are withheld shall have no effect. Upon the demand of any shareholder made before the voting begins, the election of directors shall be by ballot rather than by voice vote.

SECTION 10. PROXIES

Every person entitled to vote shares may authorize another person or persons to act by proxy with respect to such shares by filing a written proxy executed by such person or his or her duly authorized agent with the Secretary of the corporation.

A proxy shall not be valid after the expiration of eleven (11) months from the date thereof unless otherwise provided in the proxy. Every proxy continues in full force and effect until revoked by the person executing it prior to the vote pursuant thereto, except as otherwise provided in Section 705 of the California Corporations Code.

Provided, however that no shareholder of this professional corporation shall enter into a voting trust, proxy, or any other arrangement vesting another person (other than another licensed person who is a shareholder of this corporation) with the authority to exercise the voting power of any or all of his or her shares, and any such purported voting trust, proxy or other arrangement shall be void.

ARTICLE IV
DIRECTORS, MANAGEMENT

SECTION 1. POWERS

Subject to any limitations in the Articles of Incorporation and to the provisions of California law and regulations, the business and affairs of the corporation shall be managed and all corporate powers shall be exercised by, or under the direction of, the Board of Directors.

SECTION 2. NUMBER AND QUALIFICATIONS

The authorized number of Directors shall be _____ until changed by amendment to this Article of these Bylaws.

After issuance of shares, this Bylaw may only be amended to change the authorized number of directors of this corporation by approval of a majority of the outstanding shares entitled to vote; provided, however, that a Bylaw reducing the fixed number of directors to a number less than five (5) cannot be adopted unless in accordance with Article X, Section 1 of these bylaws.

Each director shall be licensed in the profession, or where permitted by Section 13401.5 of the Corporations Code, in a specified related profession.

Provided, however, that if the corporation has only one shareholder and one director, the director must be the shareholder, and if the corporation has only two shareholders and two directors, the directors must be the shareholders, in accordance with Section 13403 of the Corporations Code.

SECTION 3. ELECTION AND TENURE OF OFFICE

The directors shall be elected at the annual meeting of the shareholders and hold office until the next annual meeting and until their successors have been elected and qualified.

SECTION 4. VACANCIES

A vacancy on the Board of Directors shall exist in the case of death, resignation, disqualification, or removal of any director, or in case the authorized number of directors is increased, or in case the shareholders fail to elect the full, authorized number of directors at any annual or special meeting of the shareholders at which any director is elected. The Board of Directors may declare vacant the office of a director who has been declared of unsound mind by an order of court, or who has been convicted of a felony.

Except for a vacancy created by the removal of a director, vacancies on the Board of Directors may be filled by approval of the board or, if the number of directors then in office is less than a quorum, by (1) the unanimous written of the directors then in office, (2) the affirmative vote of a majority of the directors then in office at a meeting held pursuant to notice or waivers of notice complying with this Article of these Bylaws, or (3) a sole remaining director. Vacancies occurring on the board by reason of the removal of directors may be filled only by approval of the shareholders. Each director so elected shall hold office until the next annual meeting of the shareholders and until his or her successor has been elected and qualified.

The shareholders may elect a director at any time to fill a vacancy not filled by the directors. Any such election by written consent requires the consent of a majority of the outstanding shares entitled to vote, except that the unanimous written consent of the shareholders shall be required to fill a vacancy on the Board caused by the removal of a director.

Any director may resign effective upon giving written notice to the Chairperson of the Board of Directors, the President, the Secretary or the Board of Directors of the corporation unless the notice specifies a later time for the effectiveness of such resignation. If the resignation is effective at a later time, a successor may be elected to take office when the resignation becomes effective. Any reduction of the authorized number of directors does not remove any director prior to the expiration of such director's term in office.

Any director elected pursuant to this section shall meet the qualifications specified in Article IV, Section 2 of these bylaws.

SECTION 5. REMOVAL

Any or all of the directors may be removed without cause if such removal is approved by a majority of the outstanding shares entitled to vote, subject to the provisions of Section 303 of the California Corporations Code.

Except as provided in Sections 302, 303 and 304 of the California Corporations Code, a director may not be removed prior to the expiration of such director's term of office.

The Superior Court of the proper county may, on the suit of shareholders holding at least 10 percent of the number of outstanding shares of any class, remove from office any director in case of fraudulent or dishonest acts or gross abuse of authority or discretion with reference to the corporation and may bar from re-election any director so removed for a period prescribed by the court. The corporation shall be made a party to such action.

SECTION 6. PLACE OF MEETINGS

Meetings of the Board of Directors shall be held at any place, within or without the State of California, which has been designated in the notice of the meeting, or, if not stated in the notice or there is no notice, at the principal executive office of the corporation or as may be designated from time to time by resolution of the Board of Directors.

SECTION 7. CALL, NOTICE, AND HOLDING OF MEETINGS

Regular annual meetings of the Board of Directors shall be held without notice immediately after and at the same place as the annual meeting of shareholders. Special meetings of the Board of Directors shall be held upon four (4) days' notice by mail, or 48 hours' notice delivered personally or by telephone or telegraph. A notice or waiver of notice need not specify the purpose of any special meeting of the Board of Directors.

Special meetings of the Board of Directors may be called by the Chairperson of the Board, or the President, or Vice President, or Secretary or any two directors.

If any meeting is adjourned for more than 24 hours, notice of the adjournment to another time or place shall be given before the time of the resumed meeting to all directors who were not present at the time of adjournment of the original meeting.

SECTION 8. QUORUM AND BOARD ACTION

A quorum for all meetings of the Board of Directors shall consist of _____ of the authorized number of Directors.

Every act or decision done or made by a majority of the directors present at a meeting duly held at which a quorum is present is the act of the Board, subject to the provisions of Section 310 (relating to the approval of contracts and transactions in which a director has a material financial interest); the provisions of Section 311 (designation of committees); and Section 317(e) (indemnification of directors) of the California Corporations Code. A meeting at which a quorum is initially present may continue to transact business notwithstanding the withdrawal of directors, if any action taken is approved by at least a majority of the required quorum for such meeting.

A majority of the directors present at a meeting may adjourn any meeting to another time and place whether or not a quorum is present at the meeting.

SECTION 9. WAIVER OF NOTICE

The transactions of any meeting of the Board, however called and noticed or wherever held, are as valid as though had at a meeting duly held after regular call and notice if a quorum is present and if, either before or after the meeting, each of the directors not present signs a written waiver of notice, a consent to holding the meeting or an approval of the minutes thereof. All such waivers, consents and approvals shall be filed with the corporate records or made a part of the minutes of the meeting.

SECTION 10. ACTION WITHOUT MEETING

Any action required or permitted to be taken by the Board may be taken without a meeting, if all members of the Board shall individually or collectively consent in writing to such action. Such written consent or consents shall be filed with the minutes of the proceedings of the Board. Such action by written consent shall have the same force and effect as a unanimous vote of such directors.

SECTION 11. COMPENSATION

No salary shall be paid directors, as such, for their services, but, by resolution, the Board of Directors may allow a fixed sum and expenses to be paid for attendance at regular or special meetings. Nothing contained herein shall prevent a director from serving the corporation in any other capacity and receiving compensation therefor. Members of special or standing committees may be allowed like compensation for attendance at meetings.

ARTICLE V
OFFICERS

SECTION 1. OFFICERS

The officers of the corporation shall be a President, Vice President, a Secretary and a Treasurer, who shall be the Chief Financial Officer of the corporation. The corporation may also have such other officers with such titles and duties as shall be determined by the Board of Directors.

Each officer shall be licensed in the profession or in a specified related profession as permitted by Section 13401.5 of the Corporations Code. Provided, however, that if the corporation has only one shareholder (who is also the one director), that person shall serve as the President and Treasurer of the corporation and the other officers need not be licensed, and if the corporation has only two shareholders (who are also the directors), the two shareholders shall between them fill the offices of President, Vice President, Secretary and Treasurer, in accordance with Section 13403 of the Corporations Code.

SECTION 2. ELECTION

All officers of the corporation shall be chosen by the Board. Each officer shall hold office until his or her death, resignation, disqualification or removal or until his or her successor shall be chosen and qualified. A vacancy in any office because of death, resignation or removal or other cause shall be filled by the Board.

SECTION 3. REMOVAL AND RESIGNATION

An officer may be removed at any time, either with or without cause, by the Board subject to the provisions in Section 1 of this Article. An officer may resign at any time upon written notice to the corporation given to the Board, the President, or the Secretary of the corporation, subject to the provisions of Section 1 of this Article. Any such resignation shall take effect at the day of receipt of such notice or at any other time specified therein. The acceptance of a resignation shall not be necessary to make it effective. The removal or resignation of an officer shall be without prejudice to the rights, if any, of the officer or the corporation under any contract of employment to which the officer is a party.

SECTION 4. PRESIDENT

The President shall be the chief executive officer of the corporation and shall, subject to the direction and control of the Board of Directors, have general supervision, direction and control of the business and affairs of the corporation. He or she shall preside at all meetings of the shareholders and directors and be an ex-officio member of all the standing committees, including the executive committee, if any, and shall have the general powers and duties of management usually vested in the office of President of a corporation, and shall have such other powers and duties as may from time to time be prescribed by the Board of Directors or the Bylaws.

SECTION 5. VICE PRESIDENT

In the absence or disability of the President, the Vice Presidents, in order of their rank as fixed by the Board of Directors, of if not ranked, the Vice President designated by the Board, shall perform all the duties of the President, and when so acting, shall have all the powers of, and be subject to all the restrictions upon, the President. Each Vice President shall have such other powers and perform such other duties as may from time to time be prescribed by the Board of Directors or the Bylaws.

SECTION 6. SECRETARY

The Secretary shall keep, or cause to be kept, at the principal executive office of the corporation, a book of minutes of all meetings of directors and shareholders, with the time and place of holding, whether annual or special, and, if special, how authorized, the notice thereof given or the waivers of notice, the names of those present at directors' meetings, the number of shares present or represented at shareholders' meetings and the proceedings thereof.

The Secretary shall keep, or cause to be kept, at the principal executive office of the corporation, or at the office of the corporation's transfer agent, a share register, showing the names of the shareholders and their addresses, the number and classes of shares held by each, the number and date of certificates issued for shares, and the number and date of cancellation of every certificate surrendered for cancellation.

The Secretary shall keep, or cause to be kept, at the principal executive office of the corporation, the original or a copy of the Bylaws as amended or otherwise altered to date, certified by her or her.

The Secretary shall give, or cause to be given, notice of all meetings of shareholders and Directors required to be given by law or these Bylaws.

The Secretary shall have charge of the seal of the corporation and shall have such other powers and perform such other duties as may from time to time be prescribed by the Board or these Bylaws.

SECTION 7. TREASURER

The Treasurer shall be the Chief Financial Officer of the corporation and shall keep and maintain, or cause to be kept and maintained, adequate and correct books and records of accounts of the properties and business transactions of the corporation.

The Treasurer shall deposit monies and other valuables in the name and to the credit of the corporation with such depositories as may be designated by the Board of Directors. He or she shall disburse the funds of the corporation in payment of the just demands against the corporation as may be ordered by the Board of Directors; shall render to the President and directors, whenever they request it, an account of all his or her transactions as Treasurer and of the financial condition of the corporation; and shall have such other powers and perform such other duties as may from time to time be prescribed by the Board of Directors or these Bylaws.

In the absence or disability of the Treasurer, the Assistant Treasurers, if any, in order of their rank as fixed by the Board of Directors or, if not ranked, the Assistant Treasurer designated by the Board of Directors, shall perform all the duties of the Treasurer, and when so acting, shall have all the powers of, and be subject to all the restrictions upon, the Treasurer. The Assistant Treasurers, if any, shall have such other powers and perform such other duties as may from time to time be prescribed by the Board of Directors or the Bylaws.

SECTION 8. COMPENSATION

The salaries of the officers shall be fixed, from time to time, by the Board of Directors.

ARTICLE VI
EXECUTIVE COMMITTEES

SECTION 1

The Board may, by resolution adopted by a majority of the authorized number of directors, designate one or more committees, each consisting of two or more directors, to serve at the pleasure of the Board. Any such committee, to the extent provided in the resolution of the board, shall have all the authority of the Board, except with respect to:

a. The approval of any action for which the approval of the shareholders or approval of the outstanding shares is also required.

b. The filling of vacancies on the Board or in any committee.

c. The fixing of compensation of the directors for serving on the Board or on any committee.

d. The amendment or repeal of Bylaws or the adoption of new Bylaws.

e. The amendment or repeal of any resolution of the Board which by its express terms is not so amendable or repealable.

f. A distribution to the shareholders of the corporation, except at a rate or in a periodic amount or within a price range determined by the Board.

g. The appointment of other committees of the Board or the members thereof.

ARTICLE VII
CORPORATE RECORDS AND REPORTS

SECTION 1. INSPECTION BY SHAREHOLDERS

The share register shall be open to inspection and copying by any shareholder or holder of a voting trust certificate at any time during usual business hours upon written demand on the corporation, for a purpose reasonably related to such holder's interest as a shareholder or holder of a voting trust certificate. Such inspection and copying under this section may be made in person or by agent or attorney.

The accounting books and records and minutes of proceedings of the shareholders and the Board and committees of the Board also shall be open to inspection upon the written demand on the corporation of any shareholder or holder of a voting trust certificate at any reasonable time during usual business hours, for any proper purpose reasonably related to such holder's interests as a shareholder or as the holder of such voting trust certificate. Such inspection by a shareholder or holder of voting trust certificate may be made in person or by agent or attorney and the right of inspection includes the right to copy and make extracts.

Shareholders shall also have the right to inspect the original or copy of these Bylaws, as amended to date, kept at the corporation's principal executive office, at all reasonable times during business hours.

SECTION 2. INSPECTION BY DIRECTORS

Every director shall have the absolute right at any reasonable time to inspect and copy all books, records and documents of every kind and to inspect the physical properties of the corporation, domestic or foreign, of which such person is a director. Such inspection by a director may be made in person or by agent or attorney and the right of inspection includes the right to copy and make extracts.

SECTION 3. RIGHT TO INSPECT WRITTEN RECORDS

If any record subject to inspection pursuant to this chapter is not maintained in written form, a request for inspection is not complied with unless and until the corporation at its expense makes such record available in written form.

SECTION 4. WAIVER OF ANNUAL REPORT

The annual report to shareholders, described in Section 1501 of the California Corporations Code, is hereby expressly waived, as long as this corporation has less than 100 holders of record of its shares. This waiver shall be subject to any provision of law, including subdivision (c) of Section 1501 of the California Corporations Code, allowing shareholders to request the corporation to furnish financial statements.

SECTION 5. CONTRACTS, ETC.

The Board of Directors, except as otherwise provided in the Bylaws, may authorize any officer or officers, agent or agents, to enter into any contract or execute any instrument in the name and on behalf of the corporation. Such authority may be general or confined to specific instances. Unless so authorized by the Board of Directors, no officer, agent or employee shall have any power or authority to bind the corporation by any contract or engagement, or to pledge its credit, or to render it liable for any purpose or to any amount.

ARTICLE VIII
INDEMNIFICATION OF CORPORATE AGENTS

SECTION 1.

The corporation shall indemnify each of its agents against expenses, judgments, fines, settlements and other amounts, actually and reasonably incurred by such person by reason of such person's having been made or having been threatened to be made a party to a proceeding, to the fullest extent permissible by the provisions of Section 317 of the California Corporations Code. The corporation shall advance the expenses reasonably expected to be incurred by such agent in defending any such proceeding upon receipt of the undertaking required by subdivision (f) of such section. The terms "agent," "proceeding," and "expenses" used in this Section 1 shall have the same meaning as such terms in said Section 317 of the California Corporations Code.

ARTICLE IX
SHARES

SECTION 1. CERTIFICATES

The corporation shall issue certificates for its shares when fully paid. Certificates of stock shall be issued in numerical order, and state the name of the recordholder of the shares represented thereby; the number, designation, if any, and class or series of shares represented thereby; and contain any statement or summary required by California laws and regulations.

Every certificate for shares shall be signed in the name of the corporation by the Chairperson or Vice Chairperson of the Board or the President or a Vice President, and the Treasurer or the Secretary or an Assistant Secretary.

SECTION 2. RECORD DATE

The Board of Directors may fix a time in the future as a record date for the determination of the shareholders entitled to notice of and to vote at any meeting of shareholders or entitled to receive payment of any dividend or distribution, or any allotment of rights, or to exercise rights in respect to any other lawful action. The record date so fixed shall not be more than sixty (60) nor less than ten (10) days prior to the date of such meeting, nor more than sixty (60) days prior to any other action. When a record date is so fixed, only shareholders of record on that date are entitled to notice of and to vote at the meeting or to receive the dividend, distribution, or allotment of rights, or to exercise the rights as the case may be, notwithstanding any transfer of any shares on the books of the corporation after the record date.

ARTICLE X
AMENDMENT OF BYLAWS

SECTION 1. BY SHAREHOLDERS

Bylaws may be adopted, amended or repealed by the affirmative vote or by the written consent of holders of a majority of the outstanding shares of the corporation entitled to vote. However a Bylaw amendment which reduces the fixed number of directors to a number less than five (5) shall not be effective if the votes cast against the amendment or the shares not consenting to its adoption are equal to more than 16⅔ percent of the outstanding shares entitled to vote.

SECTION 2. BY DIRECTORS

Subject to the right of shareholders to adopt, amend or repeal Bylaws, Bylaws may be adopted, amended or repealed by the Board of Directors, except that a Bylaw amendment thereof changing the authorized number of directors may be adopted by the Board of Directors only if prior to the issuance of shares.

CERTIFICATE

This is to certify that the foregoing is a true and correct copy of the Bylaws of the Corporation named in the title thereto and that such Bylaws were duly adopted by the Board of Directors of said Corporation on the date set forth below.

Dated:_____

_____ , Secretary

APPENDIX 3

Minutes

These are to be filled out following the instructions in Chapter 6, Step 8. Also, as explained in Chapter 6, several of the resolutions contained here may not apply to your corporation. Neatly cross out resolutions not used or retype the Minutes.

Stock Issuance Receipts

Fill out one or more receipts when issuing shares to your initial shareholders as explained in Chapter 6, 14.

Receipt for Cash Payment for Shares

Acknowledgment of Cancellation of Indebtedness

Bill of Sale for Assets of a Business

Bill of Sale for Items of Property

Acknowledgment of Share Issuance for Labor Done or Services Rendered

WAIVER OF NOTICE AND CONSENT TO HOLDING

OF FIRST MEETING OF BOARD OF DIRECTORS OF

OF

_____

We, the undersigned, being all the Directors of _____, a
California corporation, hereby waive notice of the first meeting of the Board of
Directors of the Corporation and consent to the holding of said meeting at
_____, in _____, California
on _____ , _____, at _____ o'clock _.M., and consent to the
transaction of any and all business by the Directors at the meeting, including, without
limitation, the adoption of Bylaws, the election of officers, the selection of the
Corporation's fiscal year, the selection of the place where the Corporation's bank
account will be maintained, and the authorization of the sale and issuance of shares of
stock of the Corporation pursuant to 10 California Code of Regulations Section
260.105.6.

Dated: _____   _____
                                                    , Director

                                  _____
                                                    , Director

                                  _____
                                                    , Director

Director

MINUTES OF FIRST MEETING OF BOARD OF DIRECTORS

OF

_____

The Board of Directors of _____ held its first meeting on _____ , ____, at _____ o'clock _.M., at _____ _____,
California. Written waiver of notice was signed by all of the Directors.

The following Directors, constituting a quorum of the full Board, were present at the meeting:

_____

_____

_____

There were absent:

_____

_____

_____

On motion and by unanimous vote, _____ was elected temporary Chairperson and s/he then presided over the meeting. _____ was elected temporary Secretary of the meeting.

The Chairperson announced that the meeting was held pursuant to written waiver of notice signed by each of the Directors. Upon a motion duly made, seconded and unanimously carried, the waiver was made a part of the records of the meeting; it now precedes the minutes of this meeting in the Corporation's Minute Book.

ARTICLES OF INCORPORATION

The Chairperson announced that the Articles of Incorporation of the Corporation had been filed with the Secretary of the State of California on _____ , 19__. The Chairperson then presented to the meeting a certified copy of the Articles showing such filing, and the Secretary was instructed to insert the copy in the Corporation's Minute Book.

BYLAWS

There was then presented to the meeting for adoption a proposed set of Bylaws of the Corporation. The Bylaws were considered and discussed and, on motion duly made and seconded, it was unanimously

RESOLVED, that the Bylaws presented to this meeting be and hereby are adopted as the Bylaws of this Corporation;

RESOLVED FURTHER, that the Secretary of this Corporation be and hereby is directed to execute a Certificate of Adoption of the Bylaws, to insert the Bylaws as so certified in the Corporation's Minute Book and to see that a copy of the Bylaws, similarly certified, is kept at the Corporation's principal office, as required by law.

ELECTION OF OFFICERS

The Chairperson then announced that the next item of business was the election of officers. Upon motion, the following persons were unanimously elected to the office shown after their names:

_____ President

_____ Vice-President

_____ Secretary

_____ Treasurer

_____ (Chief Financial Officer)

Each officer who was present accepted his/her office. Thereafter, the President presided at the meeting as Chairperson, and the Secretary acted as Secretary.

CORPORATE SEAL

The Secretary presented to the meeting for adoption a proposed form of seal of the Corporation. Upon motion duly made and seconded, it was:

RESOLVED, that the form of corporate seal presented to this meeting be and hereby is adopted as the seal of this Corporation, and the Secretary of this Corporation is directed to place an impression thereof in the space directly below this resolution.

STOCK CERTIFICATE

The Secretary then presented to the meeting for adoption a proposed form of stock certificate for the Corporation. Upon motion duly made and seconded, it was

RESOLVED, that the form of stock certificate presented to this meeting be and hereby is adopted for use by this Corporation, and the Secretary of this Corporation is directed to annex a copy thereof to the minutes of this meeting.

ACCOUNTING PERIOD

The Chairperson informed the Board that the next order of business was the selection of the accounting period of the Corporation. After discussion and upon motion duly made and seconded, it was

RESOLVED, that the accounting period of this Corporation shall end on _____ of each year.

PRINCIPAL EXECUTIVE OFFICE

After discussion as to the exact location of the Corporation's principal executive office in the city and county named in the Bylaws, upon motion duly made and seconded, it was

RESOLVED, that the principal executive office of this Corporation shall be at _____, in _____, California.

BANK ACCOUNT

The Chairperson recommended that the Corporation open a bank account with _____. Upon motion duly made and seconded, it was

RESOLVED, that the funds of this Corporation shall be deposited with _____.

RESOLVED FURTHER, that the Treasurer of this Corporation be and hereby is authorized and directed to establish an account with said Bank and to deposit the funds of this Corporation therein.

RESOLVED FURTHER, that any officer, employee or agent of this Corporation be and hereby is authorized to endorse checks, drafts or other evidences of indebtedness made payable to this Corporation, but only for the purpose of deposit.

RESOLVED FURTHER, that all checks, drafts and other instruments obligating this Corporation to pay money shall be signed on behalf of this corporation by any _____ of the following persons:

_____

_____

_____

RESOLVED FURTHER, that said Bank be and hereby is authorized to honor and pay any and all checks and drafts of this Corporation signed as provided herein.

RESOLVED FURTHER, that the authority hereby conferred shall remain in force until revoked by the Board of Directors of this Corporation and until written notice of such revocation shall have been received by said Bank.

RESOLVED FURTHER, that the Secretary of this Corporation be and hereby is authorized to certify as to the continuing authority of these resolutions, the persons authorized to sign on behalf of this Corporation and the adoption of said Bank's standard form of resolution, provided that said form does not vary materially from the terms of the foregoing resolutions.

SALE AND ISSUANCE OF CAPITAL STOCK

The Board of Directors next took up the matters of the sale and issuance of stock to provide capital for the corporation. The Articles of Incorporation authorize the issuance of _____ shares of capital stock.

SALE AND ISSUANCE OF CAPITAL STOCK FOR CASH

Upon motion duly made and seconded, it was unanimously

RESOLVED, that this Corporation shall sell and issue an aggregate (not to exceed) _____ shares of its capital stock at a purchase price of $_____ per share, in consideration of money paid to this Corporation as follows:

Name of Purchaser	Number of Shares	Total Amount of Money
_____	_____	_____
_____	_____	_____
_____	_____	_____
_____	_____	_____
_____	_____	_____

RESOLVED FURTHER, that the appropriate officers of this Corporation be and hereby are authorized and directed to take such actions and execute such documents as they may deem necessary or appropriate to effectuate the sale and issuance of such shares for such consideration.

SALE AND ISSUANCE OF CAPITAL STOCK FOR
PROPERTY ACTUALLY RECEIVED

Upon motion duly made and seconded, it was unanimously

RESOLVED, that this Corporation shall sell and issue an aggregate of (not to exceed) _____ shares of its capital stock at a purchase price of $_____ per share, in consideration of property actually received, as follows:

Name of Purchaser	Number of Shares	Description of Property Actually Received
_____	_____	_____
_____	_____	_____
_____	_____	_____
_____	_____	_____
_____	_____	_____

RESOLVED FURTHER, that the Board of Directors of this Corporation hereby determines that the fair value of such property to the corporation in monetary terms is $_____.

RESOLVED FURTHER, that the appropriate officers of this Corporation be and hereby are authorized and directed to take such actions and execute such documents as they may deem necessary or appropriate to effectuate the sale and issuance of such shares for such consideration.

SALE AND ISSUANCE OF CAPITAL STOCK
FOR INDEBTEDNESS CANCELED

Upon motion duly made and seconded, it was unanimously

RESOLVED, that this corporation shall sell and issue an aggregate of (not to exceed) _____ shares of its capital stock at a purchase price of $_____ per share, in consideration of indebtedness canceled, as follows:

Name of Purchaser	Number of Shares	Description of Indebtedness Canceled
_____	_____	_____
_____	_____	_____
_____	_____	_____
_____	_____	_____
_____	_____	_____

RESOLVED FURTHER, that the Board of Directors of this Corporation hereby determines that the fair value of such indebtedness to this Corporation in monetary terms is $_____.

RESOLVED FURTHER, that the appropriate officers of this Corporation be and hereby are authorized and directed to take such actions and execute such documents as they may deem necessary or appropriate to effectuate the sale and issuance of such shares for such consideration.

SALE AND ISSUANCE OF CAPITAL STOCK FOR LABOR DONE

Upon motion duly made and seconded, it was unanimously

RESOLVED, that this Corporation shall sell and issue an aggregate of (not to exceed) _____ shares of its capital stock at a purchase price of $_____ per share, in consideration of labor done, as follows:

Name of Purchaser	Number of Shares	Description of Labor Done
_____	_____	_____
_____	_____	_____
_____	_____	_____
_____	_____	_____

RESOLVED FURTHER, that the Board of Directors of this Corporation hereby determines that the fair value of such labor done to this Corporation in monetary terms is $_____.

RESOLVED FURTHER, that the appropriate officers of this Corporation be and hereby are authorized and directed to take such actions and execute such documents as they may deem necessary or appropriate to effectuate the sale and issuance of such shares for such consideration.

SALE AND ISSUANCE OF CAPITAL STOCK FOR SERVICES RENDERED

Upon motion duly made and seconded, it was unanimously

RESOLVED, that this Corporation shall sell and issue an aggregate of (not to exceed) _____ shares of its capital stock at a purchase price of $_____ per share, in consideration of services rendered as follows:

Name of Purchaser	Number of Shares	Description of Services Rendered
_____	_____	_____
_____	_____	_____
_____	_____	_____
_____	_____	_____
_____	_____	_____

RESOLVED FURTHER, that the Board of Directors of this Corporation hereby determines that the fair value of such services rendered to this Corporation in monetary terms is $_____.

RESOLVED FURTHER, that the appropriate officers of this Corporation be and hereby are authorized and directed to take such actions and execute such documents as they may deem necessary or appropriate to effectuate the sale and issuance of such shares for such consideration.

SALE AND ISSUANCE OF CAPITAL STOCK FOR ASSETS OF BUSINESS

Upon motion duly made and seconded, it was unanimously

RESOLVED that this Corporation shall sell and issue an aggregate of (not to exceed) _____ shares of its capital stock at a purchase price of $_____ per share, in exchange for the assets of a business known as

_____

_____, upon delivery of these assets and execution of all such documents necessary to effect the transfer of said business to the Corporation, to the present owners of said business, as follows:

Name of Purchaser	Number of Shares	Description of Property
_____	_____	_____
_____	_____	_____
_____	_____	_____
_____	_____	_____
_____	_____	_____

RESOLVED FURTHER, that the Board of Directors of this Corporation hereby determines that the fair value of said business to this Corporation is $_____.

RESOLVED FURTHER, that the appropriate officers of this Corporation be and hereby are authorized and directed to take such actions and execute such documents as they may deem necessary or appropriate to carry out the sale and issuance of such shares for said business.

RESOLVED FURTHER, that the appropriate officers of this Corporation are authorized and directed to take any and all actions, as applicable, in connection with the proposed transfer as required by the Bulk Transfer Division of the Commercial Code.

FEDERAL S CORPORATION TAX TREATMENT

The board of directors next considered the advantages of electing to be taxed under the provisions of Subchapter S of the Internal Revenue Code of 1986, as amended. After discussion, upon motion duly made and seconded, it was unanimously

RESOLVED, that this corporation hereby elects to be treated as a Small Business Corporation for federal income tax purposes under Subchapter S of the Internal Revenue Code of 1986, as amended.

RESOLVED FURTHER, that the officers of this corporation take all actions necessary and proper to effectuate the foregoing resolution, including, among other things, obtaining the requisite consents from the shareholders of this corporation and executing and filing the appropriate forms with the Internal Revenue Service within the time limits specified by law.

COMPENSATION FOR OFFICERS

There followed a discussion concerning the compensation to be paid by the Corporation to its officers. Upon motion duly made and seconded, it was unanimously

RESOLVED, that the following annual salaries be paid to the officers of this Corporation:

President $_____

Vice President $_____

Secretary $_____

Treasurer $_____

(Chief Financial Officer)

PAYMENT AND DEDUCTION OF ORGANIZATIONAL EXPENSES

The board next considered the question of paying the expenses incurred in the formation of this corporation. A motion was made, seconded and unanimously approved, and it was

RESOLVED, that the President and the Treasurer of this corporation are authorized and empowered to pay all reasonable and proper expenses incurred in connection with the organization of the corporation, including, among others, filing, licensing, and attorney's and accountant's fees, and to reimburse any persons making any such disbursements for the corporation, and it was

FURTHER RESOLVED, that the Treasurer is authorized to elect to deduct on the first federal income tax return of the corporation the foregoing expenditures ratably over a sixty-month period starting in the month the corporation begins its business, pursuant to, and to the extent permitted by, Section 248 of the Internal Revenue Code of 1986, as amended.

QUALIFICATION OF STOCK AS SECTION 1244 STOCK

The board next considered the advisability of qualifying the stock of this corporation as Section 1244 Stock as defined in Section 1244 of the Internal Revenue Code of 1986, as amended, and of organizing and managing the corporation so that it is a Small Business Corporation as defined in that section. Upon motion duly made and seconded, it was unanimously

RESOLVED, that the proper officers of the corporation are, subject to the requirements and restrictions of federal, California and any other applicable securities laws, authorized to sell and issue shares of stock in return for the receipt of an aggregate amount of money and other property, as a contribution to capital and as paid-in surplus, which does not exceed $1,000,000.

RESOLVED FURTHER, that the sale and issuance of shares shall be conducted in compliance with Section 1244 so that the corporation and its shareholders may obtain the benefits of that section.

RESOLVED FURTHER, that the proper officers of the corporation are directed to maintain such records as are necessary pursuant to Section 1244 so that any shareholder who experiences a loss on the transfer of shares of stock of the corporation may determine whether he or she qualifies for ordinary loss deduction treatment on his or her individual income tax return.

EXEMPT OFFER AND SALE OF SHARES OF CAPITAL STOCK

It was announced that the initial issuance of shares of the Corporation's voting common stock would be exempt from qualification under 10 California Code of Regulations, Section 260.105.6. Upon motion duly made and seconded, it was unanimously

RESOLVED, that the shares of voting common stock authorized at this meeting to be sold and issued by this Corporation shall be offered and sold strictly in accordance with the terms of the exemption from qualification provided for in Section 260.105.6 of Title 10 of the California Code of Regulations.

Since there was no further business to come before the meeting, on motion duly made and seconded, the meeting was adjourned.

_____, Secretary

RECEIPT FOR CASH PAYMENT FOR SHARES

Receipt of $_____, paid by check No._____, from
_____, representing payment in full for _____ shares
of common stock of this corporation, evidenced by Certificate No.
_____, is hereby acknowledged.

Date:_____

Name of Corporation: _____

By   _____, Treasurer

ACKNOWLEDGMENT OF CANCELLATION OF INDEBTEDNESS

The receipt of _____ shares of this corporation to _____ for the cancellation by _____ of a current loan outstanding to this corporation, dated _____, with a remaining unpaid principal amount and unpaid accrued interest, if any, totaling $_____ is hereby acknowledged.

Date: _____

Name of Corporation: _____

By: _____, Treasurer

BILL OF SALE FOR ASSETS OF A BUSINESS

This is an agreement between:

_____

_____

_____

herein called "transferor(s)," and _____,a California professional corporation, herein called "the corporation."

In return for the issuance of _____ shares of stock of the corporation, transferor(s) hereby sell(s), assign(s), and transfer(s) to the corporation all right, title, and interest in the following property:

All the tangible assets listed on the inventory attached to this Bill of Sale and all stock in trade, goodwill, leasehold interests, trade names, and other intangible assets except _____ of _____, located at _____.

In return for the transfer of the above property to it, the corporation hereby agrees to assume, pay, and discharge all debts, duties, and obligations that appear on the date of this agreement on the books and owed on account of said business except _____. The corporation agrees to indemnify and hold the transferor(s) of said business and their property free from any liability for any such debt, duty, or obligation and from any suits, actions, or legal proceedings brought to enforce or collect any such debt, duty, or obligation.

The transferor(s) hereby appoint(s) the corporation as representative to demand, receive, and collect for itself any and all debts and obligations now owing to said business and hereby assumed by the corporation. The transferor(s) further authorize(s) the corporation to do all things allowed by law to recover and collect any such debts and obligations and to use the transferor's(s') name(s) in such manner as it considers necessary for the collection and recovery of such debts and obligations, provided, however, without cost, expense, or damage to the transferor(s).

Date: _____   _____
                               , Transferor

                               _____
                               , Transferor

                               _____
                               , Transferor

Date: _____   Name of Corporation: _____

By: _____
                               , President

                               _____
                               , Treasurer

BILL OF SALE FOR ITEMS OF PROPERTY

This is an agreement by _____, herein called "transferor," and _____, herein called "the corporation."

In return for the issuance and delivery of _____ shares of stock of _____, I hereby sell, assign, and transfer to the corporation all my right, title, and interest in the following property:

Date: _____

_____
, Transferor

Date: _____

Name of Corporation: _____

By:

_____
, President

_____
, Treasurer

ACKNOWLEDGMENT OF SHARE ISSUANCE FOR LABOR DONE
OR SERVICES RENDERED

This issuance of _____ shares of _____, evidenced by
Certificate No. _____ to _____ in exchange for
payment in the form of labor done or services rendered the corporation by him or her,
valued at $_____, is hereby acknowledged.

Date: _____

Name of Corporation: _____

By _____, Treasurer

APPENDIX 4

Special Provisions for Professional Corporations

This supplement is designed to provide you with specific information relating to your professional corporation. Be sure to use it in conjunction with the text. General corporation provisions applicable to all professional corporations are not included here. Most of the provisions cited in this Appendix are found in the Business and Professions Code and the California Code of Regulations.

Important: The rules listed here are subject to constant change. To be assured of accuracy, you must check with the agency supervising your profession for current regulations and procedures (including, possibly, Bylaw amendments required by your Board). We've added citations to the applicable law and regulations in case you wish to research these provisions yourself.

KEY

B & P Code	=	California Business and Professions Code
Cal. Code of Regs	=	California Code of Regulations
Corp. Code	=	California Corporations Code

Much of the information that follows on California professional boards and the requirements of each profession can be obtained in its most current form online by browsing or downloading the California Professional and Business License Handbook, available at the California Trade and Commerce Agency website at http://commerce.ca.gov/business/small/management/pub/license/index.html.

Accountancy Corporations

Website: http://www.dca.ca.gov/cba

STATUTES

Generally: B & P Code §§5000-5158; Accountancy Corps. §§5150-5158.

REGULATIONS

Generally: 16 Cal. Code of Regs. §§1-99.2; 16 Cal. Code of Regs. §§66.1-75.11 "Accountancy Corporation Rules."

LICENSING BOARD

Licensing as CPA or as Public Accountant by State Board of Accountancy (Part of Dept. of Consumer Affairs).

CERTIFICATE OF REGISTRATION REQUIRED?

Yes. Fee: $200.

ADDRESS FOR APPLICATION FOR CERTIFICATE OF REGISTRATION

2000 Evergreen St., Ste. 250, Sacramento, CA 95815. Phone: 916-263-3680. Fax: 916-263-3675.

RENEWAL OF CERTIFICATE OF REGISTRATION

Continues in effect until suspended or revoked. [16 Cal. Code of Regs. §75.11(a)].

NAMES YOU CAN USE

The name(s) must be of present, former, or prospective shareholder(s), or of persons who were associated with a predecessor person, partnership or other organization and whose name or names appeared in the name of such predecessor organization.

The B & P Code requires that either the words "Accountancy Corporation," or the word "Accountant" or "Accountants" and words or abbreviations indicating a corporation (such as: Corp.; A Professional Corporation; Inc.) be included [B & P Code §5153]. In a one-shareholder corporation, CPA or PA singular must be used in the corporation name.

EXAMPLES: Jane Doet, Accountant, A Professional Corp., Jane Doet, CPA, Incorporated.

The words "Certified Public Accountant" or the abbreviations CPA or PA can be used in the title of the corporation. However, if Certified Public Accountant or CPA is used, at least one shareholder must be a CPA—the remaining shareholders may be Public Accountants. [16 Cal. Code of Regs. §66.1] If the corporation maintains a full-time staff of at least one licensed person and one other employee, "and company" or "and associates" may be included in the corporate name [B & P Code §5153].

WHO MAY BE SHAREHOLDERS, OFFICERS, DIRECTORS

Shares may only be issued/transferred to a licensed person.1 [B & P Code §5154] "Licensed person" means licensed by the Board as a CPA or as a Public Accountant.

Each shareholder, director and officer must hold a license, except officers other than President and Treasurer in a corporation with only one shareholder may be non-licensed persons. [B & P Code §5154; Corp. Code §13403] [See also Chapter 4(E)(fn).]

SHARE TRANSFER REQUIREMENTS
Shares: Ownership and Transfer

(a) The shares of an accountancy corporation may be issued only to a licensed person[1] and may be transferred only to a licensed person[1] or to the issuing accountancy corporation.

(b) Where there are two or more shareholders in an accountancy corporation and one of the shareholders:

(1) Dies, or

(2) Becomes a disqualified person as defined in §13401(d) of the Corporations Code, for a period exceeding ninety (90) days,

*his share shall be sold and transferred to a licensed person[1] or to the issuing accountancy corporation, on such terms as are agreed upon. Such sale or transfer shall be not later than six (6) months after any such death or not later than ninety (90) days after the date he becomes a disqualified person.

(c) An accountancy corporation and its shareholders may, but need not, agree that shares sold to it by a person who becomes a disqualified person may be resold to such person if and when he again ceases to become a disqualified person.

(d) The restrictions of subsection (a) and, if appropriate, subsection (b) of this section shall be set forth in the corporation's Bylaws or Articles of Incorporation. [16 Cal. Code of Regs. §75.9]
See footnote 1.

STOCK TRANSFER CERTIFICATE LEGEND

(e) The share certificates of an accountancy corporation shall contain either:

(1) An appropriate legend setting forth the restriction of subsection (a), and where applicable, the restriction of subsection (b) [see above regulation], or

(2) An appropriate legend stating that ownership and transfer of the shares are restricted and specifically referring to an identified section of the Bylaws or Articles of Incorporation of the corporation wherein the restrictions are set forth. [16 Cal. Code of Regs. §75.9]
See footnote 1.

REPORTING REQUIREMENTS
Annual: Must be filed on or before July 31 each year (unless corporation incorporated between May 16 and July 31 of that year) and must contain information pertaining to qualifications, compliance with statutes, rules and regulations.

Fee: Set annually; not listed in regulations. Since special Board forms are sent annually, fee will be communicated then.

Special: Required within 30 days of a change related to the requirements for issuance of the certificate of registration or share ownership or share transfer (e.g., changes in shareholder, officers, directors, amendments to Bylaws or Articles of Incorporation).

Fee: Set annually; special form must be requested from Board.

Change of Address: Must be reported within 30 days. No fee.

MALPRACTICE SECURITY

Re: Claims by corporation's clients or others. What is required: Written agreement of shareholders jointly and severally guaranteeing payment of liabilities for rendering or failing to render professional services.

An executed copy of the above agreement must be furnished to the Board.

Acupuncture Corporations
Website: http://www.dca.ca.gov/acup

STATUTES

Generally: B & P Code §§4925-4979; Acupuncture Corps. §§4975-4979.

REGULATIONS

Generally: 16 Cal. Code of Regs. §§1399.400-1399.481; §§1399.470-1399.485 "Acupuncture Corporation Regulations."

LICENSING BOARD

Acupuncture Advisory Committee, Division of Allied Health Professions, Board of Medical Quality Assurance [part of Department of Consumer Affairs], 1424 Howe Avenue, Suite 37, Sacramento, CA 95825-3233. 916-263-2680.

CERTIFICATE OF REGISTRATION REQUIRED?
No. [Corp. Code §13401(b)]

Fee: Not applicable.

RENEWAL OF CERTIFICATE OF REGISTRATION
Not applicable.

NAMES YOU CAN USE

Name or names of persons:	Followed by either:	Then one of the following:
Jane Doet	Acupuncturist Acupuncture	Professional Corporation Prof. Corp. Corporation Corp. Incorporated Inc.

EXAMPLE: Jane Doet, Acupuncturist, Prof. Corp.

WHO MAY BE SHAREHOLDERS, OFFICERS, DIRECTORS

Each director, shareholder, and officer of an acupuncture corporation, other than an assistant secretary and an assistant treasurer, shall be a licensed person, except that officers other than president and treasurer in a corporation with only one shareholder may be non-licensed persons. [B & P code §4977.2; Corp. Code §13403] [See also Chapter 4(E)(fn).]

SHARE TRANSFER REQUIREMENTS

Shares: Ownership and Transfer

(a) The shares of an acupuncture corporation shall be issued only to a licensed person as defined in §13401(c) of the Corporations Code and shall be transferred only to a licensed person or to the issuing corporation.

(b) Where there are two or more shareholders in an acupuncture corporation and one of the shareholders:

(1) Dies or

(2) Becomes a disqualified person as defined in Section 13401(d) of the Corporations Code, his or her shares shall be sold and transferred to the corporation, its shareholders, or other eligible persons on such items as are agreed upon. Such sale or transfer shall not be later than six (6) months after any such death and not later than ninety (90) days after the date the shareholder becomes a disqualified person. The requirement of subsections (a) and (b) of this section shall be set forth in the acupuncture corporation's Articles of Incorporation or Bylaws.

(c) A corporation and its shareholders may, but need not, agree that shares sold to it by a person who becomes a disqualified person may be resold to such person if and when he or she again becomes an eligible shareholder.

(f) Nothing in these regulations shall be construed to prohibit an acupuncture corporation from owning shares in a nonprofessional corporation. [16 Cal. Code of Regs. §1399.477]

STOCK TRANSFER CERTIFICATE LEGEND

(d) The share certificates of an acupuncture corporation shall contain an appropriate legend setting forth the restrictions of subsection (a) and, where applicable, the restrictions of subsection (b) [see above regulation]. [16 Cal. Code of Regs. §1399.477]

REPORTING REQUIREMENTS

Not required.

MALPRACTICE SECURITY

Although B & P Code §4979 empowers the Board to make regulations regarding provision of adequate security, no such regulation has yet been published.

ARCHITECTURAL CORPORATIONS

Note: Although architects may incorporate as professional corporations or as regular business corporations, the Board of Architecture apparently does not participate in these filings (a taped message at the state Board refers you to the Secretary of State to form a professional architecture corporation). Consequently, those wishing to incorporate an architectural practice may prefer to form a regular business corporation under the California General Corporation Law—see Chapter 2, Section A. If you do form a regular business corporation, the taped message at the state Board indicates that you must comply with the following requirements:

- You must notify the board in writing of the name, date of formation of the general business corporation (see mailing address of the Board below); and

- The name of the licensed architect must be given in all instruments of service for the corporation.

Website: http://www.cab.ca.gov

STATUTES

Generally: B & P Code §§5500-5610.7; Architectural Corps. §§5610-5610.7.

REGULATIONS

Generally: 16 Cal. Code of Regs. §§100-151; no regulations yet available for architectural corporations.

LICENSING BOARD

State Board of Architectural Examiners (Part of Dept. of Consumer Affairs) 400 R Street, #4000, Sacramento, CA 95814. (916) 445-3393.

CERTIFICATE OF REGISTRATION REQUIRED?

No. [Corp. Code §13401(b)]

Fee: Not applicable

ADDRESS FOR APPLICATION FOR CERTIFICATE OF REGISTRATION

*Not applicable.

RENEWAL OF CERTIFICATE OF REGISTRATION

Not applicable.

NAMES YOU CAN USE

The name(s) must be of present, former, or prospective shareholder(s), or of persons who were associated with a predecessor person, partnership or other organization and whose name or names appeared in the name of such predecessor organization.

They must include either the words "Architectural Corporation," or the word "Architect" or "Architects" and words or abbreviations indicating a corporation (such as: Corp.; A Professional Corporation; Inc.). [B & P Code § 5610.3]

EXAMPLE: Jane Doet, Architect, A Professional Corp.

WHO MAY BE SHAREHOLDERS, OFFICERS, DIRECTORS

Each shareholder, director, and officer in an architectural corporation must hold a license, except officers other than President and Treasurer in a corporation with only one shareholder may be non-licensed persons. [B & P Code § 5610.4; Corp. Code §13403] [See also Chapter 4(E).]

SHARE TRANSFER REQUIREMENTS AND STOCK TRANSFER CERTIFICATE LEGEND

Although B & P § 5610.7 provides that the Board may adopt and enforce regulations requiring that the Bylaws of an architectural corporation include a provision for transfer of stock of a disqualified or deceased person, there are no regulations yet. Nor are there any statutes on stock transfer restrictions. Check with the Board (and see §13407 of the Corporations Code).

REPORTING REQUIREMENTS

Reports containing information pertaining to qualification and compliance with the statutes, rules and regulations of the Board shall be filed as the Board may require with a fee fixed by the Board. [B & P Code § 5610.2]

MALPRACTICE SECURITY

Although B & P Code § 5610.7 empowers the Board to adopt rules and regulations, including a provision that adequate security must be provided, there are no regulations yet.

CHIROPRACTIC CORPORATIONS
Website: N/A

STATUTES

Generally: B & P Code §§1000-1058; Chiropractic Corps. §§1050-1058.

REGULATIONS

Generally: 16 Cal. Code of Regs. §§ 301-383; §§375-383 deal with conflict of interest and are not printed in the Code; they are available from the Chiropractic Board of California. §§367.1-367.10 "Chiropractic Corporation Rules."

LICENSING BOARD

Licensing as a chiropractor is by the Chiropractic Board of California, 2710-N Gateway Oaks, Suite 100, Sacramento, CA 95833. 916-263-5355.

CERTIFICATE OF REGISTRATION REQUIRED?

Yes. Fee: $100.00

ADDRESS FOR APPLICATION FOR CERTIFICATE OF REGISTRATION

3401 Fulsom Blvd., Suite B, Sacramento, CA 95816. 916-227-2790.

RENEWAL OF CERTIFICATE OF REGISTRATION

Certificate of Registration continues in effect until it is revoked or suspended. [16 Cal. Code of Regs. §367.10(a)]

NAMES YOU CAN USE

Name or names in one of the following forms:	Followed by:	Then one of the following:
Jane T. Doet	Chiropractic	Corporation
Doet		Corp.
Robert Smythe and Jane Doet		Incorporated
Smythe & Doet		Inc.
		Professional Corporation
		Prof. Corp.

EXAMPLE: Jane Doet, Chiropractic Corp.

The name is restricted to the name or last name of one or more of the present, prospective or former shareholders.

If the word "Doctor" or "Dr." precedes a name, the word "Chiropractor" or "D.C." must immediately follow the name. [B & P Code §§1000-15]

WHO MAY BE SHAREHOLDERS, OFFICERS, DIRECTORS

All directors and shareholders must be licensed persons. [B & P Code §1051]

An assistant secretary and assistant treasurer need not be licensed persons. All other officers must be licensed, except that officers other than President and Treasurer in a corporation with only one shareholder may be non-licensed persons. [B & P Code §1055; Corp. Code §13403] [See also Chapter 4(E).]

A licensed physician, surgeon, podiatrist, psychologist, registered nurse, optometrist, marriage, family and child counselor or clinical social worker may be a shareholder, director or officer of a chiropractic corporation so long as such licensed physicians, surgeons, podiatrists, psychologists, registered nurses, optometrists, marriage, family and child counselors and clinical social workers own no more than 49% of the total shares issued by the chiropractic corporation and the number of licensed physicians, surgeons, podiatrists, psychologists, registered nurses, optometrists, marriage, family and child counselors and clinical social workers owning shares in the optometric corporation does not exceed the number of chiropractors owning shares in the corporation. [Corp. Code §13401.5.]

SHARE TRANSFER REQUIREMENTS

Shares: Ownership and Transfer

(a) The shares of a chiropractic corporation may be issued only to a licensed person and may be transferred only to a licensed person or to the issuing corporation.

(b) Where there are two or more shareholders in a chiropractic corporation and one of the shareholders:

(1) Dies, or

(2) Becomes a disqualified person as defined in §13401(d) of the Corporations Code, for a period exceeding ninety (90) days,

his/her shares shall be sold and transferred to a licensed person or to the issuing chiropractic corporation, on such terms as are agreed upon. Such sale or transfer shall be not later than six (6) months after any such death and not later than ninety (90) days after the date he/she becomes a disqualified person.

(c) A corporation and its shareholders may, but need not, agree that shares sold to it by a person who becomes a disqualified person may be resold to such person if and when he/she again ceases to become a disqualified person.

(d) The restrictions of subsection (a) and, if appropriate, subsection (b) of this section shall be set forth in the corporation's Bylaws or Articles of Incorporation. [16 Cal. Code of Regs. §367.9]

STOCK TRANSFER CERTIFICATE LEGEND

(e) The share certificates of a chiropractic corporation shall contain either:

(1) An appropriate legend setting forth the restriction of subsection (a), and where applicable, the restriction of subsection (b) [see above regulation], or

(2) An appropriate legend stating that ownership and transfer of the shares are restricted and specifically referring to an identified section of the Bylaws or Articles of Incorporation of the corporation wherein the restrictions are set forth. [16 Cal. Code of Regs. §367.9]

REPORTING REQUIREMENTS

Annual: Not required.

Special: Required within 30 days of any change of the officers, directors, shareholders, employees rendering professional services, and Articles of Incorporation. Forms provided by Board on request. [16 Cal Code of Regs. § 367.10]

Fee: $5.00

MALPRACTICE SECURITY

The corporation may provide security by means of insurance, or else the shareholder shall be jointly and severally liable for all claims by its patients arising out of its rendering or failing to render professional services.

Amounts: At least $50,000 multiplied by the number of licensed persons providing professional services for each claim. Aggregate maximum limit per policy year of at least $150,000 multiplied by the number of licensed persons providing professional services. Maximum coverage need not exceed $150,000 for each claim and $450,000 for all claims in policy year.

If insurance is provided, it must meet the above minimums.

Deductible: May not exceed $5,000 multiplied by the number of licensed persons providing professional services. [16 Cal. Code of Regs. §367.8]

CLINICAL SOCIAL WORKERS CORPORATIONS (LICENSED)
Website: http://www.bbs.ca.gov

STATUTES

Generally: B & P Code §§4990-4998.7; Licensed Clinical Social Workers Corps. §§4998-4998.7.

REGULATIONS

Generally: 16 Cal. Code of Regs. §§1873-1881; §§1850.6-1850.8 "Professional Corporations."

LICENSING BOARD

Board of Behavioral Science Examiners (part of Department of Consumer Affairs), 400 R Street, # 3150, Sacramento, CA 95814-6240. 916-445-4933.

CERTIFICATE OF REGISTRATION REQUIRED?

Yes. Fee: $100.00

ADDRESS FOR APPLICATION FOR CERTIFICATE OF REGISTRATION

See Licensing Board above.

RENEWAL OF CERTIFICATE OF REGISTRATION

Certificate of Registration continues in effect until it is revoked or suspended. [16 Cal. Code of Regs. §1850.8(a)]

NAMES YOU CAN USE

Name or names in one of the following forms:	Followed by:	Then one of the following:
Jane T. Doet Doet Robert Smythe and Jane Doet Smythe and Doet	Licensed Clinical Social Worker(s)	Professional Corporation Prof. Corp. Corporation Corp. Incorporated Inc.

EXAMPLE: Jane Doet, Licensed Clinical Social Worker, Inc.

The name(s) must be of former, present, prospective shareholder(s).

Under B&P § 4998.3, LCSWs may have a fictitious name, but it must not be false, misleading, deceptive, and the corporation must inform the patient, prior to the commencement of treatment, that the business is conducted by a licensed clinical social workers corporation.

WHO MAY BE SHAREHOLDERS, OFFICERS, DIRECTORS

Each director, shareholder, and officer of a licensed clinical social worker's corporation must be a licensed person, except that officers other than President and Treasurer in a corporation with only one shareholder may be non-licensed persons. [B & P Code §4998.4; Corp. Code §13403] [See also Chapter 4(E).]

A licensed physician, surgeon, psychologist, marriage, family and child counselor, registered nurse or chiropractor may be a shareholder, director, or officer of a licensed clinical social worker corporation so long as such physicians, surgeons, psychologists, marriage, family and child counselors, registered nurses and chiropractors own no more than 49% of the total shares issued by the licensed clinical social worker corporation and the number of physicians, surgeons, psychologists, marriage, family and child counselors, registered nurses and chiropractors owning shares in the licensed clinical social worker corporation does not exceed the number of licensed clinical social workers owning shares in such a corporation. [B & P Code §4998.4; Corp Code §13401.5]

SHARE TRANSFER REQUIREMENTS

Shares: Ownership and Transfer

(a) The shares of a licensed clinical social worker's corporation may be issued only to a licensed person and may be transferred only to a licensed person or to the issuing corporation.

(b) Where there are two or more shareholders in a licensed clinical social worker's corporation and one of the shareholders:

(1) Dies, or

(2) Becomes a disqualified person as defined in §13401(d) of the Corporations Code, for a period exceeding ninety (90) days, his/her shares shall be sold and transferred to a licensed person or to the issuing licensed clinical social workers corporation on such terms as are agreed upon. Such sale or transfer shall not be later than six (6) months after any such death and not later than ninety (90) days after the date he/she became a disqualified person.

(c) A corporation and its shareholders may, but need not, agree that shares sold to it by a person who becomes a disqualified person may be resold to such person if and when he or she again ceases to become a disqualified person.

(d) The restrictions of subdivisions (a) and, if appropriate, subdivision (b) of this section shall be set forth in the corporation's Bylaws or Articles of Incorporation. [16 Cal. Code of Regs. §1850.7]

STOCK TRANSFER CERTIFICATE LEGEND

(f) The share certificates of a licensed clinical social workers corporation shall contain either:

(1) An appropriate legend setting forth the restriction of subdivision (a), and where applicable, the restriction of subdivision (b) [see above regulation], or

(2) An appropriate legend stating that ownership and transfer of the shares are restricted and specifically referring to an identified section of the Bylaws or Articles of Incorporation of the corporation wherein the restrictions are set forth. [16 Cal. Code of Regs. §1850.7]

REPORTING REQUIREMENTS

Annual: Must be filed on or before July 31 (except those licensed on or after April 1 of that year) on a form provided by the Board. Report shall reflect the corporation's status as of the preceding June 30, and shall contain information pertaining to its qualifications and compliance with the statutes, rules and regulations. [16 Cal. Code of Regs. §1850.8(b)]

Fee: $10.00

Special: Must be filed on form provided within thirty (30) days of any change in the officers, directors, shareholders, Articles of Incorporation, or corporate name. [16 Cal. Code of Regs. §1850.8(c)]

Fee: $5.00

MALPRACTICE SECURITY

Although the B & P Code §4998.7 empowers the Board to formulate and enforce rules, including a requirement that a licensed clinical social workers corporation provide adequate security by insurance or otherwise for claims against it by its patients arising out of the rendering of professional services, no such regulation has yet been published.

DENTAL CORPORATIONS
Website: N/A

STATUTES

Generally, B & P Code §§1600-1808; Dental Corporations §§1800-1808.

REGULATIONS

Generally: 16 Cal. Code of Regs. §§1000-1089.4; §§1055-1060 "Dental Corporation Rules."

LICENSING BOARD

Licensing as dentist by State Board of Dental Examiners (part of Department of Consumer Affairs), 1432 Howe Avenue, #85B, Sacramento, CA 95825. 916-263-2300.

CERTIFICATE OF REGISTRATION REQUIRED?

Yes. Fee: $200.00

ADDRESS FOR APPLICATION FOR CERTIFICATE OF REGISTRATION

See Licensing Board above.

RENEWAL OF CERTIFICATE OF REGISTRATION

Certificate of Registration continues in effect until revoked or suspended. [16 Cal. Code of Regs. §1058(a)]

NAMES YOU CAN USE

You must choose one of these two combinations.

Name or names in one of the following forms:	Followed by one of the following:
Jane T. Doet	Dental Corporation
Doet	Dental Corp.
Robert Smythe & Jane Doet	Professional Dental Corporation
Smythe and Doet	Professional Dental Corp.
	Prof. Dental Corp.

OR

Name or names in one of the following forms:	Then:	Followed by one of the following:
Jane Doet	DDS	Corporation
Doet	(or other academic degree)	Corp.
		Incorporated
		Inc.
		Professional Dental Corporation
		Professional Dental Corp.
		Prof. Dental Corp.
		Professional Corporation
		Professional Corp.
		Prof. Corp.

EXAMPLE: Jane Doet, Dental Corp., or Jane Doet, DDS, Prof. Dental Corp.

Fictitious Names: A corporation (and an association or partnership or a group of three or more dentists) may practice under a fictitious name if it holds a valid permit for such name issued by the Board. The fictitious name must contain the family name of one or more of the past, present or prospective associates, partners, shareholders or members of the group, and one of the following: Dental Group, Dental Practice, Dental Office. [B & P Code §1701.5]

WHO MAY BE SHAREHOLDERS, OFFICERS, DIRECTORS

Each director, shareholder and officer shall be a licensed person, except officers other than President and Treasurer in a corporation with only one shareholder may be non-licensed persons. [B & P Code §1805; Corp. Code §13403] [See also Chapter 4(E).]

SHARE TRANSFER REQUIREMENTS

Shares: Ownership and Transfer

   (a) The shares of a dental corporation may be owned only by a dental corporation or by licensed dentists, hereinafter referred to as eligible shareholders, provided, however, that no issuance or transfer of shares may be made which violates the provisions of Article 3.5, Chapter 4 of Division 2 of the Code (§§1658 through 1658.7 of the Business and Professions Code).

(b) Where there are two or more shareholders in a dental corporation and one of the shareholders:

(1) Dies;

(2) Ceases to be an eligible shareholder; or

(3) Becomes a disqualified person as defined in §13401(d) of the Corporations Code, for a period exceeding ninety (90) days; his/her shares shall be sold and transferred to the corporation, its shareholders, or other eligible persons, on such terms as are agreed upon. Such sale or transfer shall be not later than six (6) months after any such death and not later than ninety (90) days after the date he/she ceases to be an eligible shareholder, or ninety (90) days after the date he/she becomes a disqualified person. The requirements of subsections (a) and (b) of this section shall be set forth in the dental corporation's Articles of Incorporation or Bylaws, except that the terms of the sale or transfer provided for in said subsection need not be set forth in said Articles or Bylaws if they are set forth in a written agreement.

(c) A corporation and its shareholders may, but need not, agree that shares sold to it by a person who becomes a disqualified person may be resold to such person if and when he/she again becomes an eligible shareholder. [16 Cal. Code of Regs. §1060]

SHARE TRANSFER CERTIFICATE LEGEND

(d) The share certificates of a dental corporation shall contain an appropriate legend setting forth the restrictions of section (a) and, where applicable, the restrictions of sections (b) and (c) [see above regulation]. [16 Cal. Code of Regs. §1060(d)]

REPORTING REQUIREMENTS

Annual: Report (on form furnished by Board) must be filed by May 31 each year, reflecting its status as of May 1. It must include information regarding qualifications and compliance with statutes, rules and regulations.

Fee: Fixed by Board.

Special: Report required within thirty (30) days of any change relating to the requirements for issuance of Certificate of Registration, share ownership and transfer, changes in directors, officers, employees performing professional services, and amendment to Bylaws and Articles of Incorporation.

Fee: Fixed by Board.

Change of Address: Must be reported "immediately" to the Board. Fee for filing address change: None. [16 Cal. Code of Regs. §1058]

MALPRACTICE SECURITY

The corporation may provide security by means of insurance, or else the shareholders shall be jointly and severally liable for all claims against the corporation arising out of its rendering or failing to render dental services.

Amounts: At least $50,000 multiplied by the number of employed licensed persons rendering dental services for each claim. Aggregate maximum limit per policy year of at least $150,000 multiplied by the number of employed licensed persons rendering dental services. Maximum coverage need not exceed $150,000 for each claim and $450,000 for all claims in a policy year.

Insurance, if provided, must meet the above minimums.

Deductible: May not exceed $5,000 multiplied by the number of licensed persons providing professional services. [16 Cal. Code of Regs. §1059]

LAW CORPORATIONS
Website: http://www.ca/bar.org

STATUTES

Generally: B & P Code §§6000-6228; Law Corporations §§6160-6172.

REGULATIONS

"Law Corporation Rules"—starting at B & P Code §6171. Rules are also available in a separate booklet available from the state bar or can be found in the California Rules of Court. [There are no regulations in the California Code of Regulations.]

LICENSING BOARD

State Bar of California, 180 Howard Street, San Francisco, CA 94105. 415-538-2360.

CERTIFICATE OF REGISTRATION REQUIRED?

Yes. Fee: $200.00

ADDRESS FOR APPLICATION FOR CERTIFICATE OF REGISTRATION

See Licensing Board above.

RENEWAL OF CERTIFICATE OF REGISTRATION

Each law corporation shall renew its certificate of registration annually at a time to be fixed by the State Bar. Renewal fee shall be fixed by the State Bar. B & P Code §6161. Check with the State Bar for further information.

NAMES YOU CAN USE

You may choose a full name or a surname. There may be more than one person's name in the corporation's name. Some examples:

Names:	Followed by an indication of corporate existence:
Jane T. Doet	Professional Corporation
Doet	Prof. Corp.
Robert Smythe and Jane Doet	Corporation
Smythe & Doet	Corp.
	Incorporated
	Inc.

EXAMPLE: Jane Doet, A Law Corp.

Name can be of one or more present, prospective, or former shareholders, or persons who were associated with a predecessor person, partnership, or other organization or whose name or names appeared in the name of such predecessor organization.

Fictitious Name: B & P Code §6161 states that an applicant for registration must submit to the State Bar all necessary and pertinent information including "any fictitious name or names which the corporation intends to use." Furthermore, the B & P Code §6171 states that with the approval of the Supreme Court, the State Bar may formulate and enforce rules and regulations which include: "(d) That the law corporation shall obtain from the State Bar and maintain current a fictitious name permit when required by the rules and regulations…" Despite this legislation, there is still some confusion as to the use of fictitious names.

We checked with the supervisor of the Incorporation Section of the State Bar and were informed that a law corporation must register its name in conformance with Law Corp. Rules IV(5) (see section above). A fictitious name permit may then be sought and used in conjunction with the officially registered corporation name. The fictitious name must clearly show that the business is a corporate entity and that the corporation is certified by the State Bar. Be sure to check with the bar before incorporating.

WHO MAY BE SHAREHOLDERS, OFFICERS, DIRECTORS

Each director, shareholder and officer must be an active member of the State Bar, except officers other than president and treasurer in a corporation with only one shareholder may be non-licensed persons. Law Corp. Rules IV(A); Corp. Code §13403] [See also Chapter 4(E).]

SHARE TRANSFER REQUIREMENTS[2]

Shares: Ownership and Transfer

[C](1) The shares of a law corporation may be owned only by (a) that corporation, or (b) by an active member of the State Bar who,

(i) is an employee or retired employee of that corporation and is not a director, officer, or shareholder of any other law corporation, and

(ii) does not practice law except on behalf of that corporation; provided, however, a member may be a shareholder although he/she or the law corporation by which he/she is employed, acts as attorney pursuant to court order or acts on behalf of a legal aid or similar organization, or is associated or employed as an attorney by another active member, law partnership, or law corporation.

(2) The shares of a law corporation owned by a person who

(a) Dies,

(b) Ceases to be an eligible shareholder, or

(c) Becomes a disqualified person as defined in §13401(d) of the Corporations Code, for a period exceeding ninety (90) days,

shall be sold and transferred to the corporation or its shareholders on such terms as are agreed upon by the corporation and its shareholders. Such sale or transfer shall occur not later than six (6) months after any such death and not later than ninety (90) days after the date he/she ceases to be an eligible shareholder or ninety (90) days after the date he/she becomes a disqualified person. The requirements of subsections (1) and (2) of this Section "C" shall be set forth in the law corporation's Articles of Incorporation or Bylaws, except that the terms of the sale or transfer provided for in said subsection (2) need not be set forth in said Articles or Bylaws if they are set forth in a written agreement.

(3) A corporation and its shareholders may, but need not, agree that shares sold to it by a person who becomes a disqualified person for any reason other than disbarment may be resold to such person if and when he/she again becomes an eligible shareholder. [Law Corporation Rules following B & P Code §6171 (or appearing in separate booklet, see card index), IV(C)]

See also footnote 2.

STOCK TRANSFER CERTIFICATE LEGEND

(4) The share certificates of a law corporation shall contain an appropriate legend setting forth the foregoing restrictions [see above regulations]. [Law Corporation Rules IV (C)]

See also footnote 2.

REPORTING REQUIREMENTS

Annual: On or before March 31 of each year every law corporation must file an annual report covering the calendar year immediately preceding on a form provided by State Bar. It must include information pertaining to qualification and compliance with statutes, rules, and regulations. Fee: Fixed by State Bar. [Law Corp Rules VI(A)(C)]

Special: Within thirty (30) days of any change relating to the requirements for issuance of Certificate of Registration (see Law Corporation Rules IV), including change in directors, officers, share ownership, employees practicing law, amendments to Articles of Incorporation and Bylaws, and notices from insurance companies of intent to cancel or terminate insurance required under IV (B) "Security" regulations. Fee: Fixed by State Bar. Law Corp Rules VI(B)(C).

MALPRACTICE SECURITY

Security for claims against the law corporation by its clients for errors or omissions arising out of the practice of law shall consist of an executed written agreement, executed by each of the shareholders, jointly and severally guaranteeing payment by the corporation.

Amount: At least $50,000 multiplied by the number of employees practicing law for each claim. Aggregate maximum limit per year of at least $100,000 multiplied by the number of employees practicing law. Maximum guaranteed need not to be more than $500,000 for each claim and $5,000,000 for all claims during the year.

Any payment required thereunder may be offset by insurance payment if the corporation has errors or omissions insurance.

Deductible: Shall not exceed $2,000 multiplied by the number of employees practicing law. [Law Corp. Rules IV(B)]

MARRIAGE, FAMILY AND CHILD COUNSELING CORPORATIONS
Website: http://www.bbs.ca.gov

STATUTES

Generally: B & P §§4980-4988.2, Marriage, Family and Child Counseling Corps. §§4987.5-4988.2

REGULATIONS

Generally: 16 Cal. Code of Regs. §§1830-1850.8; "Marriage, Family and Child Counseling Corporation Rules" §§1850-1850.8.

LICENSING BOARD

Board of Behavioral Science Examiners (part of Department of Consumer Affairs), 400 R Street, #3150, Sacramento, CA 95814-6240. Phone 916-445-4933.

CERTIFICATE OF REGISTRATION REQUIRED?

Yes. Fee: $100.00.

ADDRESS FOR APPLICATION FOR CERTIFICATE OF REGISTRATION

See Licensing Board above.

RENEWAL OF CERTIFICATE OF REGISTRATION

Certificate of Registration continues in effect until suspended or revoked. [16 Cal. Code of Regs. §1850.8(a)]

NAMES YOU CAN USE

Name or names in one of the following forms:	Then one of the following:	Then either:	Then one of the following:
Jane T. Doet	Marriage	Counseling	Professional Corporation
Doet	Family	Counselor	Prof. Corp.
Robert Smythe	Child		Corporation
and Jane Doet			Corp.
Smythe & Doet			Incorporated
			Inc.

EXAMPLE: Jane Doet, Child Counseling Corp.

The names must be the full name or surname of one or more of the present, prospective or former shareholder(s). The name must include the word, "marriage," or "family," or "child," and the word "counseling" or "counselor." [B & P Code §4987.8]

WHO MAY BE SHAREHOLDERS, OFFICERS, DIRECTORS

Each director, shareholder and officer of a marriage, family and child counseling corporation shall be a licensed person, except that officers other than president and treasurer in a corporation with only one shareholder may be non-licensed persons. [B & P Code §4987.9; Corp. Code §13403] [See also Chapter 4(E).]

A licensed physician, surgeon, psychologist, clinical social worker, registered nurse or chiropractor may be a shareholder, director or officer of a marriage, family and child counseling corporation so long as such physicians, surgeons, psychologists, clinical social workers, registered nurses and chiropractors own no more than 49% of the total shares issued by the marriage, family and child counseling corporation and the number of physicians, surgeons, psychologists, clinical social workers, registered nurses and chiropractors owning shares in the marriage, family and child counseling corporation does not exceed the number of marriage, family and child counselors owning shares in such a corporation. [B & P Code §4987.9; Corp. Code §13401.5]

SHARE TRANSFER REQUIREMENTS

Shares: Ownership and Transfer

(a) The shares of a marriage, family and child counseling corporation may be issued only to a licensed person and may be transferred only to a licensed person or to the issuing corporation.

(b) Where there are two or more shareholders in a marriage, family and child counseling corporation and one of its shareholders:

(1) Dies, or

(2) Becomes a disqualified person as defined in §13401(d) of the Corporations Code, for a period exceeding ninety (90) days, his or her shares shall be sold and transferred to a licensed person or to the issuing marriage, family and child counseling corporation, on such terms as are agreed upon. Such sale or transfer shall not be later than six (6) months after any such death and not later than ninety (90) days after the date the shareholder became a disqualified person.

(c) A corporation and its shareholders may, but need not, agree that shares sold to it by a person who becomes a disqualified person may be resold to such person if and when he/she again ceases to become a disqualified person.

(d) The restrictions of subdivision (a) and, if appropriate, subdivision (b) of this section shall be set forth in the corporation's Bylaws or Articles of Incorporation. [16 Cal. Code of Regs. §1850.7]

STOCK TRANSFER CERTIFICATE LEGEND

(f) The share certificates of a marriage, family and child counseling corporation shall contain either:

(1) An appropriate legend setting forth the restrictions of subdivision (a), and where applicable, the restrictions of subdivision (b) [see above regulation], or

(2) An appropriate legend stating that ownership and transfer of the share are restricted and specifically referring to an identified section of the Bylaws or Articles of Incorporation of the corporation wherein the restrictions are set forth. [16 Cal. Code of Regs. §1850.7]

REPORTING REQUIREMENTS

Annual: Each year on or before July 31 each marriage, family and child counseling corporation, except those licensed on or after April 1 of that year, shall file with the Board an annual report on a form provided by the Board. It shall reflect the corporation's status as of the previous June 30 and shall contain information on its qualifications and compliance with the statutes, rules and regulations. Fee: $10.

Special: Within thirty (30) days of any change of the officers, directors, shareholders, Articles of Incorporation, or corporate name, each corporation shall file a special report on a form provided by the Board. Fee: $5. [B & P Code §4987.7; 16 Cal. Code of Regs. §1850.8]

MALPRACTICE SECURITY

Although B & P Code §4988.2 authorizes the Board to formulate and enforce rules and regulations including a requirement that each corporation provide adequate security by insurance or otherwise for claims against it by its patients arising out of the rendering of professional services, no such regulation has yet been published.

MEDICAL CORPORATIONS
Website: http://www.medbd.ca.gov

STATUTES

Generally: B & P Code §§2000-2448; Medical Corps., B & P Code §§2400-2416.

REGULATIONS

Generally, 16 Cal. Code of Regs. §§1300-1353; §§1342-1349 "Professional Corporation Regulations."

LICENSING BOARD

Division of Licensing, Board of Medical Quality Assurance (part of Department of Consumer Affairs), 1426 Howe Avenue, # 54, Sacramento, CA 95825. Phone: 916-263-2344 for licensing.

CERTIFICATE OF REGISTRATION REQUIRED?

No. [Corp. Code §13401(b)]

Fee: Not applicable.

RENEWAL OF CERTIFICATE OF REGISTRATION

Not applicable.

NAMES YOU CAN USE

You must choose one of the following two combinations:

Name or names in one of the following forms:	Followed by either:
Jane T. Doet	Medical Corporation
Doet	Medical Corp.
Robert Smythe and Jane Doet	
Smythe & Doet	

Name of names in one of the following forms:	Followed by either:	Then one of the following:
Jane T. Doet	Medical Doctor	Professional Corporation
Doet	M.D.	Prof. Corp.
Robert Smythe and Jane Doet		Corporation
Smythe & Doet		Corp.
		Incorporated
		Inc.

EXAMPLE: Jane Doet, Medical Corp., or Jane Doet, M.D., Prof. Corp.

The name(s) must be of present, prospective or former shareholder(s) who are physicians, or, if any other name is used, a fictitious name permit must be applied for from the Division of Licensing of the Board of Medical Quality Assurance (BMQA).

Fictitious Names: A permit is required if name is other than the above. Must use one of the following designations (with no intervening words): Medical Group, Medical Clinic, Medical Corporation, Medical Associates, Medical Center *or* Medical Office. Fee: $50. Biennial Renewal Fee $40. [B & P Code §§ 2415, 2443; 16 Cal. Code of Regs. §§1344]

Fictitious Name Permit must be applied for on a form furnished by the Board.

Renewal of Fictitious Name Permit: All licenses (permits) expire and become invalid at 12 midnight on the last day of February of each even-numbered year, if not renewed. [B & P Code §2422]

WHO MAY BE SHAREHOLDERS, OFFICERS, DIRECTORS

Each shareholder, director and officer of a medical or podiatry corporation other than an assistant secretary or assistant treasurer must be a licensed person, except that officers other than president or treasurer in a corporation with only one shareholder may be non-licensed persons. [B & P Code §2408; Corp. Code §13401.5; Corp. Code §13403] [See also Chapter 4(E).]

A medical corporation with only one shareholder may be a shareholder of another medical corporation. The one shareholder must be licensed and may also be an officer or director of the other corporation. [B & P Code §2408]

The bylaws of a professional medical corporation may provide that the term of office of a director may be up to three years, unless the corporation has more than 200 shareholders, in which case they may provide that up to 50% of the members of the Board, plus one additional member, may have six-year terms. [Corp. Code §13403]

A licensed podiatrist, psychologist, registered nurse, optometrist, marriage, family and child counselor, clinical social worker, physicians' assistant or chiropractor may be a shareholder, director or officer of a medical corporation so long as such podiatrists, psychologists, registered nurses, optometrists, marriage, family and child counselors, clinical social workers, physicians' assistants or chiropractors own no more than 49% of the total shares issued by the medical corporation and the number of licensed podiatrists, psychologists, registered nurses, optometrists, marriage, family and child counselors, clinical social workers, physicians' assistants or chiropractors owning shares in the medical corporation does not exceed the number of physicians owning shares in such a corporation. A licensed physician, surgeon, psychologist, registered nurse, optometrist or chiropractor may be a shareholder, director or officer of a podiatry corporation so long as such physicians, surgeons, psychologists, registered nurses, optometrists and chiropractors own no more than 49% of the total shares issued by the podiatry corporation and the number of licensed physicians, surgeons, psychologists, registered nurses, optometrists and chiropractors owning shares in the podiatry corporation does not exceed the number of podiatrists owning shares in such a corporation. [16 Cal. Code of Regs. §1343(b); Corp. Code §13401.5.]

SHARE TRANSFER REQUIREMENTS

Shares: Ownership and Transfer

(a) The shares of a professional corporation shall be issued only to a licensed person as defined in §13401(c) of the Corporations Code and shall be transferred only to a licensed person or to the issuing corporation.

(b) Where there are two or more shareholders in a professional corporation and one of the shareholders:

(1) Dies; or

(2) Becomes a disqualified person as defined in §13401(d) of the Corporations Code, his or her shares shall be sold and transferred to the corporation, its shareholders or other eligible licensed persons on such terms as are agreed upon. Such sale or transfer shall not be later than six (6) months after any such death and not later than ninety (90) days after the date the shareholder becomes a disqualified person. The requirements of subsections (a) and (b) of this section shall be set forth in the professional corporation's Articles of Incorporation or Bylaws. Any sale or transfer of shares made pursuant to this section or otherwise shall be in conformity with subsection (b) of §1343.

(c) A corporation and its shareholders may, but need not, agree that shares sold to it by a person who becomes a disqualified person may be resold to such person if and when he or she again becomes an eligible shareholder. [16 Cal. Code of Regs. §1345]

STOCK TRANSFER CERTIFICATE LEGEND

(d) The share certificates of a professional corporation shall contain an appropriate legend setting forth the restrictions of subsection (a) and, where applicable, the restrictions of subsection (b) [see above regulation]. [16 Cal. Code of Regs. §1345]

REPORTING REQUIREMENTS

Not required.

MALPRACTICE SECURITY

16 Cal. Code of Regs. §1346 which provided for security for claims against a Medical Corporation was repealed in 1983 and no new regulation has been issued yet.

NURSING CORPORATIONS
Website: http://www.rn.ca.gov

STATUTES

Generally: B & P Code §§2701-2837; Nursing Corps. §§2775-2781.

REGULATIONS

Generally: 16 Cal. Code of Regs. §§1400-1485; no regulations yet available for nursing corporations.

LICENSING BOARD

State Board of Registered Nursing (part of Department of Consumer Affairs), 400 R Street, Suite 4030, Sacramento, CA 95814. 916-322-3350.

L.A. Office
107 S. Broadway, Room 8020
Los Angeles, CA 90012
213-897-3590

CERTIFICATE OF REGISTRATION REQUIRED?

No. [Corp. Code §13401(b)]

Fee: Not applicable.

RENEWAL OF CERTIFICATE OF REGISTRATION

Not applicable.

NAMES YOU CAN USE

The name of the corporation must include the word(s): "Nursing" or "Registered Nursing" and wording or abbreviations denoting corporate existence (e.g., Corp., A Professional Corporation, Inc.).

EXAMPLE: Jane Doet, Registered Nursing Corp.

WHO MAY BE SHAREHOLDERS, OFFICERS, DIRECTORS

Each shareholder, director and officer of a nursing corporation other than an assistant secretary and assistant treasurer must be a licensed person, except that officers other than president and treasurer in a corporation with only one stockholder may be non-licensed persons. [B & P Code §2779; Corp. Code §13403]. [See also Chapter 4(E).]

A licensed physician, surgeon, podiatrist, psychologist, optometrist, marriage, family and child counselor, clinical social worker, physicians' assistant or chiropractor may be a shareholder, director or officer of a nursing corporation so long as such physicians, surgeons, podiatrists, psychologists, optometrists, marriage, family and child counselors, clinical social workers, physicians' assistants or chiropractors own no more than 49% of the total shares issued by the nursing corporation and the number of the licensed physicians, surgeons, podiatrists, psychologists, optometrists, marriage, family and child counselors, clinical social workers, physicians' assistants and chiropractors owning shares in the nursing corporation does not exceed the number of nurses owning shares in such a corporation. [B & P Code §2779; Corp. Code §13401.5]

STOCK TRANSFER REQUIREMENTS AND STOCK TRANSFER CERTIFICATE LEGEND

Although B & P Code §2781 provides that the Board may adopt and enforce regulations requiring that the Bylaws of nursing corporations include a provision for transfer of stock of a disqualified or deceased person, there are no regulations at this time. Nor are there any statues on stock transfer restrictions. Check with the Board and see §13407 of the Corporations Code.

REPORTING REQUIREMENTS

Not required.

MALPRACTICE SECURITY

Although B & P Code §2781 empowers the Board to adopt rules and regulations including a requirement that each corporation provide adequate security by insurance or otherwise for claims against it by its patients arising out of the rendering of professional services, no such regulations have been published.

OPTOMETRIC CORPORATIONS
Website: http://www.optometry.ca.gov

STATUTES

Generally: B & P code §§3000-3167; Optometric Corps. §§3160-3167.

REGULATIONS

Generally: 16 Cal. Code of Regs. §§1500-1563; §§1540-1550 "Optometric Corporation Rules."

LICENSING BOARD

State Board of Optometry (part of Department of Consumer Affairs), 400 R Street, Suite 1070, Sacramento, CA 95814-6200. 916-323-8720.

CERTIFICATE OF REGISTRATION REQUIRED?

Yes. Fee: $200.00.

ADDRESS FOR APPLICATION FOR CERTIFICATE OF REGISTRATION

See Licensing Board above.

RENEWAL OF CERTIFICATE OF REGISTRATION

Certificate of Registration continues in effect until revoked or suspended. [16 Cal. Code of Regs. §1549(a)]

NAMES YOU CAN USE

Name or names in one of the following forms: Then one of the following:

Jane T. Doet

Doet

Robert Smythe & Jane Doet

Smythe & Doet

Optometric Corporation

Optometry Corporation

Corporation

Professional Corporation

Prof. Corp.

Corp.

Incorporated

Inc.

Optometric Corp.

Optometry Corp.

Professional Optometric Corporation

Professional Optometry Corporation

Professional Optometric Corp.

Professional Optometry Corp.

EXAMPLE: Jane Doet, Professional Optometry Corp.

The name or names must be of present, prospective or former shareholder(s).

The name of a former shareholder must be deleted within two years from his/her dying or ceasing to be a shareholder (by amending the Articles of Incorporation).

"Opt. D.," "O.D.," or "Optometrist(s)" may also be used if person(s) hold(s) diploma from accredited school of optometry.

Fictitious Name Permit: Form supplied by the Board; Fee: $10. Required if name does not comply with above.

A fictitious name may be used if the corporation meets the requirement of B & P Code §3125. The fictitious name must contain at least one of the following designations: "Optometry," or "Optometric."

Renewal of Fictitious Name Permit: Renewal must be made yearly. Fee: $10 (maximum).

WHO MAY BE SHAREHOLDERS, OFFICERS, DIRECTORS

Each officer, director, and shareholder must be a licensed person, except officers other than president or treasurer in a corporation with only one shareholder may be non-licensed persons. [B & P Code §3164; Corp. Code §13403] [See also Chapter 4(E).]

A licensed physician, surgeon, podiatrist, psychologist, registered nurse, or chiropractor may be a shareholder, director or officer of a optometric corporation so long as such physicians, surgeons, podiatrists, psychologists, registered nurses or chiropractors own no more than 49% of the total shares issued by the optometric corporation and the number of licensed physicians, surgeons, podiatrists, psychologists, registered nurses and chiropractors owning shares in the optometric corporation does not exceed the number of optometrists owning shares in the corporation. [Corp. Code §13401.5.]

SHARE TRANSFER REQUIREMENTS

Shares: Ownership and Transfer

(a) The shares of an optometric corporation may be issued only to a licensed person and may be transferred only to a licensed person or to the issuing corporation.

(b) Where there are two or more shareholders in an optometric corporation and one of the shareholders:

(1) Dies; or

(2) Becomes a disqualified person as defined in §13401(d) of the Corporations Code, for a period exceeding ninety (90) days, his/her shares shall be sold and transferred to a licensed person or to the issuing optometric corporation, on such terms as are agreed upon. Such sale or transfer shall not be later than six (6) months after any such death and not later than ninety (90) days after the date he/she became a disqualified person.

(c) A corporation and its shareholders may, but need not, agree that shares sold to it by a person who becomes a disqualified person may be resold to such person if and when he/she again ceases to become a disqualified person.

(d) The restrictions of subdivision (a) and, if appropriate, subdivision (b) of this section shall be set forth in the corporation's Bylaws or Articles of Incorporation. [16 Cal. Code of Regs. §1548]

STOCK TRANSFER CERTIFICATE LEGEND

(f) The share certificates of an optometric corporation shall contain either:

(1) An appropriate legend setting forth the restrictions of subdivisions (a) [see above regulation], and where applicable, the restriction of subdivision (b), or

(2) An appropriate legend stating that ownership and transfer of the shares are restricted and specifically referring to an identified section of the Bylaws or Articles of Incorporation of the Corporation wherein the restrictions are set forth. [16 Cal. Code of Regs. §1548]

REPORTING REQUIREMENTS

Annual: Must be filed on or before May 31 of each year, reflecting its status as of May 1, on a form provided by the Board. It must contain information pertaining to its qualifications and compliance with the statutes, rules, and regulations. Fee: not to exceed $50.

Special: Required within thirty (30) days of any change of the officers, directors, shareholders, places of practice, Bylaws, Articles of Incorporation, and corporate name. Fee: not to exceed $15. [16 Cal. Code of Regs. §1549]

MALPRACTICE SECURITY

The corporation may either provide insurance up to certain limits or the shareholders shall be jointly and severally liable up to the same limit for damages arising out of claims against it by its patients arising out of the rendering or failing to render optometric services.

Amounts: At least $50,000 multiplied by the number of employed licensed persons rendering optometric services per claim. Aggregate maximum limit of liability per policy year of at least $150,000 multiplied by the number of employed licensed persons rendering optometric services. Maximum coverage need not exceed $150,000 for each claim and $450,000 for all claims during the policy year.

Deductible: Shall not exceed $5,000 multiplied by the number of employed licensed persons rendering optometric services. [16 Cal. Code of Regs. §1547]

OSTEOPATHIC CORPORATIONS
Website: N/A

STATUTES

Generally: B & P Code §§2450-2459; Osteopathic Corps. §2454 "Medical Corporation with Osteopathic Physicians and Surgeons."

REGULATIONS

Generally: 16 Cal. Code of Regs. §§1665-1697 (Conflict of Interest, §1697, available from the Board); §§1665-1673 "Medical Corporation Rules." (Not the rules applicable to regular medical corporations.)

LICENSING BOARD

Osteopathic Medical Board of California, 2720 Gateway Oaks Dr., Suite 350, Sacramento, CA 95833. 916-263-3100.

CERTIFICATE OF REGISTRATION REQUIRED?

Yes. Fee: $100.00. Osteopaths who join with medical doctors still apply to this Board for their certificate. [16 Cal. Code of Regs. §1690]

ADDRESS FOR APPLICATION FOR CERTIFICATE OF REGISTRATION

State Board of Osteopathic Examiners, 921 11th Street, Suite 1201, Sacramento, CA 95814. 916-322-4306.

RENEWAL OF CERTIFICATE OF REGISTRATION

$25 each year. [16 Cal. Code of Regs. §1690(i)]

NAMES YOU CAN USE

After the name or names of the corporation, you must follow with one of these:

Medical Corporation	Corp.
Medical Corp.	Incorporated
Professional Corporation	Inc.
Prof. Corp.	Osteopathic Corp.
Corporation	Professional Corp.
Osteopathic Corporation	

EXAMPLE: Doet & Smythe, Osteopathic Corp.

Fictitious Name Permit: Required if the corporate name is other than the individual names of one or more of the shareholders. Application is made to the Board. Once the permit is obtained, a list of names and degrees (M.O., or M.D.) must be posted at the office and used on printed matter. Fee: $100.00. Renewal: $50. [16 Cal. Code of Regs. §1690]

WHO MAY BE SHAREHOLDERS, OFFICERS, DIRECTORS

All shareholders must hold a valid osteopathic physicians and surgeons certificate. [16 Cal. Code of Regs. §1670]

Each shareholder, director or officer (except as provided in Section 13403 of the Corporations Code and Section 2408 of the Code) must hold a valid physician's and surgeon's certificate, provided that a licensed podiatrist; psychologist; optometrist; physician's assistant; clinical social worker; marriage, family and child counselor or registered nurse may be a shareholder, director or officer of a medical corporation so long as such licensed persons own no more than 49% of the total shares issued by the medical corporation and the number of licensed persons owing shares in the medical corporation does not exceed the number of physicians owning shares in such a corporation.

An assistant secretary and assistant treasurer may be non-licensed persons. Officers other than the president and treasurer in a corporation with only one shareholder may be non-licensed persons.

[Cal. Code of Regs. § 1670; B & P Code §2408; Corp. Code §13403] [See also Chapter 4, Sections D & E]

SHARE TRANSFER REQUIREMENTS

Shares: Ownership and Transfer

(a) The shares of a medical corporation may be owned only by the medical corporation or by a licensed physician and surgeon, hereinafter referred to as eligible shareholders.

(b) The shares of a medical corporation owned by a person who

(1) Dies;

(2) Ceases to be an eligible shareholder; or

(3) Becomes a disqualified person as defined in §13401(d) of the Corporations Code and §1680.1(d) of these Rules, for a period exceeding ninety (90) days, shall be sold and transferred to the corporation, its shareholders, or other eligible persons, on such terms as are agreed upon by the corporation and its shareholders. Such sale or transfer shall be not later than six (6) months after any such death and not later than ninety (90) days after the date he/she ceases to be an eligible shareholder, or ninety (90) days after the date he/she becomes a disqualified person. The requirements of subsections (a) and (b) of this section shall be set forth in the medical corporation Articles of Incorporation or Bylaws, except that the terms of the sale or transfer provided for in said subsection (b) need not be set forth in said Articles or By-laws if they are set forth in a written agreement.

(c) A corporation and its shareholders may, but need not, agree that shares sold to it by a person who becomes a disqualified person may be resold to such person if and when he/she again becomes an eligible shareholder. [16 Cal. Code of Regs. §1672]

STOCK TRANSFER CERTIFICATE LEGEND

(d) The share certificates of a medical corporation shall contain an appropriate legend setting forth the foregoing restrictions [see above regulation]. [16 Cal. Code of Regs. §1672]

REPORTING REQUIREMENTS

Annual: Must be filed within thirty (30) days after the end of the fiscal year, on a form provided by the Board. It must contain information pertaining to the corporation's qualifications and compliance with the statutes, rules, and regulations. Fee: $175.

Special: Must be filed within thirty (30) days of any change of officers, directors, professional employees, share ownership, Bylaws, Articles of Incorporation, and corporate name. A copy of a notice from the insurance company of a termination or cancellation or an intent to terminate or cancel, must also be filed. Fee: $ 175.

Change of Address: Notice required immediately to the Board. Fee: None.
[16 Cal. Code of Regs. §1673]

MALPRACTICE SECURITY

The corporation may either provide insurance up to certain limits or the shareholders shall be jointly and severally liable up to the same limits for damages arising out of claims against it by its patients arising out of the rendering or failing to render medical services.

Amounts: At least $50,000 multiplied by the number of employed, licensed persons rendering medical services per claim. Aggregate maximum limit per policy year of at least $150,000 multiplied by the number of employed, licensed persons rendering medical services. Maximum coverage per claim need not exceed $150,000, and for all claims in a policy year, $450,000.

Deductible: Shall not exceed $5,000 multiplied by the number of employed, licensed persons rendering medical services.

A Certificate of Insurance issued by the insurer must be filed with the Board.
[Cal. Code of Regs. §1671]

Pharmacy Corporations

Website: http://www.pharmacy.ca.gov

STATUTES

Generally: B & P Code §§4000-4416; Pharmacy Corporations §§4120-4127.

REGULATIONS

Generally: 16 Cal. Code of Regs. §§1700-1795; No regulations yet available for pharmacy corporations.

LICENSING BOARD

State Board of Pharmacy (part of Department of Consumer Affairs), 400 R Street, #4070, Sacramento, CA 95814. 916-445-5014

L.A. Office, 107 S. Broadway, Room 8020
Los Angeles, CA 90012. 213-897-3590

CERTIFICATE OF REGISTRATION REQUIRED?

No. [Corp. Code §13401(b)]

Fee: Not applicable

ADDRESS FOR APPLICATION FOR CERTIFICATE OF REGISTRATION

Not applicable.

RENEWAL OF CERTIFICATE OF REGISTRATION

Not applicable.

NAMES YOU CAN USE

The word Pharmacist, Pharmacy or Pharmaceutical must be used. A word or abbreviation indicating corporate existence (e.g., Corp., Professional Corporation, Inc.) is also required. [B & P Code §4125]

EXAMPLE: Jane Doet, Pharmacist, Prof. Corp.

WHO MAY BE SHAREHOLDERS, OFFICERS, DIRECTORS

Each shareholder, director, and officer of a pharmacy corporation, except an assistant secretary and an assistant treasurer, must be a licensed person. [B & P Code §4124[3]] [See also Chapter 4(E).]

SHARE TRANSFER REQUIREMENTS AND STOCK TRANSFER CERTIFICATE LEGEND

Although B & P §4126 provides that the Board may adopt and enforce regulations requiring that the By-laws of a pharmacy corporation include a provision for transfer of stock of a disqualified or deceased person, there are no regulations yet. Nor are there any statutes on stock transfer restrictions. Check with the Board (and see §13407 of the Corporations Code).

REPORTING REQUIREMENTS

Not required.

MALPRACTICE SECURITY

Although B & P Code §4126 empowers the Board to adopt rules and regulations, including a provision that adequate security must be provided, there are no regulations yet.

Physical Therapy Corporations
Website: N/A

STATUTES

Generally: B & P Code §§2600-2696; Physical Therapy Corps. §§2690-2696.

REGULATIONS

Generally: 16 Cal. Code of Regs. §§1398-1399.79; §§1399.30-1399.41 "Physical Therapy Professional Corp. Regulations."

LICENSING BOARD

Physical Therapy Examining Committee, Division of Allied Health Professions, Board of Medical Quality Assurance (part of Department of Consumer Affairs), 1434 Howe Avenue, Suite # 92, Sacramento, CA 95825. 916-263-2550.

CERTIFICATE OF REGISTRATION REQUIRED?

No. [Corp. Code §13401(b)]

Fee: not applicable.

ADDRESS FOR APPLICATION FOR CERTIFICATE OF REGISTRATION

Not applicable.

RENEWAL OF CERTIFICATE OF REGISTRATION

Not applicable.

NAMES YOU CAN USE

The name of the corporation must include either "Physical Therapy," or "Physical Therapist(s)." Any wording or abbreviation indicating that it is a corporation (e.g., Corp., Professional Corporation, Inc.) is okay.

EXAMPLE: Jane Doet, Physical Therapy Corp.

WHO MAY BE SHAREHOLDERS, OFFICERS, DIRECTORS

Each shareholder, director and officer, other than the assistant secretary and assistant treasurer, shall be a licensed person, except that officers other than president and treasurer in a corporation with only one shareholder may be non-licensed persons. [B & P Code §2694; Corp. Code §13403] [See also Chapter 4(E).]

A physical therapist may be a shareholder in more than one professional corporation. [16 Cal. Code of Regs. §1399.35(b)]

SHARE TRANSFER REQUIREMENTS

Shares: Ownership and Transfer

(a) The shares of a professional corporation shall be issued only to a licensed person as defined in §13401(c) of the Corporations Code and shall be transferred only to a licensed person or to the issuing corporation.

(b) Where there are two or more shareholders in a professional corporation and one of the shareholders:

(1) Dies; or

(2) Becomes a disqualified person as defined in §13401(d) of the Corporations Code for a period exceeding ninety (90) days, his or her shares shall be sold and transferred to the corporation, its shareholders or other eligible persons on such terms as are agreed upon. Such sale or transfer shall not be later than six (6) months after any such death and not later than ninety (90) days after the date the shareholder becomes a disqualified person. The requirements of subsections (a) and (b) of this section shall be set forth in the professional corporation's Articles of Incorporation or Bylaws.

(c) A corporation and its shareholders may, but need not, agree that shares sold to it by a person who becomes a disqualified person may be resold to such person if and when he or she again becomes an eligible shareholder.

(f) Nothing in these regulations shall be construed to prohibit a professional corporation from owning shares in a nonprofessional corporation. [16 Cal. Code of Regs. §1399.37]

STOCK TRANSFER CERTIFICATE LEGEND

(d) The share certificates of a professional corporation shall contain an appropriate legend setting forth the restrictions of subsection (a) and where applicable, the restrictions of subsection (b) [see above regulation]. [16 Cal. Code of Regs. §1399.37]

REPORTING REQUIREMENTS

Not required.

MALPRACTICE SECURITY

Although B & P Code §2696 authorizes the committee to adapt regulations requiring the provision of security by insurance or otherwise, no such regulation has yet been published.

Physicians' Assistants Corporations

Website: http://www.medbd.ca.gov

STATUTES

Generally: B & P Code §§3500-3546; Physicians' Assistant Corps. §§3540-3546.

REGULATIONS

Generally: 16 Cal. Code of Regs. §§1399-500-1399.615; No regulations yet available for physicians' assistants corporations.

LICENSING BOARD

Physicians' Assistants Examining Committee, Division of Allied Health Professions, Board of Medical Quality Assurance (part of Department of Consumer Affairs), 1424 Howe Avenue, Suite 35, Sacramento, CA 95825. 916-263-2670.

CERTIFICATE OF REGISTRATION REQUIRED?

No. [Corp. Code §13401(b)]

ADDRESS FOR APPLICATIONS FOR CERTIFICATE OF REGISTRATION

Not applicable.

RENEWAL OF CERTIFICATE OF REGISTRATION

Not applicable.

NAMES YOU CAN USE

The name of the corporation must include the words "physicians' assistants" and wording or abbreviations denoting corporate existence (e.g., Corp., A Professional Corporation, Inc.). [B & P Code §3543]

WHO MAY BE SHAREHOLDERS, OFFICERS, DIRECTORS

Each shareholder, director and officer, other than the assistant secretary and assistant treasurer, shall be a licensed person, except that officers other than president and treasurer in a corporation with only one shareholder may be non-licensed persons. [B & P Code §3544; Corp. Code §13401.5; Corp. Code §13403] [See also Chapter 4(E).]

A licensed physician, surgeon, or registered nurse may be a shareholder, director or officer of a physicians' assistants corporation so long as such physicians, surgeons, or registered nurses own no more than 49% of the total shares issued by the physicians' assistants corporation and the number of the licensed physicians, surgeons, or registered nurses owning shares in the physicians' assistants corporation does not exceed the number physicians' assistants owning shares in such a corporation. [Corp. Code §13401.5]

STOCK TRANSFER REQUIREMENTS AND STOCK TRANSFER CERTIFICATE LEGEND

Although B & P §3546 provides that the Board may adopt and enforce regulations requiring that the Bylaws of a physicians' assistants corporation include a provision for transfer of stock of a disqualified or deceased person, there are no regulations at this time. Nor are there any statutes on stock transfer restrictions. Check with the Board and see §13407 of the Corporations Code.

REPORTING REQUIREMENTS

Not required.

MALPRACTICE SECURITY

Although B & P §3546 empowers the Board to adopt rules and regulations including a requirement that each corporation provide adequate security by insurance or otherwise for claims against it by its patients arising out of the rendering of professional services, no such regulations have been published.

Podiatric Corporations
Website: http://www.dca.ca.gov/bpm

STATUTES

Generally: B & P Code §§2460-2499.6; Podiatry Corps: No regulations for podiatry corporations as such. See Medical Corporation. [B & P §§2400-2416]

REGULATIONS

Generally: 16 Cal. Code of Regs. §§1399.650-1399.697; §1399.658 states that podiatrists are subject to the provisions of §§1341-1349, "Professional Corporations"—same as Medical Corporations regulations.

LICENSING BOARD

Podiatry Examining Committee, Division of Allied Health Professions, Board of Medical Quality Assurance (part of Department of Consumer Affairs), 1420 Howe Avenue, Suite 8, Sacramento, CA 95825. 916-263-2647.

CERTIFICATE OF REGISTRATION REQUIRED?

No. [Corp. Code §13401(b)]

Fee: Not applicable.

ADDRESS FOR APPLICATIONS FOR CERTIFICATE OF REGISTRATION

Not applicable.

RENEWAL OF CERTIFICATE OF REGISTRATION

Not applicable.

NAMES YOU CAN USE

You must choose one of these two combinations:

Name or names in one of the following forms: Followed by either:

Jane T. Doet
Doet
Robert Smythe & Jane Doet
Smythe & Doet

Podiatry Corporation
Podiatry Corp.

OR

Name or names in one of the following forms:	Then one of the following:	Followed by one of the following:
Jane T. Doet	Podiatrist	Professional Corporation
Doet	Doctor of Podiatric Medicine	Prof. Corp.
Robert Smythe & Jane Doet	DPM	Corporation
Smythe & Doet	MD (only if applicable)	Corp.
		Incorporated
		Inc.

EXAMPLE: Doet, Podiatry Corp., or Doet, DPM, Inc.

The name(s) must be of present, prospective, or former shareholder(s) who are podiatrists, or a fictitious name permit must be applied for from the Division of Licensing, Board of Medical Quality Assurance.

Fictitious Name Permit: Required if name is otherwise than the above samples. Must use one of the following designations (with no intervening words): Podiatrists' Group, Podiatrists' Clinic, Podiatrists' Corporation, Podiatrists' Associates, Podiatrists' Center, Podiatrists' Office, Podiatry Group, Podiatry Clinic, Podiatry Corporation, Podiatry Associates, Podiatry Center, Podiatry Office *or* Podiatry Foot Clinic.

Fee: Set by Board [B & P Code §2415].

RENEWAL OF FICTITIOUS NAME PERMIT

See Medical Corporations.

WHO MAY BE SHAREHOLDERS, OFFICERS, DIRECTORS

See Medical Corporations.

SHARE TRANSFER REQUIREMENTS

See Medical Corporations.

STOCK TRANSFER CERTIFICATE LEGEND

See Medical Corporations.

REPORTING REQUIREMENTS

See Medical Corporations.

MALPRACTICE SECURITY

See Medical Corporations.

Psychological Corporations

Website: http://www.dca.ca.gov/psych

STATUTES

Generally: B & P Code §§2900-2999; Psychological Corps. §§2995-2999.

REGULATIONS

Generally: 16 Cal. Code of Regs. §§1380-1397.40; §§1397.30-1397.40 "Psychology Corporation Regulations."

LICENSING BOARD

Psychology Examining Committee, Division of Allied Health Professions, Board of Medical Quality Assurance (part of Department of Consumer Affairs), 1422 Howe Avenue, Suite 22, Sacramento, CA 95825-3200. 916-263-2699.

CERTIFICATE OF REGISTRATION REQUIRED?

No. [Corp. Code §13401(b)]

Fee: Not applicable.

ADDRESS FOR APPLICATION FOR CERTIFICATE OF REGISTRATION

Not applicable.

RENEWAL OF CERTIFICATE OF REGISTRATION

Not applicable.

NAMES YOU CAN USE

Name or names in one of the following forms:	Then one of the following:	Followed by:
Jane T. Doet	Psychology	Professional Corporation
Doet	Psychological	Prof. Corp.
Robert Smythe &	Psychologist	Corporation
Jane Doet	Psychometry	Corp.
Smythe & Doet	Psychometrics	Incorporated
	Psychometrist	Inc.
	Psychotherapy	
	Psychotherapist	
	Psychoanalysis	
	Psychoanalyst	

EXAMPLE: Jane T. Doet, Psychology Corp.

WHO MAY BE SHAREHOLDERS, OFFICERS, DIRECTORS

Each shareholder, director and officer of a psychological corporation other than an assistant secretary and assistant treasurer must be a licensed person, except that officers other than president and treasurer in a corporation with only one stockholder may be non-licensed persons. [B & P Code §2997; 16 Cal. Code of Regs. §1397.35(b); Corp. Code §13401.5; Corp. Code §13403] [See also Chapter 4(E).]

A licensed physician, podiatrist, registered nurse, optometrist, marriage, family and child counselor, clinical social worker or chiropractor may be a shareholder, director or officer of a psychology corporation so long as these other professionals own no more than 49% of the total shares issued by the psychology corporation and the number of the other professionals who own shares in the psychology corporation do not exceed the number of psychologists owning shares in the psychology corporation. [16 Cal. Code of Regs. §1397.35(b); Corp. Code §13401.5]

A psychologist may be a shareholder in more than one psychological corporation. [16 Cal. Code of Regs. §1397.35(b)]

SHARE TRANSFER REQUIREMENTS

Shares: Ownership and Transfer

(a) The shares of a psychology corporation shall be issued only to a licensed person as defined in §13401(c) of the Corporations Code and shall be transferred only to a licensed person or to the issuing corporation.

(b) Where there are two or more shareholders in a psychology corporation and one of the shareholders:

(1) Dies; or

(2) Becomes a disqualified person as defined in §13401(d) of the Corporations Code, his or her shares shall be sold and transferred to the corporation, its shareholders or other eligible licensed persons on such terms as are agreed upon. Such sale or transfer shall not be later than six (6) months after any such death and ninety (90) days after the shareholder becomes a disqualified person. The requirements of subsections (a) and (b) of this section shall be set forth in the psychology corporation's Articles of Incorporation or Bylaws.

(c) A corporation and its shareholders may, but need not, agree that shares sold to it by a person who becomes a disqualified person may be resold to such person if and when he or she again becomes an eligible shareholder. [16 Cal. Code of Regs. §1397.37]

STOCK TRANSFER CERTIFICATE LEGEND

(d) The share certificates of a psychology corporation shall contain an appropriate legend setting forth the restrictions of subsection (a) and, where applicable, the restrictions of subsection (b) [see above regulation]. [16 Cal. Code of Regs. §1397.37]

REPORTING REQUIREMENTS

No report required.

MALPRACTICE SECURITY

Although B & P Code §2999 authorizes the committee to adopt regulations pertaining to the provision of adequate security and insurance, no such regulation has yet been published.

Shorthand Reporting Corporations/Court Reporters
Website: http://www.dca.ca.gov/crb

STATUTES

Generally: B & P Code §§8000-8047; Shorthand Reporting Corps. §§8040-8047.

REGULATIONS

Generally: 16 Cal. Code of Regs. §§2400-2471; §§2461-2468 "Shorthand Reporting Corporation Rules."

LICENSING BOARD

Court Reporters Board of California (part of Department of Consumer Affairs), 2535 Capitol Oaks Drive, Suite 230, Sacramento, CA 95833. 916-263-3660.

CERTIFICATE OF REGISTRATION REQUIRED?

No. [Corp. Code §13401(b)].

ADDRESS FOR APPLICATION FOR CERTIFICATE OF REGISTRATION

Not Applicable.

RENEWAL OF CERTIFICATE OF REGISTRATION

Not Applicable.

NAMES YOU CAN USE

Name or names in one of the following forms:	Followed by:	Or one of the following:
Jane T. Doet	Shorthand	Certified Shorthand Reporter(s)
Doet	Reporting	Professional Corporation
Robert Smythe & Jane Doet	Corporation	Certified Shorthand Reporter(s) Prof. Corp.
Smythe & Doet		Certified Shorthand Reporter(s) Corporation
		Certified Shorthand Reporter(s) Corp.
		Certified Shorthand Reporter(s) Incorporated
		Certified Shorthand Reporter(s) Inc.
		C.S.R. Professional Corporation
		C.S.R. Prof. Corp
		C.S.R. Corporation
		C.S.R. Corp.
		C.S.R. Incorporated
		C.S.R. Inc.

OR

A Professional Corporation

EXAMPLE: Jane Doet Shorthand Reporting Corporation, or Jane Doet, C.S.R. Corp.

The name(s) must be of present, former, or prospective shareholder(s) or of persons who were associated with a predecessor person, partnership, corporation or other organization and whose name or names appeared in the name of such predecessor organizations. [B & P Code §8043]

WHO MAY BE SHAREHOLDERS, OFFICERS, DIRECTORS

Each director, shareholder, and officer of a shorthand reporting corporation must be a licensed person, except that officers other than president and treasurer in a corporation with only one shareholder may be non-licensed persons. [B & P Code §8044; Corp. Code §13403] [See also Chapter 4(E).]

SHARE TRANSFER REQUIREMENTS

Shares: Ownership and Transfer

(a) The shares of a shorthand reporting corporation may be issued only to a licensed person and may be transferred only to a licensed person or to the issuing corporation.

(b) Where there are two or more shareholders in a shorthand reporting corporation and one of the shareholders:

(1) Dies; or

(2) Becomes a disqualified person as defined in §13401(d) of the Corporations Code, for a period exceeding ninety (90) days, his or her shares shall be sold and transferred to a licensed person or to the issuing shorthand reporting corporation, on such terms as are agreed upon. Such sale or transfer shall not be later than six (6) months after any such death and not later than ninety (90) days after the date he or she became a disqualified person.

(c) A corporation and its shareholders may, but need not, agree that shares sold to it by a person who becomes a disqualified person may be resold to such person if and when he or she again ceases to become a disqualified person.

(d) The restrictions of subdivision (a) and, if appropriate, subdivision (b) of this section shall be set forth in the corporation's Bylaws or Articles of Incorporation. [16 Cal. Code of Regs. §2467]

STOCK TRANSFER CERTIFICATE LEGEND

(f) The share certificates of a shorthand reporting corporation shall contain either:

(1) An appropriate legend setting forth the restriction of subdivision (a), and where applicable, the restriction of subdivision (b) [see above regulation], or

(2) An appropriate legend stating that ownership and transfer of the shares are restricted and specifically referring to an identified section of the Bylaws or Articles of Incorporation of the corporation wherein the restrictions are set forth. [16 Cal. Code of Regs. §2467]

REPORTING REQUIREMENT

Annual: Must be filed on or before July 31, unless licensed on or after May 16 of that year. The report should reflect the corporation's status as of June 30, and should include information regarding its qualifications and compliance with the statutes, rules and regulations of the Board. Fee: $30.

Special: Must be filed within thirty (30) days of any change of the officers, directors, shareholders, place of practice (i.e., change of address), Articles of Incorporation or corporate name. Fee: $50. [16 Cal. Code of Regs. §2468]

MALPRACTICE SECURITY

Although the B & P Code §8047 empowers the Board to adopt regulations requiring a shorthand corporation to provide adequate security for claims, no such regulation has yet been published.

Speech Pathology and Audiology Corporations
Website: http://www.dca.gov/spab

STATUTES

Generally: B & P Code §§2530-2539; Speech Pathology Corps. and Audiology Corps. §§2536-2539.

REGULATIONS

Generally: 16 Cal. Code of Regs. §§1399.150-1399.198; §§1399.190-1399.198 "Speech Pathology and Audiology Corporation Regulations."

LICENSING BOARD

Speech Pathology and Audiology Examining Committee, Division of Allied Health Professions, Board of Medical Quality Assurance (part of Department of Consumer Affairs), 1422 Howe Avenue, Ste. 3, Sacramento, CA 95825-3240. 916-263-2666.

CERTIFICATE OF REGISTRATION REQUIRED?

No. [Corp. Code §13401(b)]

Fee: Not applicable.

ADDRESS FOR APPLICATION FOR CERTIFICATE OF REGISTRATION

Not applicable.

RENEWAL OF CERTIFICATE OF REGISTRATION

Not applicable.

NAMES YOU CAN USE

The name of a speech pathology corporation must include one of the following terms:

Speech Pathologist

Speech Pathology

Speech Therapy

Speech Correction

Speech Correctionist

Speech Therapist

Communicology

Communicologist

Aphasiologist

Voice Therapy

Voice Therapist

Voice Pathology

Speech Clinic   Voice Pathologist
Speech Clinician   Language Therapist
Language Pathologist   Phoniatrist
Language Pathology   Logopedics
Logopedist

"or any similar titles" [B & P Code §§2538, 2530.3]

The name of an audiology corporation must include one of the following terms:

Audiologist   Hearing Clinic
Audiology   Hearing Clinician
Audiological   Hearing Therapist

"or any similar titles" [B & P Code §§2538, 2530.3]

Both audiology and speech pathology corporations shall include the word "corporation" or wording or abbreviations indicating corporate existence. [B & P Code §2538]

EXAMPLE: Jane Doet, Speech Pathology Corp., or Jane Doet, Audiology Corp.

WHO MAY BE SHAREHOLDERS, OFFICERS, DIRECTORS

Each shareholder, director, and officer of a speech pathology corporation or an audiology corporation, other than an assistant secretary and an assistant treasurer, shall be a licensed person; however, audiologists may be shareholders, officers, and directors in speech pathologist's corporations, and speech pathologists may be shareholders, officers and directors in audiology corporations. [B & P Code §2537.2; 16 Cal. Code of Regs. §1399.194; Corp. Code §13403; Corp. Code §13401.5]

Also, officers other than president and treasurer in a corporation with one shareholder may be non-licensed persons. [Corp. Code §13403] [See also Chapter 4(E).]

SHARE TRANSFER REQUIREMENTS

Shares: Ownership and Transfer

   (a) The shares of a speech pathology or audiology corporation may be issued only to a licensed person and may be transferred only to a licensed person or to the issuing corporation.

   (b) Where there are two or more shareholders in a speech pathology or audiology corporation and one of the shareholders:

       (1) Dies; or

       (2) Becomes a disqualified person as defined in 13401(d) of the Corporations Code, for a period exceeding ninety (90) days, his or her shares shall be sold and transferred to the corporation, its shareholders, or other eligible licensed persons, on such terms as are agreed upon. Such sale or transfer shall not be later than six (6) months after any such death and not later than ninety (90) days after the date the shareholder becomes a disqualified person.

(c) A corporation and its shareholders may, but need not, agree that shares sold to it by a person who becomes a disqualified person may be resold to such person if and when he or she again becomes qualified to be a shareholder.

(d) Nothing in these regulations shall be construed to prohibit a professional corporation from owning shares in a nonprofessional corporation or to prohibit a speech pathologist or audiologist from respectively owning shares in more than one speech pathology or audiology corporation.

(e) The restrictions of subdivision (a) and, if appropriate, subdivision (b) of this section shall be set forth in the corporation's Bylaws or Articles of Incorporation. [16 Cal. Code of Regs. §1399.195]

STOCK TRANSFER CERTIFICATE LEGEND

(f) The share certificates of a speech pathology or audiology corporation shall contain an appropriate legend setting forth the restrictions of subsection (a), and where applicable, the restrictions of subsection (b) [see above regulation]. [16 Cal. Code of Regs. §1399.195(c)]

REPORTING REQUIREMENTS

No report required.

MALPRACTICE SECURITY

Although §2539 of the B & P Code gives the committee the power to adopt regulations regarding security for claims, no such regulation appears.

Veterinary Corporations
Website: http://www.vmb.ca.gov

Note: Veterinarians may incorporate as professional corporations or as regular business corporations (see Chapter 2B).

STATUTES

Generally: B & P Code §§4800-4917; §§4910-4917 "Veterinary Corporations."

REGULATIONS

Generally: 16 Cal. Code of Regs. §§2000-2082; No regulations yet available for veterinary corporations.

LICENSING BOARD

Board of Examiners in Veterinary Medicine, 1420 Howe Avenue, Suite 6, Sacramento, CA 95825. 916-263-2610

CERTIFICATE OF REGISTRATION REQUIRED?

No. [Corp. Code §13401(b)]

Fee: Not applicable.

ADDRESS FOR APPLICATION FOR CERTIFICATE OF REGISTRATION

Not applicable.

RENEWAL OF CERTIFICATE OF REGISTRATION

Not applicable.

NAMES YOU CAN USE

The name of a veterinary corporation and any name or names under which it renders professional services shall include the words "veterinary corporation" or wording or abbreviations denoting corporate existence (e.g., Veterinary Professional Corporation, Veterinary Corp., Veterinary, Inc.). [B & P §4911]

EXAMPLE: Jane Doet, Veterinary Corp., or Jane Doet, Veterinary, Inc.

WHO MAY BE SHAREHOLDERS, OFFICERS, DIRECTORS

Each shareholder, director, and officer of a veterinary corporation shall be a licensed person, except that officers other than president and treasurer in a corporation with only one shareholder may be non-licensed persons. [See also Chapter 4(E).]

SHARE TRANSFER REQUIREMENTS AND SHARE TRANSFER CERTIFICATE LEGEND

Although B & P Code §4916 provides that the Board may adopt and enforce regulations requiring that the Bylaws of a veterinary corporation include a provision for transfer of stock of a disqualified or deceased person, there are no regulations at this time. Nor are there any statutes on stock transfer restrictions. Check with the Board (and see §13407 of the Corporations Code).

REPORTING REQUIREMENTS

Not required.

MALPRACTICE SECURITY

Although B & P Code §4916 empowers the Board to adopt rules and regulations including a requirement that each corporation provide adequate security by insurance or otherwise for claims against it by its patients arising out of the rendering of professional services, no such regulations have been published.

---

[1] The application form provides that if Certified Public Accountant or CPA is used in the corporate name, the ownership and transfer is restricted to CPAs *and* the Bylaws *and* the share certificates must read accordingly. As a result, such corporations will probably wish to substitute "CPA" for "licensed person" in these provisions. Also note: if you order one of the corporate kits shown at the back of the book, a legend restricting the transfer of shares to CPAs will be printed on your certificates if your corporate name includes either of these professional titles (see Chapter 6, Section E).

[2] The application form for issuance of a Certificate of Registration as a law corporation requires that two additional provisions be included in the Bylaws or Articles. One is a reference to the placing of the appropriate legend on the stock certificates setting forth the restrictions on ownership of shares (see the "Share Transfer Requirements" section above). The other refers to the prohibition of the distribution of income to a disqualified shareholder.

Thus you should include in your Bylaws or Articles the following two paragraphs, or something similar—see the application form and Rules IV(C)(4)(5):

The share certificates of this corporation must contain an appropriate legend setting forth the restrictions on ownership of shares contained in Article II of the Bylaws.

The income of this corporation attributable to its practice of law while a shareholder is a disqualified person shall not in any manner accrue to the benefit of such shareholder or his or her shares.

[3] Note that unlike the laws and regulations for the other professional corporations, the pharmacy law makes no reference to §13403 of the Corporations Code. Section 13403 says that if the corporation has only one shareholder, the shareholder need be the only director, and shall serve as President and Treasurer. The other officers need not be licensed. This omission might have been an oversight since the pharmacy law was passed in 1981 and no regulations have yet been issued. Be sure to check with the State Board of Pharmacy before you incorporate.

APPENDIX 5

How to use the forms CD-ROM

List of forms on CD-ROM

THE TEAR-OUT FORMS in Appendices 1–3 are included on a CD-ROM disk in the back of the book. This CD-ROM, which can be used with Windows computers, installs files that can be opened, printed and edited using a word processor or other software. It is NOT a stand-alone software program. Please read this Appendix and the README.TXT file included on the CD-ROM for instructions on using the forms CD.

Note to Mac users: This CD-ROM and its files should also work on a Macintosh and other operating systems. Please note, however, that Nolo cannot provide technical support for non-Windows users.

HOW TO VIEW THE README FILE

If you do not know how to view the file README.TXT, insert the forms CD-ROM into your computer's CD-ROM drive and follow these instructions:

- **Windows 95, 98 and 2000:** (1) On your PC's desktop, double-click the My Computer icon; (2) double-click the icon for the CD-ROM drive into which the forms CD-ROM was inserted; (3) double-click the file README.TXT.
- **Macintosh:** (1) On your Mac desktop, double-click the icon for the CD-ROM that you inserted; (2) double-click on the file README.TXT.

While the README file is open, print it out by using the Print command in the File menu.

A. Installing the Form Files Onto Your Computer

Word processing forms that you can open, complete, print and save with your word processing program (see Section B, below) are contained on the CD-ROM. Before you can do anything with the files on the CD-ROM, you need to install them onto your hard disk. In accordance with U.S. copyright laws, remember that copies of the CD-ROM and its files are for your personal use only.

Insert the forms CD-ROM and do the following:

1. Windows 95, 98 and 2000 Users

Follow the instructions that appear on the screen. (If nothing happens when you insert the forms CD-ROM, then (1) double-click the My Computer icon; (2) double-click the icon for the CD-ROM drive into which the forms CD-ROM was inserted; and (3) double click the file SETUP.HLP.)

By default, all the files are installed to the \Professional Corporation Forms folder in the \Program Files folder of your computer. A folder called "Professional Corporation Forms" is added to the "Programs" folder of the Start menu.

2. Macintosh Users

Step 1: If the "Professional Corporation CD" window is not open, open it by double-clicking the "Professional Corporation CD" icon.

Step 2: Select the "Professional Corporation Forms" folder icon.

Step 3: Drag and drop the folder icon onto the icon of your hard disk.

B. Using the Word Processing Files to Create Documents

This section concerns the files for forms that can be opened and edited with your word processing program. All forms and their filenames are listed at the end of this Appendix.

All word processing forms come in rich text format (these files have the extension .RTF). For example, the form for the Reservation Of Corporate Name Request discussed in Chapter 6 is on the file NAMERES.RTF. All forms and their file names are listed at the end of this Appendix.

RTF files can be read by most recent word processing programs including all versions of MS Word for Windows and Macintosh, WordPad for Windows 95, 98 and 2000, and recent versions of WordPerfect for Windows and Macintosh.

To use a form from the CD to create your documents you must: (1) open a file in your word processor or text editor; (2) edit the form by filling in the required information; (3) print it out; (4) rename and save your revised file.

The following are general instructions on how to do this. However, each word processor uses different commands to open, format, save and print documents. Please read your word processor's manual for specific instructions on performing these tasks.

DO NOT CALL NOLO'S TECHNICAL SUPPORT IF YOU HAVE QUESTIONS ON HOW TO USE YOUR WORD PROCESSOR.

Step 1: Opening a File

There are three ways to open the word processing files included on the CD-ROM after you have installed them onto your computer.

- Windows users can open a file by selecting its "shortcut" as follows: (1) Click the Windows "Start" button; (2) open the "Programs" folder; (3) open the "Professional Corporation Forms" subfolder; and (4) click on the shortcut to the form you want to work with.
- Both Windows and Macintosh users can open a file directly by double-clicking on it. Use My Computer or Windows Explorer (Windows 95, 98 and 2000) or the Finder (Macintosh) to go to the folder you installed or copied the CD-ROM's files to. Then, double-click on the specific file you want to open.

WHERE ARE THE FILES INSTALLED?

Windows Users
- RTF files are installed by default to a folder named \Professional Corporation Forms in the \Program Files folder of your computer.

Macintosh Users
- RTF files are located in the "Professional Corporation Forms" folder.

You can also open a file from within your word processor. To do this, you must first start your word processor. Then, go to the File menu and choose the Open command. This opens a dialog box where you will tell the program (1) the type of file you want to open (*.RTF); and (2) the location and name of the file (you will need to navigate through the directory tree to get to the folder on your hard disk where the CD's files have been installed). If these directions are unclear you will need to look through the manual for your word processing program—Nolo's technical support department will NOT be able to help you with the use of your word processing program.

Step 2: Editing Your Document

Fill in the appropriate information according to the instructions and sample agreements in the book. Underlines are used to indicate where you need to enter your information, frequently followed by instructions in brackets. *Be sure to delete the underlines and instructions from your edited document.* If you do not know how to use your word processor to edit a document, you will need to look through the manual for your word processing program—Nolo's technical support department will NOT be able to help you with the use of your word processing program.

EDITING FORMS THAT HAVE OPTIONAL OR ALTERNATIVE TEXT

Some of the forms have optional or alternate text:

- With optional text, you choose whether to include or exclude the given text.
- With alternative text, you select one alternative to include and exclude the other alternatives.

When editing these forms, we suggest you do the following:

Optional text

If you **don't want** to include optional text, just delete it from your document.

If you **do want** to include optional text, just leave it in your document.

In either case, delete the italicized instructions.

Alternative text

First delete all the alternatives that you do not want to include, then delete the italicized instructions.

Step 3: Printing Out the Document

Use your word processor's or text editor's "Print" command to print out your document. If you do not know how to use your word processor to print a document, you will need to look through the manual for your word processing program—Nolo's technical support department will NOT be able to help you with the use of your word processing program.

Step 4: Saving Your Document

After filling in the form, use the "Save As" command to save and rename the file because all the files are "read-only" and you will not be able to use the "Save" command. This is for your protection. IF YOU SAVE THE FILE WITHOUT RENAMING IT, THE UNDERLINES THAT INDICATE WHERE YOU NEED TO ENTER YOUR INFORMATION WILL BE LOST AND YOU WILL NOT BE ABLE TO CREATE A NEW DOCUMENT WITH THIS FILE WITHOUT RECOPYING THE ORIGINAL FILE FROM THE CD-ROM.

If you do not know how to use your word processor to save a document, you will need to look through the manual for your word processing program—Nolo's technical support department will NOT be able to help you with the use of your word processing program.

Forms on CD-ROM

File name	Form name
ARTICLES	Articles of Incorporation
MINUTES	Waiver of Notice and Consent to Holding of First Meeting of Board of Directors
RECEIPTS	Receipt for Cash Payment for Shares
	Acknowledgment of Cancellation of Indebtedness
	Bill of Sale for Assets of a Business
	Bill of Sale for Items of Property
	Acknowledgment of Share Issuance for Labor Done or Services Rendered
BYLAWS	Bylaws
COVERLET	Cover Letter to Secretary of State
NAMECHEK	Name Availability Request
NAMERES	Reservation of Corporate Name Request ■

INDEX

A

Accountants, 2/1, 3/3, 3/18, 4/6, 6/11
    consulting with, 6/1, 8/2–3
    and registered limited liability partnerships (RLLPs),
        1/2, 3/2
Accounting Period Resolution, 6/14
Accumulated earnings credit, 3/18–19
Acknowledgment of Cancellation of Indebtedness, 6/20,
    6/22-23
Acknowledgment of Share Issuance for Labor Done or
    Services Rendered, 6/28
Actuarial science services corporations, 3/3
Acupuncturists, 2/1, 4/5-6
Annual meetings, 6/12
Annual reports, 4/6
Annual Statement of Domestic Stock Corporation, 7/1
Annual Wage and Tax Statement, 7/6, 7/10
Apparent authority, 1/9
Appreciated assets
    and notes from corporation, 3/33
    taxation of gains from, 3/8, 3/21
Architects, 2/1, 3/2, 3/3, 3/18, 4/5-6, 6/10
Articles of Incorporation, 3/16, 6/1, 6/16, Appendix 1
    amendment of, 1/10
    copies, 6/7, 6/8
    and corporate name, 6/2, 6/4
    delayed filing, 6/8, 7/8
    filing, 6/7–9
    preparation, 6/4–7
    sample, 6/5–6
    sample cover letter, 6/8
    wait time, 6/9
Articles Resolution, 6/13
Assistant officers, 4/5

Attorneys. *See* Lawyers
Audiologists, 2/1, 4/3, 4/5-6

B

Bank Account Resolution, 6/14
Basis, of property, 3/31, 3/32, 3/35
Benefits. *See* Fringe benefits; Retirement plans
Bill of Sale
    for assets of a business, 6/17, 6/24–25
    for items of property, 6/26–27
Board of directors, first meeting of, 6/12–18
    See also Directors
Bonds, 3/8
Bonuses, 3/4
Borrowing funds, 3/8
    under corporate pension and profit sharing plans,
        3/9, 3/23, 5/3, 5/5–6
    from Keogh plans, 5/5-6
    See also Loans
Bulk Sales Law, 3/36, 6/17, 6/18-19
Business structures compared, 1/1–4
"Buy-out" provisions, 6/7
Bylaws, 6/1, Appendix 2
    preparation, 6/10-12
Bylaws Resolution, 6/13

C

Cafeteria plans, 5/6–7
California Administrative Code, 4/1, 6/14
California Board of Equalization, 7/11
California Bulk Sales Law, 3/36, 6/17, 6/18-19

California Business and Professions Code, 2/3, 4/1, 7/2

California Corporate Franchise tax. *See* Franchise tax

California Corporations Code, 8/2

>   apparent authority, 1/9
>
>   corporate actions benefiting directors, 1/7-8
>
>   corporate acts requiring shareholder approval, 1/10
>
>   corporate powers, 1/5
>
>   delayed filing dates for Articles of Incorporation, 6/8
>
>   directors' duties, 1/6-8
>
>   dissolution procedures, 3/37
>
>   dividend payments, 3/29
>
>   executive committees, 1/6
>
>   immunity and indemnification provisions, 1/10
>
>   labor done vs. services rendered, 6/15
>
>   names for professional corporations, 4/2, 6/2
>
>   number of directors required, 4/4
>
>   officer requirements, 4/3–5
>
>   sale or transfer of shares, 4/5
>
>   share ownership in professional corporations, 4/3
>
>   stock qualification, 4/7

California Department of Commerce, 7/3-4

California Department of Consumer Affairs, 4/1–2

California Employment Development Department (EDD), 7/9, 7/10

California Franchise Tax Board, 3/1, 3/37

California General Corporation Law, I/1, 2/3, 4/4–5

California S corporation tax election, 3/4–6

California Secretary of State

>   Articles of Incorporation, Appendix 1
>
>   contact information, 3/37, 6/1, 6/2, Appendix 1
>
>   corporate name requests, 6/2–4, Appendix 1

California Tax Form 100, 7/9

California Tax Form DE-3, 7/10

California Tax Form DE-4, 7/9

California Tax Form DE-43, 7/10

California Unemployment Insurance Code, 7/9

Capitalization, 3/13–16

Cash payment, for stock, 6/14, 6/16, 6/20, 6/22–23

C corporations, 1/1

CD-ROM forms disc, Appendix 5

Certificate of registration, 4/2, 6/28–29

Chiropractors, 2/1, 4/3

Clinical social workers, 2/1, 4/3, 4/5-6

Close corporations, 1/5, 3/28

Community property, and stock ownership, 6/19

Compensation

>   of directors, 1/7
>
>   of officers, 1/9, 6/17
>
>   of shareholder-employees, 3/4, 3/18

Compensation for Officers Resolution, 6/17

Consulting services corporations, 3/3, 3/5, 3/18

Corporate franchise tax. *See* Franchise tax

Corporate income tax. *See* Income tax

Corporate people, 1/5-11

>   *See also* Directors; Incorporators; Officers; Shareholders

Corporate powers, 1/5

Corporate records book, 6/10, 6/18

Corporate seal, 6/9-10

Corporate Seal Resolution, 6/13

Corporations

>   characteristics and types, 1/3–5
>
>   disadvantages of, 3/12–13
>
>   dissolution of, 3/36–37
>
>   and fringe benefits, 3/9–10
>
>   as legal entities, 1/3
>
>   and limited liability, 1/3, 3/1–2
>
>   order and formality of, 3/10
>
>   perpetual existence of, 1/3, 3/11
>
>   piercing the corporate veil, 3/16–17
>
>   recordkeeping, 3/12, 3/13
>
>   and taxes, 1/3, 1/4, 3/3–9, 3/11, 3/18–19. *See also* Tax headings
>
>   *See also* specific types of corporations

D

Death

>   and continuation of business, 1/3, 3/11
>
>   of shareholders in professional corporations, 3/11, 4/5

Death benefits, 3/10, 3/22

Debentures, 3/8

Debt capital, vs. equity capital, 3/14–15

Debt to equity ratios, 3/15

Deeds transfers, resources, 6/26

Deficiency dividends, 3/20

Defined benefit plans, 3/9, 5/3, 5/4

Defined contribution plans, 5/3, 5/4-5

Dentists, 2/1, 3/5, 4/3, 4/6

Depositing taxes, 7/6, 7/8

Directors, 1/6–8

    annual meeting of, 6/12

    corporate decisions benefiting, 1/6–8

    first meeting of, 6/12–18

    immunity and indemnification of, 1/10

    number required, 4/4

    in professional corporations, 4/3-4

    special unemployment and disability insurance rules, 7/10

    and workers' compensation coverage, 7/11

Disability insurance, 3/10, 7/10

Dissolution of corporation, 3/36–37

Dividend income, reporting, 7/7-8

Dividends

    deficiency dividends, 3/20

    and directors of professional corporations, 1/9

    dividend treatment of excessive salaries, 3/18

    double taxation of, 3/3–4

    restrictions on payment of, 3/29

Doctors, 2/1, 3/5

    See also Medical corporations

Domestic corporations, 1/4

Domestic Stock Corporation Statement, 7/1

Double taxation, 3/3–4, 3/6

E

EDD (Employment Development Department), 7/9, 7/10

Election of Officers Resolution, 6/13

Employee benefits. *See* Fringe benefits; Retirement plans

Employee-owner, IRS definition of, 3/26

Employee stock ownership plans, 3/23

Employee's Withholding Exemption Certificate, 7/5

Employer Identification Number, 7/5

Employer registration forms, 7/9

Employment contracts, 3/17, 3/18

Employment taxes

    California, 7/9

    federal, 7/5–6

    resources, 7/2

Engineering corporations, 3/3

Entity Classification Election, 3/6

Equity capital, vs. debt capital, 3/14–15

Estimated tax payments

    California, 3/4

    federal, 7/7-8

Executive committees, 1/6

Exempt Sale of Common Stock Under 10 California Administrative Code Resolution, 6/14

F

Federal Employer Identification Number (FEIN), 7/5

Federal S Corporation Tax Treatment Resolution, 6/17

Federal Unemployment Tax (FUTA), 7/6-7

FICA tax. *See* Social Security tax

Fictitious Business Name Statement, 7/2–3

Fictitious corporate names, 4/3, 6/4

Fiduciaries of the corporation, 1/6, 1/7, 1/8–9, 1/10

"52-53 week" tax year, 3/25

Filing fees, 3/12, 6/1

Financial advice, 8/2–3

Fiscal year, 3/11, 3/23, 3/26, 3/27

"500 series" securities rules, 4/8

Foreign corporations, 1/4

Forms disc, how to use, Appendix 5

401(k) plans, 5/2, 5/6-7

Franchise tax, 3/4

    annual tax return, 7/9

    delaying payment, 3/4, 7/8

    estimated tax return, 7/8–9

    minimum payments, 3/4, 3/12

    and S corporations, 3/5

Fringe benefits, 1/3, 3/4, 3/9–10

    cafeteria plans, 5/6–7

    IRS publications, 5/1

    restrictions for S corporations, 3/6, 3/10, 3/22

    See also Retirement plans

FUTA tax, 7/6-7

G

General Corporation Law, I/1, 2/3, 4/4–5

General Utilities doctrine, repeal of, 3/8

Guarantees, of director and officer obligations, 1/8, 1/9

H

Health clubs, 3/5

Health insurance, 3/10, 3/22

Health services corporations, 3/3, 3/5, 3/18
  See also Medical corporations; specific medical pro-
    fessions

I

Immunity and indemnification, 1/8, 1/9, 1/10, 6/11
Income, reallocation of, 3/17
Income splitting, 3/6
Income tax, 3/3–6
  California corporate. *See* Franchise tax
  California personal, 7/9, 7/10
  deferral of, via fiscal tax year election, 3/11, 3/26,
    3/27
  federal corporate, 3/3, 7/7-8
  federal individual, 3/3–4, 7/5-6
  individual and corporate rates and payments com-
    pared, 3/6–7
Incorporation
  advantages, 2/2
  capitalization, 3/13–16
  costs, I/1, 3/12–13, 6/7–8
  of preexisting business. *See* Preexisting businesses
  See also Corporations
Incorporators, 1/6
Indemnification and immunity, 1/8, 1/9, 1/10, 6/11
Independent contractors, 7/5, 7/9
Individual Retirement Arrangements (IRAs), 5/2
Insurance
  California unemployment and disability, 7/10
  as fringe benefit, 3/10
  malpractice, 3/2, 4/5-6, 7/12
  personal liability coverage for directors or officers,
    1/8, 1/9
  private commercial coverage, 7/12
  workers' compensation, 7/11
Internal Revenue Code. *See* IRC
Internal Revenue Service. *See* IRS
Intrastate offering exemption, 4/7–8
IRAs (Individual Retirement Arrangements), 5/2
IRC
  Section 248 (deduction of organization expenses),
    6/17–18
  Section 269A restrictions, 3/17
  Section 351, 3/30–33, 3/35–36
  Section 444 rules, 3/27

  Section 448(d)(2) (flat tax rate for personal service
    corporations), 3/3, 3/5
  Section 469 (material participation rules), 3/23
  Section 535(c)(2)(B) (accumulated earnings credit),
    3/18–19
  Section 543(a)(7) (personal service contract income),
    3/19
  Section 1244 stock, 3/29–30
IRS
  dividend treatment of excessive salaries paid to
    shareholder-employees, 3/18
  and income tax deferral, 3/11
  online address for forms requests, 7/2
  phone number for forms requests, 7/2
  retirement/benefit plan qualification, 5/7
  unpaid taxes and limited liability, 3/1
  See also Tax headings
IRS Form 940, 7/7
IRS Form 941, 7/6
IRS Form 1040, 7/7-8
IRS Form 1040, Schedule E, 7/7-8
IRS Form 1120, 7/7
IRS Form 1128, 3/27
IRS Form 2553, 3/24, 7/4-5
IRS Form 8832, 3/6
IRS Form SS-4, 7/5
IRS Form W-2, 7/6
IRS Form W-3, 7/6
IRS Form W-4, 7/5, 7/9
IRS publications, 7/2
  IRAs, 5/2
  Keogh plans, 5/2-3
  retirement plans, 5/1
  S corporations, 3/20

J

Joint ownership of stock, 6/19

K

Keogh plans, 3/9, 5/1, 5/2-3, 5/4, 5/5-6
Key employees, top-heavy retirement plans, 5/6

L

Law corporations, 3/3, 3/18, 4/3, 4/6, 6/11
Law libraries, 8/2
Lawyers, I/1, 2/1, 3/2
    and registered limited liability partnerships, 1/2
    selecting and consulting with, 6/1, 8/1–2
Leases, transferring to corporation, 6/25
Legal research, 8/2
Legal services group plans, 3/10
Liabilities of preexisting business, assumption by
    corporation, 3/33, 3/34–35, 3/36
Liability
    of corporation, for acts of officers, 1/9
    for malpractice, 1/2, 1/3, 1/10, 3/2, 4/5-6, 5/1
    and nonprofit corporations, 1/4–5
    of partners, 1/2
    of shareholders, 1/3, 3/13
    of sole proprietors, 1/1
    See also Limited liability; Personal liability
Licensing, 4/1–2
    state requirements, resources, 7/3-4
Life insurance, 3/10, 3/22
Limited liability, 1/3, 3/1–2
    and professional corporations, 2/2, 3/2
    registered limited liability partnerships, 1/2, 2/1, 3/2,
      3/6
    See also Liability; Personal liability
Limited liability companies (LLCs), 1/2, 3/6
Limited partnerships, 1/2
Liquidation of assets, taxation of gains, 3/8
LLCs. See Limited liability companies
Loans
    cancellation of, in return for stock, 6/16, 6/26–27
    as capital for corporation, 3/14–15, 3/16
    to directors, 1/8
    to officers, 1/9
    and securities law, 3/16
    See also Borrowing funds; Promissory notes
Losses
    and S corporations, 3/6, 3/20–21, 3/22
    Section 1244 treatment for stock losses, 3/29–30
    and transfer of assets to corporation, 3/35–36

M

Malpractice
    indirect participation in, 3/2
    liability for, 1/2, 1/3, 1/10, 3/2, 4/5-6, 5/1
    required security for claims, 4/5-6
Marriage, family, and child counselors, 2/1, 4/3, 4/5-6
Married shareholders, and taking title to stock, 6/19
Material participation, 3/22, 3/23
Medical corporations, 4/3, 6/11
    See also Health services corporations; Specific medi-
      cal professions
Meetings, 3/16–17, 6/12
    first board of directors meeting, 6/12–18
Minutes, of first meeting of board of directors, 6/13–18
Money-purchase pension plans, 5/4–5
Mortgages, and property transfers to corporations, 6/26
Moscone-Knox Professional Corporation Act, I/1, 2/3

N

Names for professional corporations, 4/2–3, 6/2–4
    availability and reservation requests, 6/2–4,
      Appendix 1
    Fictitious Business Name Statement, 7/2–3
    rules for specific professions, Appendix 4
Non-calendar tax year. See Fiscal year
Nonprofit corporations, 1/4–5
Nonpublic offering exemption, 4/7
Non-stock corporations, 1/4
Notes. See Promissory notes
Notice of Sales of Securities, 4/8
Nurses, 2/1, 3/5, 4/3, 4/5-6, 6/10

O

Officers, 1/8–10, 4/3–5
    Compensation for Officers Resolution, 6/17
    special unemployment and disability insurance rules,
      7/10
    and workers' compensation coverage, 7/11
One-shareholder professional corporations, 4/4–5, 7/10
Optometrists, 2/1, 4/2, 4/3, 4/6
Ordinary loss treatment for stock losses, 3/29–30

Organization expenses, resolution for payment and
     deduction of, 6/17–18
Osteopaths, 2/1, 4/3, 4/6

P

Partnerships, 1/1–2, 1/3, 3/6, 5/3
     compared to S corporations, 3/25
     dissolution of, 7/4
     of incorporated professionals, 2/2, 3/2
     resources, 1/3
     See also Registered limited liability partnerships
Passive income sources, 3/19
Payment and Deduction of Organization Expenses
     Resolution, 6/17–18
Pension plans. SeeRetirement plans
Performing arts corporations, 3/3
Perpetual existence of corporations, 1/3, 3/11
Personal holding company penalty tax, 3/19–20
Personal liability, 1/1, 1/2
     of directors, 1/8, 1/10
     for liabilities of prior business, 3/36
     of promoters, 1/6
     of shareholders in undercapitalized corporations,
          3/13
     and signing of corporate documents, 6/29
     See also Liability; Limited liability
Personal service contracts, 3/19
Personal service corporations
     federal corporate tax rate, 3/3, 3/5
     IRC Section 269A restrictions, 3/17
     IRS definition of, 3/26
     tax year rules, 3/11, 3/26, 3/27
Pharmacists, 2/1, 4/5-6, 6/10
Pharmacy Corporation Law, 4/5
Physical therapists, 2/1, 4/3, 4/5-6
Physicians, 2/1, 3/5
     See also Medical corporations
Physicians' assistants, 2/1, 4/3, 4/5-6, 6/10
Piercing the corporate veil, 3/16–17
Podiatrists, 2/1, 4/3
Preexisting businesses
     dissolving, 7/3-4
     incorporating, 3/21, 3/34–36, 6/18-19
     stock issuance in return for assets of, 3/33, 6/16,
          6/17, 6/23–25

Principal Executive Office Resolution, 6/14
Professional boards, 4/1–2
     and annual reports, 4/6
     and certificates of registration, 4/2, 6/28–29
     and fictitious names, 4/3, 7/2, Appendix 4
     and officer positions, 4/3–5
     and security for malpractice claims, 4/5-6
     and stock certificates, 6/10
Professional Corporation Act, 4/4
Professional corporations, 1/5
     advantages of, 2/2
     and death of shareholders, 3/11, 4/5
     directors and officers in, 4/3–5
     legal address, 6/11
     and limited liability, 2/2, 3/2
     names for, 4/2–3, 6/2–4
     as partners, 2/2, 3/2
     required annual reports, 4/6
     required security for malpractice, 4/5-6
     restrictions on corporate powers, 1/5
     restrictions on share ownership, 3/11, 3/28, 4/5
     shareholders in, 3/11, 4/3
     special provisions for specific professions,
          Appendix 4
     state licensing board requirements, 3/12, 4/2
     stock qualification exemption, 4/7
     transferring shares, 4/5
     See also Corporations; Personal service corporations;
          specific professions
Professions permitted to incorporate as regular business
     corporations or professional corporations, 2/1
Professions permitted to use fictitious corporate names,
     4/3
Professions required to incorporate as professional
     corporations, 2/1
Profit sharing plans, 5/5
Promissory notes, 3/8, 3/14, 3/15, 3/16
     stock issuance in exchange for, 3/33, 6/16
Promoters, 1/6
Property taxes, Proposition 13 reassessments, 6/26
Property transfers, 3/34
     in exchange for stock, 3/30–33, 6/14-15, 6/16,
          6/26–27
     resources, 6/26
     tax implications, 3/30–36
Proposition 13 tax reassessments, 6/26
Psychologists, 2/1, 4/3, 4/5-6

Q

Quorum rules, 6/12

R

Reallocation of income, 3/17

Real property, transferring to corporation, 3/30–31, 3/34, 6/26

Receipt for Cash Payment for Shares, 6/22

Recordkeeping, 3/12, 3/13
    corporate records book, 6/10, 6/18

Registered limited liability partnerships (RLLPs), 1/2, 2/1, 3/2, 3/6

Rental property, corporation as new tenant, 6/26

Reservation of Corporate Name Request, 6/3, Appendix 1

Resolutions, at first board meeting, 6/13–18

Retirement plans, 3/9, 3/12, 5/1–7
    borrowing from, 3/9, 3/23, 5/3, 5/5–6
    corporate plan types, 5/3–5
    custodial vs. trustee plans, 5/7
    401(k) plans, 5/2, 5/6-7
    Individual Retirement Arrangements (IRAs), 5/2
    IRS publications, 5/1, 5/2, 5/3
    IRS qualification, 5/7
    Keogh plans, 3/9, 5/1, 5/2-3, 5/4, 5/5-6
    Roth IRAs, 5/2
    S corporation restrictions, 3/23
    SEP (Simplified Employee Pension) plans, 5/3
    SIMPLE plans, 5/2
    top-heavy plans, 5/3, 5/6

Right of first refusal, 1/7

RLLPs. See Registered limited liability partnerships

Roth IRAs, 5/2

S

Salaries, of shareholder-employees, 3/4, 3/18

Sale and Issuance of Capital Stock Resolution, 6/14

Sales and use tax, 7/11

S corporations, 1/1, 3/6, 3/20–25
    and accumulated earnings credit, 3/18
    California election, 3/4–6
    compared to partnerships, 3/25
    federal election, 3/24, 7/4-5

    Federal S Corporation Tax Treatment Resolution, 6/17
    and pass-through of losses, 3/6, 3/20–21, 3/22
    pros and cons, 3/20–23
    qualification requirements, 3/24
    required tax return filing, 7/7
    restrictions on fringe benefits, 3/6, 3/10, 3/22
    revocation or termination of S corporation status, 3/24–25
    and taxability of gains from appreciated assets, 3/8, 3/21
    tax advantages, 3/7–8
    tax year rules, 3/23, 3/26, 3/27

SEC. See Securities and Exchange Commission

Secretary of State. See California Secretary of State

Section 351 tax-free exchange treatment, 3/30–33, 3/35–36

Section 444 rules, 3/27

Section 1244 Stock Resolution, 6/18

Section 1244 stock treatment, 3/29–30

Securities Act of 1933, 4/7

Securities and Exchange Commission (SEC), 4/7–8

Securities law
    and debt capitalization, 3/16
    federal, and initial stock offerings, 4/7–8

Self-employment tax, 3/20
    See also Social Security tax

Seller's Permit, 7/11

SEP (Simplified Employee Pension) plans, 5/3

Service mark searches, 6/4

Services, stock issuance in exchange for, 3/32–33, 6/16, 6/27–28

Shareholder-employees
    dividend treatment of excessive salaries, 3/18
    employment contracts for, 3/17, 3/18

Shareholders, 1/10-11
    annual meeting of, 6/12
    approval of transactions benefiting directors, 1/8, 1/10
    married, and taking title to stock, 6/19
    in professional corporations, 3/11, 4/3
    reporting of dividend and employment income, 7/7-8
    rights of, 1/10-11
    special unemployment and disability insurance rules, 7/10
    of undercapitalized corporations, personal liability, 3/13

Shareholders' agreements, 3/28

Shareholder's derivative suit, 1/11

Shares of stock. *See* Stock

Shorthand reporters, 2/1, 4/5-6

Sick pay, 3/10

Signing of corporate documents, 6/29

SIMPLE plans, 5/2

Small business corporation, defined, 3/30

Social Security tax, 3/8, 3/12, 7/5-6

    See also Self-employment tax

Sole proprietorships, 1/1, 1/3, 3/6, 5/3

Spas, 3/5

Speech pathologists, 2/1, 4/3, 4/5-6

State Board of Equalization, 7/11

State licensing boards. *See* Professional boards

State Withholding Allowance Certificate, 7/9

Stock

    Exempt Sale of Common Stock Resolution, 6/14

    number of shares authorized, 6/16

    sale of, 3/28

    Section 1244 Resolution, 6/18

    Section 1244 treatment, 3/29–30

    taking title to, 6/19

    transfers of, 3/28, 4/5, 6/7

Stock bonus and ownership plans, 3/23

Stock Certificate Resolution, 6/13

Stock certificates, 6/10

    distributing, 6/20, 6/22–28

    filling out, 6/19-20

    sample, 6/21

Stock corporations, 1/4

Stock issuance, 6/18–28

    for assets of preexisting business, 3/33, 3/34, 6/16,
       6/17, 6/23–25

    for cash, 6/14, 6/16, 6/20, 6/22–23

    for future services, 6/16

    for indebtedness canceled, 6/15, 6/16, 6/20, 6/22–23

    initial offering exemptions, 4/7–8

    for labor done or services rendered, 3/32–33,
       6/15-16, 6/27–28

    for promissory notes, 3/33, 6/16

    for property received, 3/30–33, 6/14-15, 6/16,
       6/26–27

    Sale and Issuance of Capital Stock Resolution, 6/16

Stock qualification exemption, 4/7

Targeted benefit pension plans, 5/5

Taxes and taxation

    accumulated earnings credit, 3/18–19

    California corporate franchise tax. *See* Franchise tax

    and corporations, 1/3, 1/4, 3/3–9, 3/11, 3/18–19

    election of corporate tax treatment by non-corpora-
       tions, 3/6

    employment. *See* Employment taxes

    of gains from appreciated assets, 3/8, 3/21

    of gains from liquidation of a corporation, 3/8

    income tax. *See* Income tax

    and limited liability companies, 1/2, 3/6

    and nonprofit corporations, 1/4

    and partnerships, 1/2, 1/3, 3/6, 3/25

    personal holding company penalty tax, 3/19–20

    Proposition 13 property tax reassessment, 6/26

    and registered limited liability companies, 1/2, 3/6

    sales and use tax, 7/11

    and S corporations. *See* S corporations

    Section 1244 treatment of stock losses, 3/29–30

    self-employment tax, 3/20

    Social Security tax, 3/8, 3/12, 7/5-6

    and sole proprietorships, 1/1, 1/3, 3/6

    tax advantages of debt capital, 3/15

    unpaid, and limited liability, 3/1

    See also IRC; IRS

Tax forms

    California, 7/8–11

    federal, 7/4–8

    See also California Tax Forms; IRS Forms

Tax-free exchange treatment, 3/30–33, 3/35–36

Tax rates

    California corporate franchise tax, 3/4, 3/5

    federal corporate income tax, 3/3, 3/5

    individual and corporate compared, 3/6–7

Tax Reform Act, 5/1

Tax year, 3/23, 3/25–27, 6/14

    and deferral of income tax, 3/11, 3/26, 3/27

Top-heavy retirement plans, 5/3, 5/6

Trademark/trade name searches, 6/4

Transmittal of Income and Tax Statements, 7/6

25test, for fiscal tax year election, 3/27

Two-shareholder professional corporations, 4/5

U

Unemployment insurance, California, 7/10
Unemployment tax, federal, 7/6-7
U.S. Department of Labor, 5/5-6
U.S. Patent and Trademark Office, website, 6/4

V

Veterinarians, 2/1, 4/5-6, 6/10
Voting rules, 6/12

W

Wage and Tax Statement, 7/6, 7/10
Waiver of Notice and Consent to Holding of First Meeting
    of Board of Directors, 6/13
Withholding of taxes, 7/5-6, 7/9, 7/10
Withholding Returns
    California, 7/10
    federal, 7/6
Workers' compensation insurance, 7/11

CATALOG

...more from Nolo

	PRICE	CODE

BUSINESS

Avoid Employee Lawsuits (Quick & Legal Series)	$24.95	AVEL
⊙ The CA Nonprofit Corporation Kit (Binder w/CD-ROM)	$49.95	CNP
▣ Consultant & Independent Contractor Agreements (Book w/Disk—PC)	$24.95	CICA
▣ The Corporate Minutes Book (Book w/Disk—PC)	$69.95	CORMI
The Employer's Legal Handbook	$39.95	EMPL
Firing Without Fear (Quick & Legal Series)	$29.95	FEAR
▣ Form Your Own Limited Liability Company (Book w/Disk—PC)	$44.95	LIAB
▣ Hiring Independent Contractors: The Employer's Legal Guide (Book w/Disk—PC)	$34.95	HICI
▣ How to Create a Buy-Sell Agreement & Control the Destiny of your Small Business (Book w/Disk—PC)	$49.95	BSAG
▣ How to Form a California Professional Corporation (Book w/Disk—PC)	$49.95	PROF
▣ How to Form a Nonprofit Corporation (Book w/Disk —PC)—National Edition	$44.95	NNP
⊙ How to Form a Nonprofit Corporation in California (Book w/CD-ROM)	$44.95	NON
▣ How to Form Your Own California Corporation (Binder w/Disk—PC)	$39.95	CACI
▣ How to Form Your Own California Corporation (Book w/Disk—PC)	$39.95	CCOR
▣ How to Form Your Own New York Corporation (Book w/Disk—PC)	$39.95	NYCO
⊙ How to Form Your Own Texas Corporation (Book w/CD-ROM)	$39.95	TCOR
How to Write a Business Plan	$29.95	SBS
The Independent Paralegal's Handbook	$29.95	PARA
Leasing Space for Your Small Business	$34.95	LESP
Legal Guide for Starting & Running a Small Business, Vol. 1	$29.95	RUNS
▣ Legal Guide for Starting & Running a Small Business, Vol. 2: Legal Forms (Book w/Disk—PC)	$29.95	RUNS2
Marketing Without Advertising	$22.00	MWAD
▣ Music Law (Book w/Disk—PC)	$29.95	ML
Nolo's California Quick Corp (Quick & Legal Series)	$19.95	QINC
Nolo's Guide to Social Security Disability	$29.95	QSS
Nolo's Quick LLC (Quick & Legal Series)	$24.95	LLCQ

▣ Book with disk
⊙ Book with CD-ROM

		PRICE	CODE
⊙	Open Your California Business in 24 Hours (Book w/CD-ROM)	$24.95	OPEN
▣	The Partnership Book: How to Write a Partnership Agreement (Book w/Disk—PC)	$39.95	PART
	Sexual Harassment on the Job	$24.95	HARS
	Starting & Running a Successful Newsletter or Magazine	$29.95	MAG
	Tax Savvy for Small Business	$34.95	SAVVY
	Wage Slave No More: Law & Taxes for the Self-Employed	$24.95	WAGE
▣	Your Limited Liability Company: An Operating Manual (Book w/Disk—PC)	$49.95	LOP
	Your Rights in the Workplace	$29.95	YRW

CONSUMER

Fed Up with the Legal System: What's Wrong & How to Fix It	$9.95	LEG
How to Win Your Personal Injury Claim	$29.95	PICL
Nolo's Everyday Law Book	$24.95	EVL
Nolo's Pocket Guide to California Law	$15.95	CLAW
Trouble-Free Travel...And What to Do When Things Go Wrong	$14.95	TRAV

ESTATE PLANNING & PROBATE

	8 Ways to Avoid Probate (Quick & Legal Series)	$16.95	PRO8
	9 Ways to Avoid Estate Taxes (Quick & Legal Series)	$24.95	ESTX
	Estate Planning Basics (Quick & Legal Series)	$18.95	ESPN
	How to Probate an Estate in California	$39.95	PAE
⊙	Make Your Own Living Trust (Book w/CD-ROM)	$34.95	LITR
	Nolo's Law Form Kit: Wills	$24.95	KWL
▣	Nolo's Will Book (Book w/Disk—PC)	$34.95	SWIL
	Plan Your Estate	$39.95	NEST
	Quick & Legal Will Book (Quick & Legal Series)	$21.95	QUIC

FAMILY MATTERS

Child Custody: Building Parenting Agreements That Work	$29.95	CUST
Child Support in California: Go to Court to Get More or Pay Less (Quick & Legal Series)	$24.95	CHLD
The Complete IEP Guide	$24.95	IEP

▣ Book with disk
⊙ Book with CD-ROM

	PRICE	CODE
Divorce & Money: How to Make the Best Financial Decisions During Divorce	$34.95	DIMO
Do Your Own Divorce in Oregon	$29.95	ODIV
Get a Life: You Don't Need a Million to Retire Well	$24.95	LIFE
The Guardianship Book for California	$34.95	GB
⦿ How to Adopt Your Stepchild in California (Book w/CD-ROM)	$34.95	ADOP
A Legal Guide for Lesbian and Gay Couples	$25.95	LG
⦿ The Living Together Kit (Book w/CD-ROM)	$34.95	LTK
Nolo's Pocket Guide to Family Law	$14.95	FLD
Using Divorce Mediation: Save Your Money & Your Sanity	$21.95	UDMD

GOING TO COURT

	PRICE	CODE
Beat Your Ticket: Go To Court and Win! (National Edition)	$19.95	BEYT
The Criminal Law Handbook: Know Your Rights, Survive the System	$29.95	KYR
Everybody's Guide to Small Claims Court (National Edition)	$18.95	NSCC
Everybody's Guide to Small Claims Court in California	$24.95	CSCC
Fight Your Ticket ... and Win! (California Edition)	$24.95	FYT
How to Change Your Name in California	$34.95	NAME
How to Collect When You Win a Lawsuit (California Edition)	$29.95	JUDG
How to Mediate Your Dispute	$18.95	MEDI
How to Seal Your Juvenile & Criminal Records (California Edition)	$34.95	CRIM
Mad at Your Lawyer	$21.95	MAD
Nolo's Deposition Handbook	$29.95	DEP
Represent Yourself in Court: How to Prepare & Try a Winning Case	$29.95	RYC

HOMEOWNERS, LANDLORDS & TENANTS

	PRICE	CODE
California Tenants' Rights	$24.95	CTEN
▣ Contractors' and Homeowners' Guide to Mechanics' Liens (Book w/Disk—PC)—California Edition	$39.95	MIEN
The Deeds Book (California Edition)	$24.95	DEED
Dog Law	$14.95	DOG
⦿ Every Landlord's Legal Guide (National Edition, Book w/CD-ROM)	$44.95	ELLI

▣ Book with disk
⦿ Book with CD-ROM

		PRICE	CODE
	Every Tenant's Legal Guide	$26.95	EVTEN
	For Sale by Owner in California	$29.95	FSBO
	How to Buy a House in California	$29.95	BHCA
	The Landlord's Law Book, Vol. 1: Rights & Responsibilities (California Edition)	$44.95	LBRT
⊙	The California Landlord's Law Book, Vol. 2: Evictions (Book w/CD-ROM)	$44.95	LBEV
	Leases & Rental Agreements (Quick & Legal Series)	$24.95	LEAR
	Neighbor Law: Fences, Trees, Boundaries & Noise	$24.95	NEI
⊙	The New York Landlord's Law Book (Book w/CD-ROM)	$39.95	NYLL
	Renters' Rights (National Edition—Quick & Legal Series)	$19.95	RENT
	Stop Foreclosure Now in California	$34.95	CLOS

HUMOR

29 Reasons Not to Go to Law School		$12.95	29R
Poetic Justice		$9.95	PJ

IMMIGRATION

How to Get a Green Card		$29.95	GRN
U.S. Immigration Made Easy		$44.95	IMEZ

MONEY MATTERS

▫	101 Law Forms for Personal Use (Quick & Legal Series, Book w/Disk—PC)	$29.95	SPOT
	Bankruptcy: Is It the Right Solution to Your Debt Problems? (Quick & Legal Series)	$19.95	BRS
	Chapter 13 Bankruptcy: Repay Your Debts	$29.95	CH13
▫	Credit Repair (Quick & Legal Series, Book w/Disk—PC)	$18.95	CREP
▫	The Financial Power of Attorney Workbook (Book w/Disk—PC)	$29.95	FINPOA
	How to File for Chapter 7 Bankruptcy	$29.95	HFB
	IRAs, 401(k)s & Other Retirement Plans: Taking Your Money Out	$24.95	RET
	Money Troubles: Legal Strategies to Cope With Your Debts	$24.95	MT
	Nolo's Law Form Kit: Personal Bankruptcy	$16.95	KBNK

▫ Book with disk
⊙ Book with CD-ROM

ORDER 24 HOURS A DAY
Call 800-992-6656 • www.nolo.com • Mail or fax the order form in this book

	PRICE	CODE
Stand Up to the IRS	$29.95	SIRS
Surviving an IRS Tax Audit (Quick & Legal Series)	$24.95	SAUD
Take Control of Your Student Loan Debt	$24.95	SLOAN

PATENTS AND COPYRIGHTS

	PRICE	CODE
◉ The Copyright Handbook: How to Protect and Use Written Works (Book w/CD-ROM)	$34.95	COHA
Copyright Your Software	$24.95	CYS
Domain Names	$24.95	DOM
▣ Getting Permission: How to License and Clear Copyrighted Materials Online and Off (Book w/Disk—PC)	$34.95	RIPER
How to Make Patent Drawings Yourself	$29.95	DRAW
The Inventor's Notebook	$34.95	INOT
Nolo's Patents for Beginners (Quick & Legal Series)	$29.95	QPAT
▣ License Your Invention (Book w/Disk—PC)	$39.95	LICE
Patent, Copyright & Trademark	$29.95	PCTM
Patent It Yourself	$49.95	PAT
Patent Searching Made Easy	$29.95	PATSE
The Public Domain	$34.95	PUBL
◉ Software Development: A Legal Guide (Book w/ CD-ROM)	$44.95	SFT
Trademark: Legal Care for Your Business and Product Name	$39.95	TRD
The Trademark Registration Kit (Quick & Legal Series)	$19.95	TREG

RESEARCH & REFERENCE

	PRICE	CODE
Legal Research: How to Find & Understand the Law	$34.95	LRES

SENIORS

	PRICE	CODE
Beat the Nursing Home Trap: A Consumer's Guide to Assisted Living and Long-Term Care	$21.95	ELD
The Conservatorship Book for California	$44.95	CNSV
Social Security, Medicare & Pensions	$24.95	SOA

▣ Book with disk
◉ Book with CD-ROM

Order Form

Name

Address

City

State, Zip

Daytime Phone

E-mail

Item Code	Quantity	Item	Unit Price	Total Price

Method of payment

☐ Check ☐ VISA ☐ MasterCard
☐ Discover Card ☐ American Express

Subtotal	
Add your local sales tax (California only)	
Shipping: RUSH $8, Basic $3.95 (See below)	
"I bought 3, ship it to me FREE!"(Ground shipping only)	
TOTAL	

Account Number

Expiration Date

Signature

Shipping and Handling

Rush Delivery—Only $8

We'll ship any order to any street address in the U.S. by UPS 2nd Day Air* for only $8!

* Order by noon Pacific Time and get your order in 2 business days. Orders placed after noon Pacific Time will arrive in 3 business days. P.O. boxes and S.F. Bay Area use basic shipping. Alaska and Hawaii use 2nd Day Air or Priority Mail.

Basic Shipping—$3.95

Use for P.O. Boxes, Northern California and Ground Service.

Allow 1-2 weeks for delivery. U.S. addresses only.

For faster service, use your credit card and our toll-free numbers

Order 24 hours a day

Online	www.nolo.com
Phone	1-800-992-6656
Fax	1-800-645-0895
Mail	Nolo.com
	950 Parker St.
	Berkeley, CA 94710

Visit us online at
www.nolo.com

Ex Libris® is a registered trademark of Julius Blumberg, Inc.
Portfolio is our name for the Syndicate® Kit, a registered trademark
of Julius Blumberg, Inc.

The Corporations Code and regulations for each profession require special printing of professional share certificates. We have developed special California Professional Share Certificates for each profession containing the appropriate legend. Provide us with the specific profession and profession number from the list to the right and we will print your certificates with the appropriate legend.

Nolo, in cooperation with Julius Blumberg, Inc. offers two superior corporate kits. The Ex Libris® Kit features a high quality 3-ring looseleaf vinyl binder with your corporate name embossed on the spine. The Portfolio Kit features a handcrafted, simulated red and black leather binder with your corporate name embossed in gold on the spine. You are not required to have a corporate kit, but many people find it is a convenient addition.

The Ex Libris® and Portfolio Kits include:

- **Corporate Records Book**. The primary difference between the two books is described above.

- 20 numbered, lithographed **Stock Certificates** with professional-looking green borders printed with your corporate name and the appropriate stock legend for your profession.

- **Corporate Seal**. This is a solid metal tool designed to imprint the name of your corporation on corporate documents.

- Eight-page **Stock Transfer Ledger (share register)** bound in a separate section.

- Mylar coated **Index Tabs** with these five important divisions: Articles of Incorporation, Bylaws, Minutes, Share Certificates and Transfer Ledger.

- **Corporate Record Tickler**, an exclusive form that records information pertinent to the corporation (principal shareholders/directors, registered agent, annual meetings, etc.) and serves as a reminder for review of minutes and tax materials.

- 50 pages of quality bond **Minute Paper**.

Profession	Profession Number
Accountancy	3.1
Acupuncture	3.2
Architecture	3.2A
Audiology	3.3
Chiropractic	3.4
Dentistry	3.5
Law	3.6
Licensed Clinical Social Worker	3.7
Marriage, Family or Child Counseling	3.8
Medical (physicians and/or surgeons only)	3.9
Nurses	3.9A
Optometric	3.10
Osteopathic	3.11
Pharmacy	3.12
Physical Therapy	3.13
Physicians' Assistants	3.13A
Podiatry (podiatrists only)	3.14
Psychology	3.15
Shorthand Reporting	3.16
Speech Pathology	3.17
Veterinary	3.18

CALIFORNIA PROFESSIONAL CORPORATIONS WITH COMMON SHARE STOCK CERTIFICATES

Profession*   **Profession Number***

Indicate only one profession. If your corporation intends to engage in more than one profession, these kits will not work for you (see Chapter 6, Step 5). Select the profession number from the list on the facing page. We will imprint the appropriate legend on your share certificates.

Year of Incorporation _____, CA

Name of Corporation (print exactly as on Articles of Incorporation)   45

☐☐☐

☐☐☐

Put one character per space (including punctuation and spaces); be sure capital and lower case letters are clear

☐ **Ex Libris Kit**   ☐ **Portfolio Kit**
   $119.95 $139.95 .... $ _____

Long corporate names (over 45 characters) cost an additional $25.00 .... $ _____

SUBTOTAL .... $ _____

California residents add your local sales tax (8.25%) .... $ _____

Delivery charges
Regular $10 shipping within 12-15 business days/Rush $25 shipping within 4 business days. All delivery dates are calculated from the day we receive your order

be sure to check one: ☐ $10.00 **or** ☐ $25.00 .... $ _____

TOTAL ENCLOSED ....$ _____

Ship to:

Name: _____

Street Address **(no PO boxes)** _____

City _____ State _____ Zip _____

Phone _____

Send to:
NOLO
950 Parker Street
Berkeley CA 94710

Prices are subject to change without notice.
Fax with credit card number to: 510-548-5902.
Sorry, we do not accept telephone orders for corporate kits.

Extra stock certificates cost $45.00 in groups of 20. Make sure to ask for Item 7CA3.1 and specify your California profession, as explained above. Extra Corporate Seal: $30 each, plus the corporate kit shipping price.

Take 2 Minutes
& Give Us Your 2 cents

Your comments make a big difference in the development and revision of Nolo books and software. Please take a few minutes and register your Nolo product—and your comments—with us. Not only will your input make a difference, you'll receive special offers available only to registered owners of Nolo products on our newest books and software. Register now by:

PHONE
1-800-992-6656

FAX
1-800-645-0895

EMAIL
cs@nolo.com

or **MAIL** us
this registration card

REMEMBER:
Little publishers have big ears. We really listen to you.

fold here

NOLO

REGISTRATION CARD

NAME _____ DATE _____

ADDRESS _____

_____

CITY _____ STATE _____ ZIP _____

PHONE _____ E-MAIL _____

WHERE DID YOU HEAR ABOUT THIS PRODUCT? _____

WHERE DID YOU PURCHASE THIS PRODUCT? _____

DID YOU CONSULT A LAWYER? (PLEASE CIRCLE ONE)   YES   NO   NOT APPLICABLE

DID YOU FIND THIS BOOK HELPFUL?   (VERY)   5   4   3   2   1   (NOT AT ALL)

COMMENTS _____

_____

_____

_____

WAS IT EASY TO USE?   (VERY EASY)   5   4   3   2   1   (VERY DIFFICULT)

DO YOU OWN A COMPUTER? IF SO, WHICH FORMAT? (PLEASE CIRCLE ONE)   WINDOWS   DOS   MAC

❑ If you do not wish to receive mailings from these companies, please check this box.
❑ You can quote me in future Nolo promotional materials. Daytime phone number _____.

PROF 6.2

fold here

- -

Place
stamp here

nolo
950 Parker Street
Berkeley, CA 94710-9867

Attn: PROF 6.2